Cultural Studies and Political Economy

Critical Media Studies

Series Editor
Andrew Calabrese, University of Colorado

This series covers a broad range of critical research and theory about media in the modern world. It includes work about the changing structures of the media, focusing particularly on work about the political and economic forces and social relations which shape and are shaped by media institutions, structural changes in policy formation and enforcement, technological transformations in the means of communication, and the relationships of all these to public and private cultures worldwide. Historical research about the media and intellectual histories pertaining to media research and theory are particularly welcome. Emphasizing the role of social and political theory for informing and shaping research about communications media, Critical Media Studies addresses the politics of media institutions at national, subnational, and transnational levels. The series is also interested in short, synthetic texts on key thinkers and concepts in critical media studies.

Titles in the series

Governing European Communications: From Unification to Coordination
by Maria Michalis
Knowledge Workers in the Information Society edited
by Catherine McKercher and Vincent Mosco
The Laboring of Communication: Will Knowledge Workers of the World Unite?
by Vincent Mosco and Catherine McKercher
Punk Record Labels and the Struggle for Autonomy: The Emergence of DIY
by Alan O'Connor
Cultural Studies and Political Economy: Toward a New Integration
by Robert Babe

Cultural Studies and Political Economy

Toward a New Integration

Robert E. Babe

LEXINGTON BOOKS

A division of
ROWMAN & LITTLEFIELD PUBLISHERS, INC.
Lanham • Boulder • New York • Toronto • Plymouth, UK

LEXINGTON BOOKS

A division of Rowman & Littlefield Publishers, Inc.
A wholly owned subsidiary of The Rowman & Littlefield Publishing Group, Inc.
4501 Forbes Boulevard, Suite 200
Lanham, MD 20706

Estover Road
Plymouth PL6 7PY
United Kingdom

British Library Cataloguing in Publication Information Available

Library of Congress Cataloging-in-Publication Data

[Babe, Robert E.
Cultural studies and political economy : toward a new integration / Robert E. Babe.
p. cm. — (Critical media studies)
Includes bibliographical references and index.

ISBN-13: 978-0-7391-2366-9 (cloth: alk. paper)
ISBN-13: 978-0-7391-3198-5 (e-book)

1. Economics—Sociological aspects. 2. Cultural industries—Social aspects. 3. Mass media—Economic aspects. I. Title.
HM548.B33 2009
306.3'4—dc22

2008031566

Printed in the United States of America

∞™ The paper used in this publication meets the minimum requirements of American National Standard for Information Sciences—Permanence of Paper for Printed Library Materials, ANSI/NISO Z39.48–1992.

To Bill

The besetting danger is not so much of embracing falsehood for truth, as of mistaking part of the truth for the whole.

Raymond Williams, *Culture and Society*, 66

Contents

Acknowledgments

In 2002, as editor of *Topia: Canadian Journal of Cultural Studies,* Professor Jody Berland of York University invited me to prepare a series of annual columns on political economy and cultural studies. Five columns appeared between 2003 and 2006. In a very real sense, the present book began with that invitation. As editor, Professor Berland touched up the prose of those contributions. All have been revised (and given new titles) for presentation here as chapters 4 through 8. I gratefully acknowledge permission to republish.

Edward Comor graciously read and commented on an early version of the manuscript. In addition, he coauthored the original version of chapter 8. Edward's wisdom, energy, and generosity are greatly appreciated.

Mike Babe graciously consented to be my copy editor; his diligence and stellar performance are most respected.

Sandra Braman, Kostas Gouliamos, and James Winter read and commented on portions of the present manuscript. All have been pillars of support over the years. Forty years ago Warren J. Samuels opened the field of intellectual history to me, and he has been an inspiration ever since.

Part One

GENEALOGIES

Introduction to Part I

Culture Is Our Business.[1] Marshall McLuhan's evocative maxim can be understood at two levels, at least.

First and most obviously, cultural industries manufacture, buy, sell, and distribute symbolic wares for money. These symbolic wares—likened to pieces of toast by a former chairman of the Federal Communications Commission[2]—pass through a series of production nodes (for books: text preparation, editing, typesetting, printing, binding, distribution, marketing, retail; for stage plays: scripting, financing, assemblage of props, facilities and performers, direction, rehearsal, insurance, marketing, performance). Value is added at each stage of the production process, as is true of all commodity production—including toasters and pieces of toast. Cultural artifacts, then, McLuhan's aphorism implies, are to be understood as commodities. That they are more than mere commodities—a term inappropriately implying final consumption, few if any externalities, and presuming the ubiquity of private, not public goods[3]—does not gainsay their status or treatment primarily as commodity in our political-economic system.

Second, and even more poignantly, McLuhan's dictum can be construed as implying that cultural artifacts are means to fabricate, support, reinforce, condone, justify, or extend the fundamental organization of the consumer society. "We *make* consumer culture" would be an accurate paraphrase of this second interpretation. By this rendering, the production and distribution of cultural (symbolic) wares are understood to create and reinforce the psychic ground of, or more philosophically the ontology for, *a culture of consumption*. Cultural products that pass the market "test" of success by achieving high sales—top-grossing movies, books on the bestseller list, sound recordings at the top of the charts, TV shows winning the ratings sweeps, the painting that sets a record at an auction—all these are admired, acclaimed, and in turn promoted for their success in the marketplace, illustrating by example the doctrine of *consumer sovereignty* and validating the meaning of success in a pecuniary culture.[4]

As well, *within* their narratives and visual representations, symbolic wares often depict the ontology of consumerism—product placements in movies being but one example of a surreptitious if not always subtle mode of persuasion. Furthermore, popular songs, famous paintings, literary allusions, star athletes, and celebrities increasingly are used by advertisers to help brand products, again affirming the nexus of popular culture and the broader political economy.

McLuhan's "mentor,"[5] economic historian and media theorist Harold Adams Innis (1894–1952), went further. Innis maintained that throughout the course of human history, cultures, cultural artifacts, and cultural processes have generally supported, and were supported by, their society's predominant mode of economic and political organization. Within each civilization or society, according to Innis, there is and always has been a symbiosis between economy/polity on the one hand and the *dominant* culture/mode of communication on the other. If and when these grow out of synch, Innis maintained, transformation, transition, or even revolution follows. Later in the book, we will look more closely at Innis' media thesis.

Culture is our business, *and* business is our culture. Few today would deny at least some interactivity between culture/cultural artifacts and the economy/polity. Nonetheless, in the scholarly fields of communication and media studies, there has been, famously, a split—indeed, an at times bitter rift—between those analyzing the economic, financial, policy, and power dimensions of cultural production and practice ("political economists") versus "cultural studies" scholars. *Cultural studies* may be loosely defined as the multidisciplinary study of culture across various social strata, where *culture* refers to arts, knowledge, beliefs, customs, practices, and norms of social interaction. *Studies in political economy of media*, in contrast, focus on the economic, financial, and political causes and consequences of culture. Exploring the rift—the causes, dimensions, consequences, and possible resolution—is the central topic of this book.

I argue here that in their formative years, political economy of media and cultural studies were fully integrated, consistent, and mutually supportive, but the poststructuralist turn in cultural studies caused media studies to split into hostile political economy and cultural studies camps. I also claim that that split today, however, is no greater than the current division within cultural studies itself—between poststructuralism and cultural materialism—those terms being defined below.

Reintegrating cultural studies and political economy is of some urgency. On the one hand, to study culture without taking into account either the influence of the political-economic base or the political-economic consequences of cultural activities, is to be naïve in the extreme. These oversights can cause one to misconstrue oppression as pluralism, persuasion as democracy, and elite control as popular freedom. They also can entail a flight from lived conditions into the safe haven of language or discourse, making thereby the pursuit of social justice (as but one example) impossible. On the other hand, to overemphasize the political-economic determinants to the neglect of human volition and freedom is equally detrimental. Denying or belittling human agency is tantamount to denigrating human dignity and to fatalistically understate the possibility of social reform. This book argues that there is a balance, a dialectical middle ground, that must be sought after, achieved, and maintained. And that middle ground is precisely what the writers featured in this book, Harold Innis, Theodor Adorno, Raymond Williams, Richard Hoggart, and E. P. Thompson, all achieved through their *cultural materialism*. And, that is precisely what was lost in cultural studies' poststructuralist turn. Moreover, that is precisely what needs to be retrieved today, by reintegrating political economy and cultural studies. I will argue that this retrieval will facilitate both the pursuit of social justice and the quest for environmental health.

The antagonisms between political economy and cultural studies are well known. In a 1987 article in the journal *Communication*, Kevin Robins and Frank Webster noted that cultural studies and political economy had become "polarized, even antagonistic."[6] The authors added: "There has been a grumbling, often tacit but occasionally explicit, state of intellectual belligerence between the advocates of cultural studies and those of political economy."[7]

According to Robins and Webster, from a cultural studies perspective, political economists engage in economic reductionism: they one-sidedly concentrate on economic factors which they presume *determine* the cultural (ideological) effects of media, without inquiring into the ideological and interpretive practices of audiences. Conversely, to some political economists, cultural studies scholars are mired in hermeneutics, deconstruction, semiotics, rhetoric, and other modes of textual analysis. Absorbed by their high abstractions and entangled in their presuppositions concerning the self-referentiality of language, cultural studies scholars seem aloof from and possibly oblivious to power plays, injustices, oppression, and suffering in the real, material world.[8]

Rancor surfaced at the 1993 meetings of the International Communication Association in Washington, D.C., and hostilities continued as a "Colloquy" in the March 1995 issue of *Critical Studies in Mass Communication.* There,

Lawrence Grossberg and James Carey, championing their understanding of cultural studies, faced off against Nicholas Garnham and Graham Murdock, who represented critical political economy. According to the journal's associate editor, Oscar Gandy, Jr., the Colloquy was Grossberg's idea, a way he thought to transfer the debate from the extemporaneous platform of a live conference to the less volatile and less evanescent medium of the printed page.[9] Less evanescent, the published symposium certainly was; reduction in volatility, however, is quite another matter. Gandy reports that Angela McRobbie, invited as discussant on account of her feminist perspectives on cultural studies, bowed out, "so outraged and insulted" had she been "by Garnham's initial draft." Likewise, Carey fumed at what he termed Garnham's "condescending attitude toward cultural studies," adding that "these are tones of bitter divorce, not a search for a friendly reconciliation or a merger of intellectual labor."[10] In fact, even the published final edit is laced, from both sides, with epithets, insults, and innuendo. Grossberg, for example, accused Garnham of intentionally misrepresenting the founders of British cultural studies, and then closed his contribution with the following caustic volley: "So I must decline the invitation [proffered in the title of Garnham's article] to reconcile, and point out that we don't need a divorce because we were never married."[11] The claim, "we were never married," is a major object of analysis and criticism in part I of this book.

Over a decade later, the fields remain riven. Janice Peck, for example, wrote in 2006 that political economy and cultural studies "have arrived at an uneasy truce born of having divided up the world—and their respective objects of inquiry—into the putatively separate realms of 'economy' and 'culture.'"[12] Richard Lee, similarly, speaks not of two, but of three solitudes, maintaining that inquiry into economic, political, and cultural matters "face off [as] mutually exclusive superdisciplines."[13] Making the impasse even more ironic and unfortunate is the fact that, as Eileen Meehan observes, the camps share, or at least claim to share, the same "critical valuation" of capitalism and its cultural processes. There should be, in other words, substantial common ground. Nonetheless, Meehan asks rhetorically, "Is dialogue between cultural studies and political economy possible?"[14]

What, then, has prevented or inhibited many political economy and cultural studies scholars from entering, or re-entering, into sustained and fruitful dialogue? One explanation might be the propensity to specialize, even to such an extent that academic specialties become noncommunicative. In chapter 1 I review the emergence in the eighteenth century of political economy from moral philosophy, and as well I recount the split between economics and political philosophy/political science in the late nineteenth and early twentieth centuries—to the effect that today's mainline economics ("neoclassicism") is undertaken in a manner that acknowledges little or no connection to either the system of morality (other than market "morality"[15]) or the system of power. One could argue that the same pressures for specialization have caused cultural studies and political economy of media to go their separate ways, in which case (re)integration could be achieved through concerted efforts at interdisciplinarity.[16] Indeed, as noted by Andrew Calabrese, in recent years political economists have shown greater interest in researching audiences (audiences as commodity, audiences as objects of surveillance, and audience segmentation as means of inclusion and exclusion)—audiences traditionally being the domain of cultural studies. Likewise among some cultural theorists there is a growing interest in policy analysis, criticism, and intervention—domains traditionally dominated by political economy.[17] Calabrese is hopeful that this new common ground of research focus may lead to "more fruitful dialogue, and even collaboration, between practitioners of political economy and cultural studies."[18]

I argue here, however, that difference in subject matter is a lesser, indeed inessential factor behind the rift. Cultural studies, after all, is self-consciously interdisciplinary, and political economy is an approach applied to many fields of inquiry, not just media and communication. The real issues, rather, I will argue, are ontological, political, and ideological. As elaborated particularly in chapter 3, I view the main combatants at the Colloquy, namely Garnham and Grossberg, as flailing away on largely superficial issues, masking or diverting attention from the deeper, ontological divide; in chapter 4, I then address deep-set political/ideological differences. For now, however, it may suffice to support the claim by one example symptomatic of a deep ontological divide. As just noted, Grossberg contended (quite inaccurately, I believe) that cultural studies and political economy were never very close, and he expressed no desire for them to draw closer now. Indeed, the main title of his Colloquy paper, "Cultural Studies *vs.* Political Economy," is in telling contrast to Garnham's title, "Political Economy *and* Cultural Studies." Grossberg's position, however, is in keeping with poststructuralists' distrust of big theories ("grand narratives"), and their approval of diversity, inconsistency, contradiction, and antithesis.[19] *Pluralism* in and inconsistencies among points of view, poststructuralists claim, undermines concentrated power, and hence far from being regretted is to be celebrated. In contrast, the unification or integration of diverse knowledge was a principal aim of the Enlightenment, and Garnham (with political economists generally) retains that desire.[20] Rather than attempting to undermine or de-authenticate scientific/instrumental knowledge through deconstruction and other strategies, as poststructuralists are wont to do, political economists are more inclined *to use* that knowledge, albeit in more equitable, more democratic, more humane, and more ecologically benign ways. Hence, they recommend restructuring institutions in terms of accountability and lines of control, so that instrumental knowledge (scientific, social scientific, technological, psychological, social-psychological, financial, rhetorical, and so on) will be so deployed. Some, such as Harold Innis, have recommended, too, that instrumental knowledge be counterbalanced (as opposed to de-authenticated) by other types of knowledge—moral, aesthetic, historical, communal.

Part I of this book, among other things, contradicts Grossberg's assertion that cultural studies and political economy were never very close. In fact, as we will see, political economy was fully integrated in the writings of the British authors commonly acknowledged as inaugurating cultural studies—Raymond Williams, Richard Hoggart, and E. P. Thompson. That finding alone, developed in chapter 2, is sufficient to overturn Grossberg's contention. But also, as shown in chapter 1, cultural studies and political economy were highly integrated in inaugural political economy writings, too. In that regard, I turn to Harold Innis and Theodor Adorno. In doing so, I depart from conventional thinking, but as developed in chapter 1 these writers unquestionably were first off the mark in developing political economy analyses of media; they predated the English cultural studies theorists, too, by a number of years. In any event, and this is the far more important point, all of these figures—Innis, Adorno, Williams, Hoggart, Thompson—point to means whereby political economy and cultural studies can be (re)integrated today, and hence for that reason alone they are worth studying together.

Even among those who agree that integration (or rather, *re*-integration) between political economy and cultural studies is desirable, however, there is controversy. Some maintain that culture "contains," or is much larger than merely the economy and polity, that not only are important aspects of cultural production, transmission, and interpretation separate from markets, classes, and other predominantly economic/political categories, but that political economy should be regarded at most as a subfield within cultural studies; integration for these scholars means absorption of political economy by cultural studies.[21] Others contend, however, that the economy "contains" culture, that the pursuit of the material means of existence touches all major belief systems and modes of understanding and acting; these writers consequently speak of a *political economy of culture*.[22] The median and dialectical position (*cultural materialism*), which I will argue characterized *both* critical political economy and cultural studies at their beginnings, acknowledges mutual interaction and mutual dependency in the *systems theory* sense among culture, economy, and polity/policy.

It was in a spirit of reconciliation between cultural studies and political economy that in the fall of 2002 Professor Jody Berland invited me to prepare annual political economy columns for *Topia: Canadian Journal of Cultural Studies*, with a view also to stimulating policy- and political economy-related submissions. Five columns appeared between the spring of 2003 and the fall of 2006, revised versions of which are gathered here. Before moving forward, however, it is essential to recount from whence we have come. Chapters 1 and 2, therefore, present brief "genealogies" of political economy and cultural studies, respectively. Together, these chapters establish the integrated nature of political economy and cultural studies in the formative years, and by implication point to means of reintegrating them now. Chapter 3 revisits the Colloquy, and looks at related materials, to determine the main lines of opposition separating political economy and cultural studies. It is proposed that it was the poststructuralist turn in cultural studies that instigated the separation. Chapter 4, therefore, reviews the beginnings of American poststructuralist cultural studies, and places that within the genealogy of mainstream American media/communication thought; the argument is made that poststructuralism is quite consistent with, and is indeed the latest manifestation of, the historic inattention of mainstream American media scholarship toward considerations of inequality. Given the historical background of part I, part II—"Portals for Dialogue"—suggests three means whereby political economy and cultural studies can be reintegrated: recognizing money as a culturally biased medium of communication, contemplating the time-space dialectic of communication media, and foregrounding what I term the "dialectic of information." The final chapter of part II, however, which compares and contrasts the media thought of Harold Innis and poststructuralist Mark Poster, is less optimistic; it shows that poststructuralism is fundamentally at odds with these three "portals," and hence also with the prospect of reintegrating political economy and cultural studies. A final chapter addresses the issues at a new level.

NOTES

1. Marshall McLuhan, *Culture is Our Business* (New York: McGraw Hill, 1970).
2. For FCC commissioner, Mark Fowler, "Television is just another appliance. It's a toaster with pictures. . . . Why is there this national obsession to tamper with this box of transistors and tubes when we don't do the same for *Time* magazine?" Mark Fowler, Interview in *Reason* magazine, 1 November 1981.
3. Cultural "commodities" are not usually used up, as are normal consumer goods; books, sound recordings, films, carvings, paintings, and so forth, endure after being processed by users, meaning that they are more analogous to capital items than they are to consumer goods. Live performances, too, linger, perhaps attenuated, perhaps reinterpreted, in human minds—with unforeseen consequences, some of which may

be to influence future cultural productions. As well, cultural "commodities" may affect indirectly those without direct exposure to the cultural artifact, the very definition of an "externality" or third-party effect. These properties make cultural goods ill-suited for mainstream economics—one reason among several for preferring political economy to neoclassical analyses of media and cultural industries. See Robert E. Babe, *Communication and the Transformation of Economics* (Boulder, CO: Westview Press, 1995).

4. Edward Comor, *Consumption and the Globalization Project: International Hegemony and the Annihilation of Time* (New York: Palgrave Macmillan, 2008).

5. McLuhan described himself as a "disciple" of Innis, and referred to his own most scholarly tome, *The Gutenberg Galaxy*, as but "a footnote to the observations of Innis." James Carey once quipped that the Canadian contribution to media studies would have been far more impressive had the Innis-to-McLuhan lineage been in the opposite direction. Elsewhere I have argued that McLuhan turned Innis on his head by emphasizing biases in reception (eye vs. ear) as opposed to biases in transmission (space vs. time), in effect de-politicizing Innis. See Robert E. Babe, *Canadian Communication Thought: Ten Foundational Writers* (Toronto: University of Toronto Press, 2000), chapter 11. See also the discussion at the conclusion of chapter 7 regarding the integration of the media theories of Innis and McLuhan.

6. Kevin Robins and Frank Webster, "The Communications Revolution: New Media, Old Problems," *Communication* 10, no.1 (1987): 72.

7. Robins and Webster, "The Communications Revolution," 72.

8. Robins and Webster, "The Communications Revolution," 72.

9. Oscar H. Gandy, "Colloquy," *Critical Studies in Mass Communication* 12, no.1 (1995): 60.

10. James W. Carey, "Abolishing the Old Spirit World," *Critical Studies in Mass Communication* 12, no. 1 (1995): 82.

11. Lawrence Grossberg, "Cultural Studies vs. Political Economy: Is Anybody Else Bored with this Debate?" *Critical Studies in Mass Communication* 12, no. 1 (1995): 80.

12. Janice Peck, "Why We Shouldn't Be Bored with the Political Economy Versus Cultural Studies Debate," *Cultural Critique* 64 (2006): 92.

13. Richard E. Lee, *Life and Times of Cultural Studies* (Durham, NC: Duke University Press, 2003), 2.

14. Eileen R. Meehan, "Commodity, Culture, Common Sense: Media Research and Paradigm Dialogue," *The Journal of Media Economics* 12, no. 22 (1999): 150.

15. Jane Jacobs, *Systems of Survival: A Dialogue on the Moral Foundations of Commerce and Politics* (New York: Vintage, 1994).

16. This possibility was raised by three of the four participants in the Colloquy. Carey and Grossberg maintained, however, that specialization is not just an explanation for the separation, but that it also provides justification for keeping the fields separate. Murdock, representing political economy, dissented, urging that specialization needs to be overcome.

17. Andrew Calabrese, "Toward a Political Economy of Culture," in *Toward a Political Economy of Culture: Capitalism and Communication in the Twenty-First Cen-*

tury, ed. Andrew Calabrese and Colin Sparks (Lanham, MD: Rowman and Littlefield, Publishers, 2004), 9. This is not to say that consumption has not figured prominently in political economy. According to Innis, as we will see, for society to focus on consumption is tantamount to present-mindedness; for Raymond Williams, present-mindedness means a decline in class consciousness.

18. Calabrese, "Toward a Political Economy of Culture," 9.

19. See, for example, Frank Webster, *Theories of the Information Society* (London: Routledge, 1995), 163–92.

20. Introducing his edited collection dedicated to Garnham, Calabrese described Garnham's thirty-year scholarly career as "an intelligent and sustained appeal to the Enlightenment project." See Calabrese, "Toward a Political Economy of Culture," 9.

21. See, for example, Richard Maxwell, "Political Economy Within Cultural Studies," in *A Companion to Cultural Studies,* ed. Toby Miller (Oxford: Blackwell Publishing, 2001), 116–38.

22. For example, Calabrese, "Toward a Political Economy of Culture."

Chapter One

Genealogy of Political Economy

TWO POLITICAL ECONOMIES[1]

Classical Political Economy

Dating from the Scottish Enlightenment, *political economy* is the scholarly discourse studying power relations affecting the production, distribution, and consumption of wealth, income, and resources—including information and communication resources.[2] Adam Smith's *The Wealth of Nations* (first edition, 1776) is often regarded as the inaugural text.[3] Smith defined his discipline, *political oeconomy*, as a "branch of the science of a statesman or legislator" helping governments set conditions to stimulate economic growth.[4] His subject was *political* economy because it was within the context of statecraft that he studied economic processes and relations. Smith was a radical in his day as his liberal doctrine of wealth creation through competition, specialization (division of labor), and freer international trade challenged the received tenets of mercantilism. Once the industrial capitalist class attained dominance, however, Smith and his successors (David Ricardo, Thomas Malthus, James Mill, Jeremy Bentham) became voices for the new establishment.

A notable feature of classical political economy was its narrowed focus—its participation, one might say, in the division of scholarly labor. Following the precedent set at Glasgow University by his predecessor and mentor, Francis Hutcheson, Smith taught political economy as a distinct and severable component of moral philosophy, the other parts being natural theology, jurisprudence, and ethics (the focus of Smith's other renowned tome, *The Theory of Moral Sentiments*).[5] According to some, *The Wealth of Nations* and *Moral Sentiments* were meant by Smith to be interdependent in the sense that *Moral Sentiments* sets out the ethical framework for a market economy, while

The Wealth of Nations describes the operations of such an economy.[6] But none of this is at all clear from reading Smith, who seldom cross-referenced the two works.[7] And for good reason! They are fundamentally inconsistent. *Wealth of Nations* celebrates "self-love" as the engine of economic prosperity and denigrates altruism for interfering with wealth creation; *Moral Sentiments,* conversely, lauds empathy (what Smith termed *sympathy*) as the highest of human virtues, and claims that sympathy is in no way compatible with self-love.[8] In writing separate and essentially inconsistent books, Smith figured prominently in separating political economy from moral philosophy.[9] Furthermore, Smith redefined political economy as the study of wealth generation, as opposed to the study of wealth distribution (economic justice), which had been the central problematic for Aristotle, Thomas Aquinas, and other of his precursors[10]—again pointing to his role in segregating political economy from moral philosophy.

A second distinguishing characteristic of classical political economy is the *labor theory of value*, which was developed most notably by Smith, David Ricardo, and Karl Marx. Arguably, it was Marx's claim—that if labor is the source of value, then workers should rightfully receive that value—that caused mainline political economists (to become known simply as economists) to struggle in the late 1800s for a new *theory of value*, one less prone to spotlighting injustices in the distribution of wealth and income, and hence less threatening to established power.

Neoclassical Economics

The new mainstream position, developed in the late nineteenth and early twentieth centuries and still *de rigueur* today, is neoclassicism. *Neoclassical economics* proposes that value derives not from labor, but from consumer "tastes and preferences." This new, or neoclassical, approach makes no reference to class (*everyone,* after all, is a "consumer"), and thereby *consumer sovereignty* became enshrined as the discipline's new axial presupposition and principle.[11]

As with any axiom, however, the rightness or justness of consumer sovereignty itself is seldom questioned. Nor are the nature and composition of consumer tastes and preferences assessed. Rather, in the words of Nobel laureates George Stigler and Gary Becker, "*De Gustibus non est disputandum*;"[12] literally, tastes are not to be disputed. Although the production and consumption (i.e., the supply and demand) of cultural goods and services *are* addressed by the neoclassical paradigm, they are treated solely as commodities, produced and purchased in the marketplace to satisfy *preexisting* tastes and preferences, not as factors which through use might alter consumer wants and desires (through invidious imitation, habituation, or addiction, for example[13]). Nor are persuasion and deeper psychological forms of indoctrination to be studied as influencing tastes and preferences. Nor are tastes and preferences to be judged as to their soundness.[14] Rather, they are to be sovereign.

This new or neoclassical economics departed from classical political economy in yet another, perhaps even more fundamental way. Continuing in the vein established by Stanley Jevons[15] and other founders (Leon Walras, Vilfredo Pareto, Francis Edgeworth, Alfred Marshall), it abstracts from the social, political, institutional, and cultural setting. Economics became essentially a mathematical-deductive system—in stark contrast to classical political economy, which was fully engaged with the cultural/political/economic environment.[16]

CONTEMPORARY POLITICAL ECONOMY

The "New" (Chicago) Political Economy

Although by 1900 neoclassicism had replaced classical political economy as the economics orthodoxy, political economy in various guises persisted, albeit often at the margins, and today can be a vibrant alternative approach to economic and social analysis. Unfortunately, at present, contending forces vie for the title, and hence political economy can connote even antithetical approaches. One such contender is the Chicago School, also known as *the new* or *positive political economy*, which aspires to reclaim the name of its classical predecessor even while extending neoclassical methods[17] into myriad new applications. Leading exponents have included Gary Becker, Richard Posner, Ronald Coase, and George Stigler. Becker, for example, applied neoclassical modes of analysis to family planning, discrimination, marriage, divorce, suicide, addiction, and crime,[18] while Coase gained fame by proposing the commodification of pollution as the preferred "solution" to environmental woes.[19] According to the Chicago theorists, most if not all areas of life "are subject to the analysis of maximizing or calculations of advantage,"[20] making neoclassicism eminently suited for such extensions.

However, certain areas do remain out of bounds for these "new" political economists. As noted by Samuels, conservative political economists do not deploy neoclassical theory and its understanding of the self-interested use of state power to investigate the origin of private property,[21] likely because such study could undermine the basic neoclassical postulate that property is inviolable. Nor do they, as we have seen, address persuasion and other factors influencing tastes and preferences, again in all likelihood because that type of investigation would undermine the axiom of consumer sovereignty.[22] Through the doctrine of *Pareto optimality,*[23] moreover, the new political economists eschew assessing the distribution of wealth and income as that, they claim, would require value judgments on their part, which would be contrary to their aim of providing "positive" or value-neutral analyses.[24] Professing an unwillingness or inability to make interpersonal utility comparisons, the new political economists cannot even approve measures that would benefit millions if but one person would become less well off as a result. The ultra-conservative stance of the new political economy is readily apparent.

Critical Political Economy

The *new* political economy is to be contrasted with a second contemporary approach—namely, *critical* political economy. The term, *critical*, originated with the Institute of Social Research, established in 1923 at the University of Frankfurt. Upon the appointment of Max Horkheimer as director in 1930, the Institute turned from its initially "hard-nosed brand" of Marxism; rather than presuming strict economic determinism, it began taking seriously "the claims of culture and consciousness."[25] This transformation, according to Martin Jay, entailed shifting the focus from society's socio-economic *base* to its cultural *superstructure*.[26] Stephen Crook proposes that it was by injecting Marxism with Freudianism that the critical theorists were able to turn from "the rigidities . . . of their earlier reductionist accounts."[27] We will have occasion below to spend considerable time on the issue of economic determinism and interactions between base and superstructure, as that has proved contentious in contemporary media studies generally and has figured prominently in the split between political economy and cultural studies. For now, though, three points seem essential. First, as just noted, after 1930 critical theorists at the Frankfurt School eschewed the hard economic determinisms ("vulgar" Marxism[28]) characterizing the early Frankfurt School as well as Chicago/neoclassical political economy! Second, the Frankfurt theorists denied that knowledge can ever be "value-free, a position distinguishing them again from conservative (Chicago) political economists";[29] hence, they self-consciously *appraised* (critiqued) both social/economic conditions and practices, and mainstream theorizing about those practices and conditions. Among the normative criteria they explicitly invoked was fairness in the distribution of wealth and income. Finally, they maintained that culture is key to understanding power relations in society, and hence this second wave of critical theorists often addressed mass media, thereby inaugurating *critical media studies*. It was much later (as we will see) that critical political economy and cultural studies went their separate ways. With the Frankfurt School of the 1930s and 1940s, there was no such division.

In a classic article first published in 1941, Paul Lazarsfeld (a founder and practitioner *par excellence* of *administrative media studies*) cast further light on *critical* media-related studies. Lazarsfeld distinguished between "administrative" media research (research carried out at the behest of large organizations, generally to help them improve the effectiveness with which they used media), and "critical" media research. In making the distinction, Lazarsfeld had Max Horkheimer and Theodor Adorno firmly in mind, the latter for a time being a colleague of Lazarsfeld's at Princeton. Lazarsfeld suggested four major differences. First, unlike administrative research, critical media research supplies a broad, often historical context. Second, it addresses the "general role of our media of communication in the present social situation." Third, it develops "a theory of the prevailing social trends of our time." Fourth, it insists on "ideas of basic human values according to which all actual or desired effects should be appraised."[30] It is this last-mentioned dimension—the appraisal of actual circumstances and practices in light of enduring human values and ideals—that makes the term, "critical," so apt.

Unmentioned by Lazarsfeld but also characterizing critical media research are its dialectical mode of analysis,[31] its interdisciplinarity,[32] its negative stance toward both concentrated power and instrumental reason,[33] its attempt to integrate philosophy and social analysis,[34] and its focus on the social totality.[35] Practically speaking, a researcher's self-positioning as administrative or critical will have a significant bearing on the choice of research projects, Lazarsfeld himself being a prime example as illustrated by his refusal to study the relationship between the U.S. Congress, the Federal Communications Commission, and the broadcasting companies because (as he confided to his memoirs) "a budding research institute is dependent on the media and must try to avoid losing their support."[36]

CRITICAL MEDIA STUDIES

Today, however, and this is of course the main point, critical media studies is split in two. There is both a *critical political economy*, which has a materialist and generally social science orientation, and a *critical cultural studies*, which is more closely aligned with the arts, literature, and humanities. In a very real sense, the Frankfurt School birthed both these modes of critical media analysis. This chapter traces through the beginnings of critical political economy of media, while chapter 2 addresses cultural studies.

ORIGINS OF CRITICAL POLITICAL ECONOMY OF MEDIA

Within critical political economy of media, there are two major approaches (see figure 1.1). One stems from Marxism, with Theodor W. Adorno (1903–1969) of the Frankfurt School, I argue here, being foundational. A virtue of Adorno's approach to media studies is that it fully integrates critical political economy and cultural studies.

Adorno, however, is seldom identified as an inaugurator of critical political economy of media. There are likely three main reasons for this neglect. First, Adorno is (justifiably) associated more with the arts and humanities than with the social sciences. He was, after all, a musician, a musicologist, a philosopher, and an aesthete; he ruminated on Beethoven, Wagner, Kierkegaard, Spengler, Nietzsche, Hegel, jazz, and the philosophy of music. Hence, he is associated more with cultural studies than political economy, and indeed is celebrated, with others of the Frankfurt School, as a founder of cultural studies.[37] In terms of volume, if not necessarily importance, his writings on aesthetics do indeed dwarf his contributions to political economy. Second, Adorno's most renowned essay on the political economy of media, namely "The Culture Industry: Enlightenment as Mass Deception," is a chapter in a book (*Dialectic of Enlightenment*, coauthored with Max Horkheimer) dedicated to critiquing instrumental reason. Unfolding the political economy of media in that book was but a means to a larger end. Third, both the essay and the book, although written in California, were initially published in German (1947, with a mimeographed version circulating in 1944); the essay was not published in English until 1972.

This is not so say, however, that Adorno was without influence with regard to a nascent literature on the political economy of media. His essay, "The Stars Come Down to Earth," on the astrology column of the *Los Angeles Times,* was written in English in 1952–1953, and it draws repeated connections to the larger and more general outputs of the culture industry. Adorno's editor, J. M. Bernstein, proposed that "most of the central tenets of his theory of the *culture industry*" were formulated in his earlier essay of 1938, "On the Fetish Character in Music and the Regression of Listening."[38] It was noted previously that Lazarsfeld had Adorno and Horkheimer firmly in mind when distinguishing in 1941 between administrative and critical media studies. George Gerbner, C. Wright Mills, and others were likewise influenced by Horkheimer and Adorno.

But initial influence aside (and after all, the essential point here is that Adorno was not and is not influential enough!), it is indisputably a fact that Adorno (with Horkheimer) *invented* the analytical construct, *the culture industry*, and did so to help describe and investigate the consequences of mass producing culture for purposes of profit. As Andrew Fagan notes, Adorno was likely the first to identify the entertainment industry as a major site of elite domination within contemporary capitalist societies, and first to connect that domination with broader structures of political-economic power.[39] Adorno himself, years later, affirmed that the term *culture industry* likely was used for the first time in *The Dialectic of Enlightenment*.[40] In brief, Adorno inaugurated political economy studies of media.

Deborah Cook concurs: "Adorno's attempt [was] to develop one of the first critiques of the political economy of the culture industry using Marx's ideas about capitalist modes of production and the commodity form."[41] Cook characterizes Adorno's *culture industry* as being "geared to profit-making, controlled by centralized interlocking corporations, and staffed with marketing and financial experts, management, and production teams, technicians, 'star' reporters, writers, actors, musicians, and other creative talent."[42]

J. M. Bernstein, who compiled several of Adorno's essays on the culture industry into a book, described culture industry this way: "The culture industry, which involves the production of works for reproduction and mass consumption, thereby organizing 'free' time, the remnant domain of freedom under capital in accordance with the same principles of exchange and equivalence that reign in the sphere of production outside leisure, presents culture and the realization of the right of all to the gratification of desire while in reality continuing the negative integration of society."[43] Why "negative integration"? Because the culture industry effects a series of falsifications: pseudo-individuality replaces individuality, pleasure is confused with happiness, consensus is mistaken for freedom.[44] Adorno understood commercial mass media as inculcating and reinforcing tendencies of psychological dependence and social conformity.

Although certainly inspired by Marxism, and today still generally considered a Marxist,[45] in the present book I refer to Adorno as "*neo*-Marxist"—due to his heightened attention to the symbolic or cognitive *superstructure*, to his abandoning such basic tenets as class warfare between capital and labor to focus instead on elite-mass conflicts, and to his denial of the doctrine of inevitable progress through the working out of the materialist dialectic. For Adorno, the fulfillment of capitalism was not socialism or communism, but fascism, since fascism "continued reason's work of domination through integration and unification."[46] As noted by Stephen Crook, "Adorno saw the commodified American culture of mass-consumption, movies, jazz and radio serials as putting into play the same basic psychodynamic principles that formed the basis of fascism: psychological dependency and social conformism."[47] If some contemporary critical political economists have reverted to a more "vulgar" Marxism since the time of Adorno, that does not gainsay the point that at this point of origin (Adorno-Horkheimer), critical political economy of media was "*neo*-Marxist."

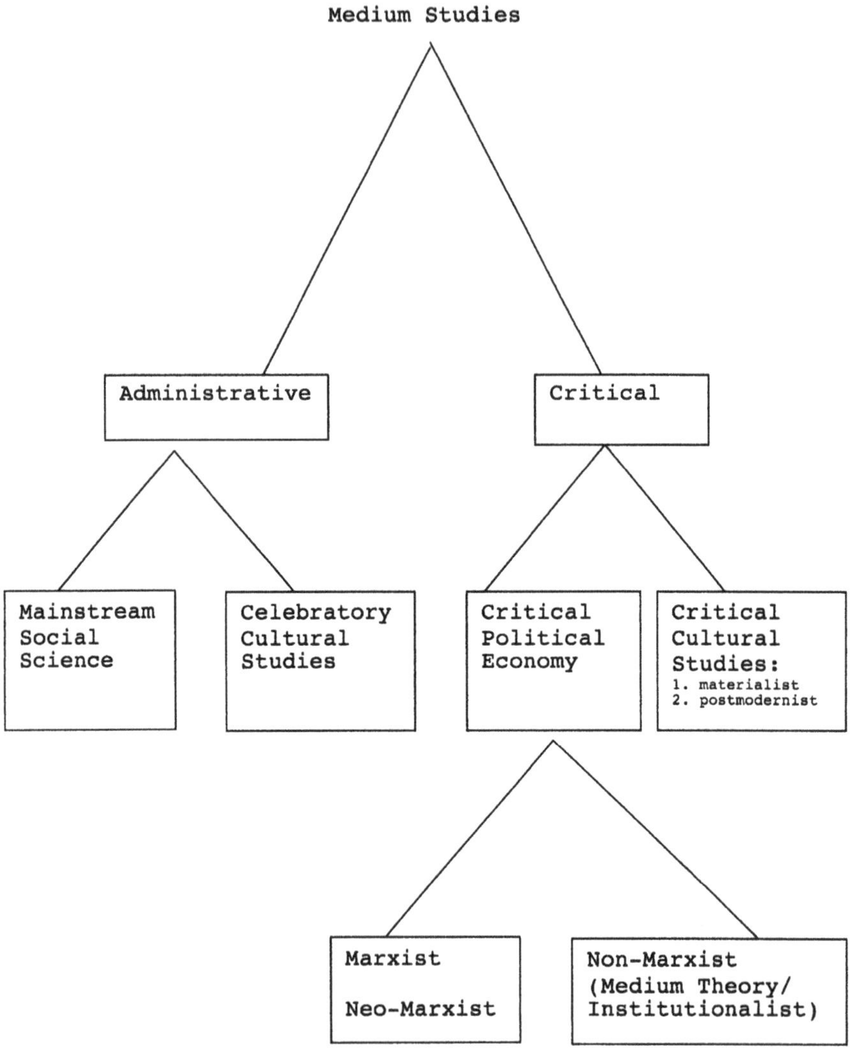

Figure 1.1. Typology of Media/Communication Studies. Media Studies has both administrative and critical camps, which are in turn divided into arts/humanities ("cultural studies") and social science ("political economy").

The second stream of critical political economy, a non-Marxian ("institutionalist") approach, also known as *communication in history* and as *medium theory*, was inaugurated by a Canadian economic historian, Harold Adams Innis (1894–1952). Innis took his PhD in economics from the University of Chicago (1920), where he became familiar with, among other writings, the works of maverick political economist Thorstein Veblen, to whom Innis was much indebted.[48] Indeed, among Innis' earliest publications is a tribute to Veblen.[49] Begrudgingly, Innis also acknowledged certain affinities with Marx: "Much of this will smack of Marxian interpretation," he wrote, "but I have tried to use the Marxian interpretation to interpret Marx; there has been no systematic pushing of the Marxian conclusion to its ultimate limit, and in pushing it to its limit, showing its limitations."[50]

Like Adorno, however, Innis, too, is seldom singled out as a founder of critical political economy of media. Here again, I can propose possible explanations. First, Innis was Canadian. He worked at the margin of the U.S. center. Elsewhere I have speculated whether John Kenneth Galbraith, like Innis an economist of Scottish ancestry and born in close proximity to Innis in rural southwestern Ontario, would have attained international acclaim had he chosen to spend his career at the University of Toronto instead of Harvard, or to advise Canadian prime ministers instead of U.S. presidents.[51] Second, Innis turned to media studies only late in his abbreviated life, focusing for most of his career on Canadian economic history. Third, while certainly paying attention to contemporary media, particularly advertising and news systems, Innis' canvass was far grander than is usual among political economists; he wrote about media practices and media control in ancient Greece, Rome, China, Babylon, Sumer, and Egypt, as well as in medieval Europe and (then-contemporary) America. Hence, many think of him as a historian of media, rather than as a political economist.

Nonetheless, Innis' credentials as an inaugurator of political economy approaches to media studies, like those of Adorno, are impeccable. Innis was likely the first to proclaim that, to persist, political-economic power needs to control the media of communication. He emphasized the struggle to control media, which for him was part and parcel of the struggle for political-economic dominance. He related shifts in media technologies to changes in the distribution of political and economic power, both domestically and internationally. He invented the term "monopolies of knowledge" to represent not only concentration of media ownership and control, but also of the knowledges circulating in society as they affect people's perceptions and understandings. He coined the term "information industries" to highlight the economic/industrial dimensions of cultural production. He related industrial processes generally, such as the quest for economies of scale and mass marketing, to the production and distribution of culture through such constructs as "the mechanization of knowledge." Moreover, Innis' analyses of the political-economic dimensions of media and changes in media technologies and patterns of media control were fully integrated to such cultural categories as conceptions of time, conceptions of space, education, literacy, the news and mass entertainment, and the mass production of culture. All this he accomplished between 1946 and 1952.

Innis' innovative contributions have been acknowledged. According to Professor Paul Heyer, for example, Innis founded *medium theory,* also known as *communication and history*—the practice of placing media of communication at the very center of historical analysis.[52] American media scholar, James W. Carey, likewise credited Innis with founding "the modern studies that now exist under the banner of media imperialism,"[53] surely an aspect of political economy. Innis inspired an extensive and still burgeoning literature.[54]

Nonetheless, it is safe to say that, outside of Canada, Innis remains marginal. Reasons for this marginality, though, while of interest, are really beside the point. The important issues are whether he *deserves* to be credited with (co-)founding political-economic approaches to media studies, and even more importantly, what have been the repercussions of his neglect. As with Adorno, I propose here that Innis seamlessly weaved together aspects of what are now known as cultural studies and political-economic analyses of media, and that rescuing both scholars from the inattention they have unjustifiably received in this regard could go a long way toward reestablishing conversations between cultural studies and political economy—to the betterment of both fields.

Although theoretical similarities (I will argue) abound between Innis and the founding members of the Frankfurt School, in terms of biography their differences could hardly be greater. Innis was a farm boy, who grew up in a staunchly Baptist household virtually bereft of books. He attended a one-room school in rural southwestern Ontario for his primary education. Moreover, for most of his life Innis remained untouched by literature, music, and the arts. "I never heard him quote a line of poetry," remarked friend and fellow historian, Arthur Lower, "and I suspect that to him poetry would have appeared not worth a serious man's attention."[55] Innis enlisted in World War I but, injured at Vimy Ridge, returned home, in his own words a "psychological casualty," and as well a rather embittered agnostic.

Although securing a PhD from Chicago after the war, and a teaching position in the Department of Political Economy at the University of Toronto, and despite receiving the acclaim of his peers (he is the only Canadian, apart from Galbraith, then at Harvard, to become President of the American Economics Association) Innis humbly described himself as a "dirt economist." He actually visited the regions he wrote about to mingle with the miners, trappers, lumberjacks, and fishers. As a component of his research for his book, *The Fur Trade in Canada,* he canoed down the Peace River to Lake Athabasca and, by the Slave River, to Great Slave Lake, and then down the Mackenzie. According to biographer Donald Creighton, Innis attained thereby a knowledge of the northlands "such as none of his contemporary Canadian scholars would ever possess."[56] Members of the Frankfurt School, in contrast, almost to the man, were sons of well-to-do European Jewish businessmen (in Adorno's case, only one parent was Jewish) who fled German fascism in the 1930s for the United States. In their writings, they often forsook praxis in the name of theoretical "purity."[57] According to Martin Jay, Adorno and his coauthor Max Horkheimer combined "a rigorous philosophical mind with a sensibility more aesthetic than scientific."[58] Nor did Adorno ever abandon "his cultural elitism,"[59] and "despite the fervent expressions of solidarity with the proletariat . . . at no time did [Adorno or other members] of the Institut affect the life-style of the working class."[60]

What the Frankfurt scholars did share with Innis, though, and evidently decisively so, even at the height of their renown, was a lingering sense of marginality, a condition that might be termed that of the "insider-outsider."[61] Thorstein Veblen, himself a classic example, described that condition as it applied to Jewish intellectuals.[62] Innis, too, however, was resolutely an outsider, even when acknowledged at the highest echelons of Canadian, if not indeed international, scholarship. He was a lifelong dissenter who railed against concentrations of power, the mechanization of knowledge, and the totalitarian nature of "our way of life."

Another plausible candidate for point of origin of critical political economy of media is the University of Illinois at Urbana–Champaign, where Dallas W. Smythe in 1948–1949 began teaching the first course in the United States on the political economy of communication.[63] Initially (early-to-mid-1950s), Smythe's focus in his published work, however, was confined to content analyses of commercial television programming as undertaken for the National Association of Educational Broadcasters.[64] While radical for the time (this was the McCarthy era, after all), this research did not approach the scope or the radical critique of his later writings, the turning point undoubtedly being his 1957 monograph, *The Structure and Policy of Electronic Communication*. Smythe's seminal article, "On the Political Economy of Communications," appeared in 1960, and his book on the political economy of media, *Dependency Road,* in 1981, many years after he had left Illinois for the University of Saskatchewan at Regina. Several of the major constructs developed in *Dependency Road*—the "consciousness industry,"[65] the commodification of culture, audience-as-commodity, the consumption of entertainment as extended work time, conflicts between individual psychological needs and requirements of the socio-economic system—are anticipated in Horkheimer and Adorno's work of the late 1930s and 1940s. While Smythe without doubt made immense contributions to the political economy of communication, in terms of beginnings stronger cases can be made for both Adorno and Innis.

ADORNO

Through their concept of *the culture industry* (that is, enterprises engaged in the mass production, reproduction, and distribution for profit of cultural artifacts[66]), Adorno and Horkheimer laid the foundation for neo-Marxian analyses of media. For these authors, to adequately understand culture, it is insufficient merely to depict general relations between various cultural products (say, musical genres) and social life. Rather, one needs to explore how cultural products help organize society (allocate leisure time and promote passivity and conformity in audiences, for example), and address in detail the production, reproduction, distribution, exchange, and consumption of cultural commodities.[67]

In what follows, I summarize Adorno's seminal contributions to a nascent political economy of media. Some of his descriptions will seem dated, referring as they often do to media products of the 1940s and earlier, but the connections he forged between cultural production and power remain as pertinent as ever. The goal here is not to canvass the full corpus of Adorno's work.[68] Nor is Adorno presented necessarily as an archetype for the entire Frankfurt tradition. Rather, the point is simply that in formulating and forwarding the culture industry as an important analytical category, Adorno (with Horkheimer) helped introduce a Marxian-inspired political economy mode of media analysis, major aspects of which were later elaborated by successor political economists, and he did so in such a way as to integrate what are today regarded as critical political economy and cultural studies.

Commodification of Culture

In his 1944 essay with Horkheimer entitled "The Culture Industry" (published in English in 1977), and in articles compiled posthumously as a book bearing the same title, Adorno claimed that cultural production had by then become an industrial process akin to other industrial processes. The "culture industry," like other industries, he proposed, produces and purveys commodities for profit in response to market conditions, including revenues, costs, market structures, marketing/advertising, competition, and so on. For Adorno, "Culture now impresses the same stamp on everything; films, radio and magazines make up a system which is uniform as a whole and in every part."[69]

Adorno is criticized these days for insisting that the culture industry produces sameness in cultural commodities. Postmodernists[70] particularly point to the seemingly enormous range of cultural commodities from which individuals can select to construct and reconstruct personal "identities."[71] However, as noted by Stephen Crook, using mass-produced commodities to construct "identities" or "lifestyles" actually entails a good deal of conformity, and hence this practice can be understood as affirming Adorno's essential position: "The successful adoption of a lifestyle is only possible, only recognizable as such on the basis of conformity," Crook writes. Indeed, he goes further to suggest that "postmodernizing change might be seen as intensifying, rather than relaxing, pressures toward dependency and conformism through the demand for information."[72]

For Adorno, the culture industry has become a "totality" through which "the whole world is made to pass,"[73] so much so that it now controls both "high" and "low" art, obscuring or effacing demarcations that for centuries had delimited the two.[74] In previous eras, according to Adorno, high art served the noble function of critique by providing "negative knowledge of the actual world."[75] (Prime examples of this, one might interject, were the Dadaist painters and sculptors of the 1920s in Weimar Germany, prior to the tight state control of art for propagandistic purposes.[76]) Fulfilling the important role of critique was possible, according to Adorno, only because and to the extent that artists were free from pressures to conform. To be sure, in both the Middle Ages and the Renaissance there had often been a "unity of style," as influenced by the respective structures of social power. Nonetheless, Adorno insisted, the truly great artists frequently transcended conformist pressures. However, contemporaneous with the rise of mass media, which is to say with the birth of the culture industry, "high art" became transformed. Retaining still perhaps vestiges of its venerable critical function, high art now, for the most part, reveals "obedience to the social hierarchy;" it has become little more than mere style.[77] Contemporary high art is renowned less for its "autonomous essence," or for its "own specific content and harmonious formation," than for its money value attributable to its role as status symbol.[78] Adorno and Horkheimer summarized: "The prestige seeker replaces the connoisseur. . . . No object [today] has an inherent value; it is valuable only to the extent that it can be exchanged."[79]

"Low" or popular art likewise is diminished, in Adorno's view. No longer the authentic voice of working people, low art has been taken over and commodified by the culture industry. Through easy replication, mass distribution, and centralized administration, mass culture is packaged "as a commodity for narcissistic consumption,"[80] depriving individuals "from coming to consciousness of themselves as subjects."[81]

Dialectic of Art

Music, like all art, for Adorno, is intrinsically dialectical. On the one hand, music is "the immediate manifestation of impulse;" on the other, it is "the locus of its taming."[82] By expressing impulse, for instance, impulse is "tamed."

The "disciplining function" of music has long been known. But, in the age of the culture industry, the contradictions are taken to a new level. When working people made their own music, it rebelled against conventions and oppression through "impulse, subjectivity and profanation;" when music is produced by the culture industry, however, "the listener is converted, along his line of least resistance, into the acquiescent purchaser. . . . Representatives of the opposition to the authoritarian schema become witnesses to the authority of commercial success."[83] Music complements the reduction of people to silence, filling "the pockets of silence that develop between people moulded by anxiety, work and undemanding docility."[84]

Adorno and Horkheimer chose the term *the culture industry* rather than *mass culture* to emphasize that non-elite culture for the most part no longer arises spontaneously from the grass roots; nor is it to be understood as the contemporary form of popular culture.[85] Rather, they insisted, the outputs of the culture industry are consciously and purposefully manufactured by elites whose intent is to make money.[86] Whereas authentic popular culture, for Adorno, is not merely rebellious but is also an "expression of suffering and contradiction [whereby people attempt] to maintain a grasp on the idea of the good life,"[87] outputs of the culture industry falsely insist that "the good life" is attainable here and now, that by conforming to the consumptionist ethic happiness is available immediately.

Control of Consciousness

Commercial media, then, Adorno claimed, impose "civilizational constraints" on cultural commodities by removing rebelliousness or calls to dissent previously characterizing popular culture.[88] In contrast to genuinely working class songs and other cultural artifacts, one might note, commercial media rarely call for picketing or boycotting; rather, voting (for pre-selected and heavily marketed candidates) is set forth as the hallmark of democratic expression.[89]

In his analysis of the astrology column of the *Los Angeles Times,* for instance, Adorno pointed to its essentially conservative ideology, its justifying of the status quo, and its promulgating social conformity.[90] The column implicitly urged readers to adjust themselves "to the commands of the stars at given times," emphasizing thereby "the individual's powerlessness" in the face of cosmic design, which the column compensated for "with suggestions of unexpected good fortune, assistance and the like."[91] Adorno's editor, J. M. Bernstein, adds, "What holds for astrology exemplifies the culture industry generally from advertising to film and television."[92] One wishes that Adorno might have lived long enough to unfold the conformity-inducing function of lotteries!

As a means of promoting conformity, Adorno and Horkheimer remarked that radio was clearly an advance over the telephone, as it turns "all participants into listeners. . . . No machinery of rejoinder has been devised."[93] (Since Adorno's time, of course, talk radio—ostensibly a two-way forum—has become the rage; arguably listeners who call in, however, are often little more than sounding boards for the radio host.) For Adorno and Horkheimer, technological innovations of all sorts, not just mass media, deepen elite control over society: "A technological rationale *is* the rationale of domination itself."[94]

Curtailing controversy by controlling discussion of basic issues is not the only means whereby the culture industry strengthens the already powerful. Also important is the diversionary function of entertainment. According to Horkheimer and Adorno, in what might be seen as an unduly puritanical declaration but one nonetheless pinpointing an important elite strategy and typical audience response:

> Pleasure always means not to think about anything, to forget suffering even where it is shown. Basically it is helplessness. It is flight; not, as is asserted, flight from a wretched reality, but from the last remaining thought of resistance. The liberation which amusement promises is freedom from thought and from negation.[95]

According to Adorno, the culture industry constructs reality for its audiences. Referring to the movies of the 1940s but anticipating by decades the enculturation studies of George Gerbner and colleagues (see chapter 4 in this volume), Horkheimer and Adorno remarked on "the old experience of the movie-goer, who sees the world outside as an extension of the film he has just left. . . . The illusion [prevails] that the outside world is the straightforward continuation of that presented on the screen."[96] Adorno later qualified these remarks, writing:

> What the culture industry presents people with in their free time . . . is indeed consumed and accepted, but with a kind of reservation, in the same way that even the most naïve theatre or filmgoers do not simply take what they behold there for real. . . . It is not quite believed in. It is obvious that the integration of consciousness and free time has not yet completely succeeded.[97]

Regarding the more contemporary scene, a development, arguably, has been the culture industry's frequent depictions of poststructuralist positions: for instance that artifice, simulation, or hyperreality are everywhere and are virtually indistinguishable from the real, or have displaced the real. Such is the common thread linking otherwise disparate movies like *Last Year at*

Marienbad, Wag the Dog, The Truman Show, The Matrix trilogy, *Pleasantville, The Island, The Purple Rose of Cairo,* and *Stranger Than Fiction.* On the one hand, one could argue that in drawing attention to simulations, these films foster a more critical, more discerning audience, one less likely to be "duped," to quote Lawrence Grossberg. Another possibility, however, is that the films, although undoubtedly amusing and perhaps thought provoking, essentially propagate positions forwarded by scholars like Jean Baudrillard and Mark Poster, *viz.* that since we are now "submerged"[98] in simulations and the hyperreal, truth has become an anachronous concept.[99] If this latter interpretation predominates, then the culture industry can be viewed as responding to audiences' lingering doubts, which Adorno had noted, by proposing that authenticity itself is a romantic and outmoded concept.

Horkheimer and Adorno suggested also that the leisure industry prolongs and extends work, because "entertainment" often attunes workers into fitting the requirements of capitalist society.[100] Adorno gave sports as an example, speculating that the physical exertion and "functionalization" of the body in team activity subtly train people into modes of behavior required by the work place.[101] "Sports," he wrote, "is not play but ritual in which the subjected celebrate their subjection; they parody freedom in their readiness for service, a service which the individual exacts from his own body." The athlete, he continued, plays the role of the master by inflicting on his "slave" (his own body) "the same injustice he has already endured at the violent hands of society."[102] Sports as indoctrination has been the subject of several studies since the time of Adorno.[103] More generally, Adorno declared that experiences of mass culture are "inevitably after-images of the work process itself . . . so profoundly does mechanization determine the manufacture of leisure goods."[104]

More generally, Adorno claimed that centralized administration had transformed mass culture "into a medium of undreamed of psychological control."[105] This it accomplished through positive and negative messages, prescriptions, taboos, schemata, and stereotypes. Stereotypical images and schematized themes, Deborah Cook explains, enlarging on Adorno, "prevent individuals from thinking beyond the given."[106] She claims Adorno was among the first to compare the products of the culture industry with Nazi propaganda, arguing that in both cases stereotypes and schemata play upon the emotions and irrational impulses of mass audiences in order to undermine their critical and rational thought.[107]

For Adorno, products of the culture industry are layered with meanings, with the hidden layers often being the more important as they bypass the defenses of the consciousness.[108] He wrote: "Probably all the various levels in mass media involve *all* the mechanisms of consciousness and unconsciousness stressed by psychoanalysis."[109] Layers of meanings, indeed, constituted one of several portals whereby Adorno introduced Freudian categories into his analysis. Whereas layers of meaning are used by the culture industry to "handle" audiences, multiplicity of meanings also implies that the culture industry can never take for granted the effects intended for audiences.[110]

Matters for Adorno, however, are yet more complex. For example, whereas "heterodox ideology" is often used by the culture industry to attract interest, in the end orthodoxies are invariably promoted. Often the more sensationalist a newspaper is, for example, the more conservative its orientation. Adorno remarked that tabloid newspapers often use excesses to attract circulation, but in the end affirm a conventional "moral of the story."[111] Likewise, many feature films today contain "excesses" to attract audience interest, but in the end they support existing distributions of political and economic power (*Pearl Harbor, Armageddon,* and *Independence Day,* for example). It is also likely, however, that a critical cinema is much more evident in our day than it was in Adorno's—*Fahrenheit 911, The Corporation, Blood Diamond, Syriana,* and *Manufacturing Consent* being prime examples.

Political Economy of Art and Knowledge

While cultural monopolies may appear to be strong, according to Adorno and Horkheimer, in fact they are weak: they "cannot afford to neglect their appeasement of the real holders of power if their sphere of activity in mass society . . . is not to undergo a series of purges."[112] The authors here may have had in mind purges against critical artists in Nazi Germany (Bertoldt Brecht, Fritz Lang, the Berlin Dadaists and Expressionists, for instance), but closer to home they became only too familiar with American intolerance during the Red Scare of the 1950s and beyond.

In addition to political/military repressions and pressures, of course, there are also the corporations—what Raymond Williams termed "extra-parliamentary formations of political and economic power,"[113] which include the great financial institutions and transnational corporations. Indeed, Horkheimer and Adorno provided a rudimentary description of the entanglement of cultural monopolies and larger political-economic structures: "The dependence of the most powerful broadcasting company [NBC] on the electrical industry [GE], or of the motion picture industry on the banks, is characteristic of the whole sphere, whose individual branches are themselves economically interwoven."[114] In making these claims Horkheimer and Adorno were prescient, as one of the major activities of present day critical political economy is mapping lines of control over concentrated media by advertisers and large industrial structures, by the military, and by governments.[115]

Adorno wrote also of "servile intellectuals"[116] who downplay the control aspects of the culture industry and celebrate instead its fun and democratic veneer. *Uses and gratifications* theorists, for example, insist that audiences, not media companies, are in control as audiences purportedly select from a vast array of media offerings in accordance with their pre-existing needs and preferences (the doctrine of consumer sovereignty). One such "need" is to be entertained, and we just saw Adorno's riposte to that. Another is to perceive order or pattern to an otherwise chaotic existence. Adorno acknowledged that need, too, but claimed the media's *covert* response is to inculcate ideology. He explained:

> The concepts of order which it [the culture industry] hammers into human beings are always those of the status quo. They remain unquestioned, unanalysed and undialectically presupposed. . . . The power of the culture industry's ideology is such that conformity has replaced consciousness.[117]

In the face of all this, Adorno contended, the public remains largely placid. Although not unaware of the deceptions inherent in the proffers of the culture industry, he suggested, people tend to view the fleeting gratifications as adequate compensation.[118] On the other hand, as noted previously, he also claimed that people's "deep unconscious mistrust" keeps them from construing the world entirely in accordance with the culture industry's representations.[119]

Instrumental Reason

Equally problematic, according to Horkheimer and Adorno, is the *instrumental reason* of western culture generally and of modern science in particular. Whereas philosophical convention since the Enlightenment has counterposed reason and domination, due to reason's capacity to undermine dogma and superstition, Adorno maintained that reason itself is thoroughly entangled with domination—not just of nature, as Francis Bacon had proposed, but also of other people, and even of the self:

> Knowledge, which is power, knows no obstacles: neither in the enslavement of men nor in compliance with the world's rulers. . . . What men want to learn from nature is how to use it in order wholly to dominate it and other men.[120]

At this point Adorno again turned to Freudian psychoanalytical theory. The Enlightenment's insistence on the rule of reason, he attested, leads to the repression of all sorts of irrational drives, desires, fears, instincts, and sensory experiences. Horkheimer and Adorno drew on the myth of Odysseus to illustrate the conflicted human condition in the age of Enlightenment.[121] The culture industry is, of course, well aware of repressions, and uses this knowledge to exact compliance on the part of audiences.

Adorno and Horkheimer also associated the Enlightenment with the rise of selfish individualism, at the expense of solidarity and community, a tendency most certainly played upon and amplified by the commercial media. "Whoever resigns himself to life without any reference to self-preservation," they remarked, "would, according to the Enlightenment . . . regress to prehistory [i.e., to mythic consciousness]."[122] For Adorno, Spinoza's dictum—the drive to self-preservation is the primary virtue—was the cardinal rule of Enlightenment morality.

Adorno and Horkheimer insisted also that Enlightenment rationality erodes meaning, as formula (algorithm) substitutes for concept.[123] Moreover, the "Enlightenment has put aside the classical requirement of thinking about thought. . . . Mathematical procedure became, so to speak, the ritual of thinking."[124] This is most unfortunate as *reflexivity* for Adorno should be an important aspect of scholarship. Contemporary science and reason, then, for Adorno and Horkheimer, are hardly roads to emancipation. But, unfortunately, in the age of capitalism, neither are the arts, for reasons noted earlier.

As we will see shortly, Harold Innis shared Adorno's distrust of the Enlightenment. Ironically, that same distrust characterizes, indeed motivates, poststructuralists. It is not this overriding concern with regard to the Enlightenment, then, that separates the founding political economists from poststructuralists; rather, as we shall see, it is their dichotomous responses.

Essentials of a Critical Political Economy

Contained in these brief excerpts and summaries are some of the fundamentals for critical political economy of media and culture. These fundamentals include: the claim of marked asymmetries in the distribution of communicatory power; an emphasis on the oppression, manipulation, and control through media by an elite; the notion of domination of media as a prerequisite to attaining and maintaining political-economic power; media as devices for influencing if not controlling consciousness and limiting resistance; economic power as affecting cultural production, including both scholarship and commercial culture; transformations wrought by commodification (exchange value suppressing use value); critique of science, technology, and instrumental reason; creative arts as a possible but waning key to critical understanding; emphasis on the social totality; and the importance of contradiction, reflexivity, and dialectics.

The role of dialectics in Adorno's political economy deserves particular emphasis. As noted above, Adorno maintained that historically, prior to the rise of the culture industry, tension or opposition between both high and low culture on the one hand and established power on the other was continually in play. In the contemporary period, although the dialectic of capital-labor may have waned, class conflict—now between elite and mass—continues apace. Despite the ubiquity and the seeming acceptance of the proffers of the culture industry, the general public (the mass) possesses at least a latent capacity to see through the dissimulations and deceptions. Belief in this "unconscious distrust" is what motivated Adorno to "expose the socio-psychological implications and mechanisms [so that] the public at large may be sensitized to the nefarious effect of some of these mechanisms."[125] Borrowing from Freud, Adorno insisted that each individual's psychological needs and drives are in fundamental conflict with the socio-economic order, that while the culture industry both "solicits and represses the instincts" in order to encourage conformity with the prevailing economic system, it can never be fully successful.[126] Repression, of course, implies latent conflict. Indeed, by his continual invocation of Freudian psychology, one might say that Adorno's analyses are riddled with conflict, which is to say *dialectics*. For example, the pervasiveness of commodity exchange tends to transform people's interpersonal relations into relations between things, contradicting deep-seated needs for meaningful interpersonal contact, if not indeed a sense of community.[127]

Perhaps most fundamentally, though, as Martin Jay suggests, the whole Frankfurt enterprise was in fact dialectical in the sense of being "contrapuntal." It opposed closed philosophical systems. It was "essentially open-ended, probing, unfinished."[128] Critical Theory consisted of "a series of critiques of other thinkers and philosophical traditions."[129] In this section we have reviewed Adorno's oppositional (dialectical) stance toward classical Marxism, instrumental reason, scientism and the Enlightenment, popular culture, and the culture industry. The implication is that even Adorno's own analyses should be subject to critique, in accordance with the dynamism of the dialectic.

INNIS AND MEDIUM THEORY[130]

From the mid-1940s to the early 1950s, Canadian economic historian Harold Adams Innis inaugurated a non-Marxist (institutionalist) stream of critical political economy within media studies. In fact, Innis made *two* exceptional contributions to scholarship. In addition to *medium theory*, Innis was the architect also of what is now known as the *staples thesis* of Canadian economic development. I will address each, beginning with the staples thesis.

The Staples Thesis

According to the staples thesis of Canadian economic development, the extraction or processing of staples or natural resources (first fish, then fur, timber, wheat, and minerals) transformed environments, with important consequences for people's thought structures, social organization, and activities. In *The Cod Fisheries,* for example, Innis noted that the fish trade, centered on submerged land masses forming multitudinous bays and harbors along the Atlantic coast of North America, induced decentralized control. Prior to settlement, law and order were enforced in each harbor by an "admiral," the sea captain whose ship was first to arrive in the spring. Initially, settlements established on the basis of the European demand for fish were limited to coastal areas, resulting in their isolation from the continent's interior. The shift westward of the fur trade and the subsequent development of the timber trade, however, encouraged more complete settlement, particularly in areas of the St. Lawrence River. In Newfoundland, however, geography and climate severely constrained agricultural development, and so specialization in cod continued.[131]

According to Innis, the rise to predominance of a new staple, in combination with technological change, invariably produced a "period of crisis." Adjustments needed to be made and new patterns of social interaction developed.[132] Groups controlling the new staple and the new technology ascended to power, while the influence of the group associated with the old staple and the old technology waned.

In *The Fur Trade in Canada* Innis emphasized the disruption or imbalance resulting when previously separate civilizations come into closer contact. Fur (beaver pelts), in a sense, was a medium bringing "a relatively complex civilization" into contact with "a much more simple civilization"[133]—with dramatic consequences. Concentrating on fur production meant that European settlers lacked the motivation to develop indigenous manufacturing.[134] Moreover, the infrastructure (transportation, trade, finance) and government activities were subordinated to the production of staples for export rather than being developed to encourage a broader economic and social base. As Di Norcia, interpreting Innis, summarizes, "hinterland economies . . . are rigidly biased in favour of resources and their depletion."[135] The weakness of the colonies resulting from heavy specialization in staples also necessitated "reliance upon military support from the mother country."[136]

The medium of fur also had a drastic impact on indigenous peoples. In exchange for furs, native peoples acquired "iron goods" such as hatchets, knives, scissors, needles, and most significantly muskets,[137] greatly disrupting their ways of life. Guns, for instance, which replaced bows and arrows, required both periodic repair and a steady flow of parts and ammunition, making aboriginal people continuously dependent on Europeans. Rifles changed hunting practices drastically, diminishing to the point of virtual disappearance the supply of beavers in territories opened to the hunt. They also escalated the level of hostility among the various tribes which now competed for control over the prime hunting territories.[138] Innis lamented,

> The history of the fur trade is the history of contact between two civilizations, the European and the North American. . . . Unfortunately the rapid destruction of the food supply and the revolution in the methods of living accompanied by the increasing attention to the fur trade by which these products were secured, disturbed the balance which had grown up previous to the coming of the European. The new technology with its radical innovations brought about such a rapid shift in the prevailing Indian culture as to lead to wholesale destruction of the peoples concerned by warfare and disease.[139]

Innis did not propose staples as working their effects unidirectionally, or in isolation of other forces. His analysis, rather, concerned interactions among staples, the technologies used to harvest and transport them, and the geographic characteristics of the regions. These three factors—staples, geography, and technology—intersected to form distinct "amalgams."[140] As Alexander John Watson summarizes, Innis' staples thesis is "more complex, more universal, and less rigidly deterministic than commonly accepted; Innis never uses the staple as anything more than a focusing point around which to examine the interplay of cultures and empires."[141]

From Staples to Media

Innis' staples thesis prefigured his more renowned medium thesis in numerous ways. First, as just noted, staples may be regarded as media for bringing into contact previously isolated civilizations and biasing their relations in terms of dominance and dependence, and mediating also to the dual dialectic of continuity vs. change, and control over unbounded space vs. local control. Just as a change to a different staple accompanied new patterns of political-economic control, for Innis so too do new media usher in a new regime and alter the time-space organization of society. Second, as noted by Paul Heyer, ocean transport favored staples that were light and valuable (such as fur), whereas primary inland waterways favored bulk commodities (such as lumber and minerals), paralleling Innis' analysis of the physical properties of time-binding and space-binding communication media,[142] to be addressed below. Likewise, as Watson interpreting Innis noted, since "each staples-transportation system contains an unused capacity,"[143] the ensuing instability foreshadowed the *biases* featured in Innis' media studies. Third, the imperial centers of Innis' staples writings (England, France, USA) occupy a role equivalent to *monopolies of knowledge* in his media writings. Fourth, for Heyer, studying the pulp and paper staple opened "a door to the newly emergent field of communication studies; [Innis] simply followed pulp and paper through its subsequent stages: newspapers and journalism, books and advertising."[144] Marshall McLuhan made a similar suggestion, writing:

> Innis made the further transition from the history of staples to the history of the media of communication quite naturally. Media are major resources like economic staples. In fact, without railways, the staples of wheat and lumber can scarcely be said to exist. Without the press and the magazine, wood pulp could not exist as a staple either.[145]

Finally, as proposed first by Robin Neill, the staples and media theses are connected through Innis' continuing concern for *value*: "Through institutional formation," Neill wrote, "values [according to Innis] are embodied in the structure of economic activity, and therefore an explanation of economic advance is impossible unless the determinants of values can be specified."[146] Initially, Innis located these "determinants" in staples, albeit as interacting with geography, modes of extraction, modes of transportation, and with foreign demand. In his media writings, however, Innis proposed a more central role for transportation and communication: "The values that constitute society," Neill wrote, "are a set of judgments that, to a significant degree, are structured by the dominant means of transportation and communication; that is to say, the medium is the message."[147]

Medium Theory

In his introduction to *Empire and Communications,* first published in 1950, Innis gave a brief summary of what is today known as *medium theory*.[148] Innis claimed the physical attributes of media (their heaviness and durability, and elsewhere he mentioned also their capacity to store messages and their ease or difficulty in being encoded), cause them to be biased either toward supporting control through time (as exercised by religious leaders and others invoking custom, tradition, local culture, continuity, myth, collective memory, and ultimate meaning), or control over space (as exercised by large corporations, governments, and the military, all of which are intent on administering ever-larger territories in the present). Paper, for example, being lighter and more tractable than stone or parchment, and with the larger messaging capacity, is the more space-binding medium; in conjunction with the printing press, paper becomes more space-binding still. An alternative formulation of this space-time dialectic is *being vs. becoming*.[149]

However, as Edward Comor and others have noted, Innis was no technological or media determinist.[150] He maintained, rather, that a medium's influence in terms of space or time can be understood only within "the social-economic context of [its] use."[151] For example, Innis initially thought that radio, due to its reliance on sound and its apparent recalling of the oral tradition, would counterbalance the space bias of the newspaper. Given the commercial context of American media, however, Innis soon realized that radio amplifies the space bias of the press, rather than neutralizing it.[152] Similarly, although paper was invented in China centuries before its use became common in Europe, the political-economic conditions in ancient China coupled with the absence of a phonetic alphabet meant that paper did not have the dramatic space bias in China that it later had in Europe. Innis carefully selected such terms and phrases as "bias," "hastens," "facilitates," and "helps to define," to indicate that media emphasize, but do not determine.[153]

The absence of hard technological determinism in Innis' writings is illustrated as well by his stance toward scholarship. On the one hand, Innis believed, scholars (like everyone else) are affected by the biases of their era as supported particularly by the predominant media of communication. In fact, he expressed great concern that the universities were being captured by the "present-mindedness" characterizing military and corporate communications. On the one hand, it is lucrative for universities and scholars to work on behalf of the economically dominant interests. On the other, writing—the very means of scholarship—tends toward space bias and present-mindedness. Hence, in his preface to *Empire and Communications*, he cautioned, "All written works, *including this one*, have dangerous implications to the vitality of an oral tradition and to the health of a civilization."[154] And again, later in the same work: "The letter killeth and the concern has been with the diverse means by which different types of letters bring about their deadly results."[155] In brief, writing, and hence scholarship, have an inherent and potentially deadly bias.[156] However, Innis' response, obviously, was not to quit writing. Nor was it to try to de-authenticate theories and other "grand narratives." Rather, he endeavored to take the inherent bias of writing into account and compensate for it—a practice known as *reflexivity*: "Thought in the social sciences," Innis wrote, "grows by the development and correction of bias."[157] An important aspect of scholarship for Innis, then, was recognizing and adjusting for the biases that the means of communication present and encourage.[158]

Innis was also cognizant of his bias as an economist. In the preface to *The Bias of Communication* he confided: "With the bias of an economist I may have extended the theory of monopoly to undue limits." He then justified his approach, however, by claiming that "it is part of the task of the social scientist to test the limits of his tools and to indicate their possibilities,"[159] indicating yet another way whereby one can take his or her biases into account. Elsewhere he noted also the propensity of economists to overestimate the capacity of markets to resolve all sorts of problems, particularly in cases where "the social scientist is paid for obtaining such an appreciation."[160]

In addition to reflexivity and the pushing of concepts to their limits, Innis attempted to become aware of and to account for bias also by following the example of the classical Greeks in advocating balance between extremes. In particular, Innis emphasized both the desirability and difficulty of attaining, *and maintaining,* tension or balance between space and time as societal organizing principles (and, by implication, between the classes or groups supporting these divergent principles). He assuredly did not favor ultimate victory of one over the other (which would terminate the dialectic). Rather, he regarded in apocalyptic terms the current imbalance whereby space is overwhelming time. Innis' "balance," then, was not one of harmony or stability; rather, it was dynamic, ever shifting, wrought by struggle and tension, achieved through countervailing power or opposition. According to Robin Neill, Innisian balance means competition; "its opposite is monopoly."[161]

Innis followed the Greeks also in insisting that knowledge and power are normally in opposition. However, he approached this contradiction dialectically, so to speak.[162] On the one hand, he recognized that knowledge workers require the protection of the police, the state, and the military in order to do their work.[163] Moreover, he accepted Francis Bacon's dictum that knowledge is power, which is to say that applied knowledge empowers people. In both these senses, there is no opposition between knowledge and power. But as well, and seemingly in contradiction to the foregoing, Innis wrote: "Power and its assistant, force [are] the natural enemies of intelligence."[164] And again: "Force is no longer concerned with [the scholar's] protection and is actively engaged in schemes for his destruction."[165] In other words, Innis proposed a fundamental contradiction between knowledge and power. How, then, can these two views be reconciled?

For Innis, the flowering of intellectual and artistic creativity and freedom is possible only when political and economic power loosen their grip. He proposed that a creative high point in the life cycle of civilizations occurs when each is entering its death throes, for then knowledge workers and artists are freer to pursue truth, be creative, and engage in critical work. Another opportunity is when a new medium of communication, normally introduced from the margin by groups aspiring to power, challenges, eventually perhaps to supplant, an older medium. In *Empire and Communications* he surveyed civilizations, both ancient and modern, to show linkages among changing media, transformations in knowledge, and shifts in power. For Innis, only at rare intervals were space- and time-biased media truly in balance or in tension, thereby permitting the flowering of knowledge unencumbered by "monopolies." One such period was the golden age of Greece, when Plato inscribed the hitherto oral Socratic dialogues.[166]

For the contemporary period, Innis proposed a recursive (non-determinist, dialectical) relationship among culture, knowledge, and political-economic power. On the one hand, political-economic power exerts influence over science, affecting scientific research agendas and possibly causing scientists to distort their findings; on the other, even when impeccably carried out, science disfigures culture.

To illustrate the first claim, recall scientists in the employ of tobacco,[167] drug,[168] and certain oil companies,[169] who for pecuniary reasons apparently skewed "findings" concerning health or environmental consequences of their benefactors' activities and products.[170] Innis himself proposed that "the bias of economics . . . makes the best economists come from powerful countries,"[171] indicating that in his view mainstream economics favors the wealthy in their contestations with the poor. He drew attention also to the close conjuncture between science and the military, writing: "The universities are in danger of becoming a branch of the military arm."[172] The irony and tragedy of science, as he saw it, was that once it became free from the monopolies controlling time (a victory represented symbolically, perhaps, by Galileo's ultimate victory in his contestations with the Church), science succumbed to the monopolies controlling space (the military and commercial organizations).[173]

Much more could and should be said about this aspect of Innis' political economy of knowledge thesis, and I pursue that general theme further in chapter 4. Now, however, I turn to the second issue: how science acts recursively on culture. Innis wrote,

> The impact of science on cultural development has been evident in its contribution to technological advance, notably in communication and in the dissemination of knowledge. In turn it has been evident in the types of knowledge disseminated; that is to say, science lives its own life not only in the mechanism which is provided to distribute knowledge but also in the sort of knowledge which will be distributed.[174]

The manifestation, the making concrete, of scientific knowledge in new technologies is obvious enough: Internet, satellites, television, radio, and other "mechanisms . . . to distribute knowledge" may inspire awe just by their very *presence*, irrespective of content or the ostensible "messages." The evolving media infrastructure may well affect also one's view regarding the strength and nature of the existential constraints imposed by time and space.[175] Innis' second point, namely that new media are inherently biased or selective in the types of messages they transmit, is a more nuanced claim, and warrants elaboration.

In Innis' mind the space bias of contemporary society, that is, its undue emphasis on *being,* also referred to as *present-mindedness*—its disregard of traditions on the one hand, and insouciance concerning the future on the other—is associated strongly with "mechanized" media, defined as media that result from applied science. This space bias, not being offset to any large extent by oral dialectic (his favorite time-binding medium), engenders difficulties in understanding.

For Innis, the inventions of the mechanical printing press and the paper machine heralded the onset of mechanization in knowledge production and distribution.[176] Mechanization in knowledge production (as in other production), he observed, gives rise to both an "obsession with specialization"[177] and to dogged pursuit of economies of scale,[178] inducing thereby the rise of the "information industries."[179] (Very likely this is the first time this term, now a commonplace, appeared in print). In referring to mechanization of knowledge and of media, Innis had in mind not only larger presses and larger print runs, but as well larger class sizes in universities,[180] the use of mechanical instruments including books as teaching aids,[181] the discouragement of oral dialogue and the concomitant decline of critical, creative thought,[182] insistence on the efficacy of formulaic knowledge,[183] and perhaps most importantly undue emphasis on the present and on the transitory ("present-mindedness"). Citing Laski, Innis wrote sardonically, "Education . . . became the art of teaching men to be deceived by the printed word."[184]

Innis also insisted that organized force normally controls not just scholarship and education, but also popular culture, which he sometimes termed "the vernacular." He wrote: "The success of organized force is dependent on an effective combination of . . . the vernacular in public opinion with technology [or media of communication] and science."[185] Indeed, he claimed, once science had enfeebled religion "as an anchorage," the state (and, we could add, corporations) became "more dependent on cultural development."[186] It is in the area of "cultural development" that Innis' analysis and commentaries on press systems are particularly poignant and merge with Adorno's analysis of the culture industry.

"Freedom of the press" as guaranteed by the U.S. Constitution, Innis suggested dryly, *narrowed* the "marketplace of ideas."[187] Innis' coupling of freedom of the press with the growth of monopolies of knowledge on the face of it seems absurd, and so warrants further scrutiny. Innis had several things in mind. First, freedom of the press meant, in part, freedom of press owners to do as they pleased—even to combine into the monopolistic Associated Press news system and to enter into restrictive covenants with the telegraph company, Western Union; in other words, freedoms enjoyed by press systems included, for a time, the freedom to engage in monopolistic business practices.

Second, the freedom to publish, affirmed by the First Amendment, is a right possessed by owners of the press to publish what they wish, and *pari passu* to exclude viewpoints and spokespersons as the owners see fit.[188] Consequently, Innis correctly observed that the First Amendment fostered "a narrowing of the range from which material is distributed and a widening of the range of reception, so that large numbers receive, but are unable to make any direct response."[189] And again, reminiscent of Horkheimer and Adorno, Innis declared, "Those on the receiving end of material from a mechanized central system are precluded from participation in healthy, vigorous, and vital discussion."[190] Hence, in shoring up the rights of the powerful, the First Amendment, at least relatively, reduced the rights of the general public.

Third, the enormous growth in the press combined with press freedom, meant that increasingly newspaper production enjoyed large economies of scale, further serving to reduce the number of smaller, independent voices and simultaneously inducing the larger presses to seek out the lowest common denominator among readers.[191] As Innis explained, "Hearst resorted to new devices to increase circulation, ranging from larger headlines to sensationalism in the Spanish-American war, large salaries to attract staff from Pulitzer, features, and comic strips."[192] Since Innis' time, a new word has been coined—*infotainment*—marking the ubiquity of practices analogous to those bemoaned by Innis over half a century ago.

Fourth, to increase circulation, and thereby the utility of newspapers to advertisers, prices to charged readers were lowered, with advertising making up the shortfall. This meant in turn that advertisers began exerting significant (monopolistic) control over editorial content. Muckraking in the financial field disappeared, according to Innis, as advertisers were concerned, rather, "with constant emphasis on prosperity."[193] Indeed, for Innis, "advertising became monopolistic in relation to a monopolistic press and imposed its influence on political, social and economic life," resulting in "maladjustments" which Innis associated first with the boom of the nineteen twenties, followed by the depression of the thirties.[194]

Fifth, through copyright, "news became a vendible commodity,"[195] as newspapers attained the freedom to "own" the news. The establishment of a property right in the news strengthened the Associated Press' news monopoly and constrained the free flow of information and ideas.

Sixth, the press became a vehicle for molding public opinion through devious, even subliminal means. "Success in the industrialized newspaper," Innis wrote, "depends on constant repetition, inconspicuous infiltration, increasing appeal to the subconscious mind, and the employment of acts of attrition in molding public opinion.[196] For Innis, "the art of making and slanting news" had become a basic skill at which employees of advertisers and publishers needed to become adept if they hoped to succeed.[197]

Finally, and most importantly in Innis' view, in exercising its freedoms the press helped promote a space-biased culture and monopoly of knowledge, neglecting time in the sense of continuity and time as duration:

> The type of news essential to an increase in circulation, to an increase in advertising, and to an increase in the sale of news was necessarily that which catered to excitement. A prevailing interest in orgies and excitement was harnessed in the interests of trade.[198]
>
> [Newspaper] bias culminated in an obsession with the immediate. Journalism, in the words of Henry James, became a criticism of the moment at the moment.[199]
>
> In the United States the dominance of the newspaper led to large-scale development of monopolies of communication in terms of space and implied a neglect of problems of time.[200]
>
> Time has been cut into pieces the length of a day's newspaper.[201]

For Innis, an undue emphasis on space and lack of concern for time (duration, continuity) is the tragic flaw of our contemporary civilization. He exclaimed, "The balance between time and space has been seriously disturbed with disastrous consequences to Western civilization."[202] What, then, are some of the "disastrous consequences"? Innis proposed the following:

- The "atomization" of society by the "pulverizing" effects of machine industry; that is, the rise in hedonistic individualism at the expense of community.[203]
- War, as attention in space-bound societies is riveted on capturing and controlling additional space and the accompanying resources.[204]
- Lapse of democracy, due both to the decline in oral debate[205] and the "obsession of the press with the immediate," making public opinion "unreliable."[206]
- Instability. According to Innis, stability is dependent upon "an appreciation of a proper balance between the concepts of space and time."[207]
- Lapse of morality. Innis cites Wyndham Lewis: "The modern 'clerks' consider everything only as it exists *in time,* that is as it constitutes a succession of particular states, a 'becoming,' a 'history,' and never as it presents a state of permanence beyond time,"[208] which is to say ideals and enduring values.
- The waning of the university as an island of free thought.[209]

- Erosion of meaning. Innis declared: "The essence of living in the moment and for the moment is to banish all individual continuity."[210]
- Secular totalitarianism. Innis wrote: "The disappearance of time monopolies facilitated the rapid extension of control by the state and the development of new religions evident in fascism, communism, *and our way of life*."[211]

In Innis' view, then, popular culture and science, the vernacular and the scholarly, are usually cut from the same cloth, more often than not reinforcing one another, emphasizing the present to the neglect of time as duration and as a sense of the future. There being little or no contradiction between scholarship and popular culture in this regard, they comprise in combination the monopoly of knowledge of our day. Together they serve military and commercial force, and in Innis' terms, drive out understanding.

INNIS, ADORNO, AND CRITICAL POLITICAL ECONOMY OF MEDIA

It is unlikely that Innis, who died in 1952, was familiar with the work of Adorno, and even less likely that Adorno was familiar with that of Innis. Nonetheless, striking parallels abound. By identifying some of the common elements, the essentials of a critical political economy of media become manifest. Judith Stamps was perhaps the first to suggest affinities between Innis and Adorno.[212]

To begin, both writers adopted materialist perspectives on media and culture. Running through Innis' writings, from his staples thesis to medium theory, is the conviction that material environments affect cultures, including thought systems and social organization, and that these in turn reshape material environments. In contrast to Innis, Adorno's political economy concerned mainly contemporary mass media. Nonetheless, Adorno's analysis is equally materialist. Like Innis, Adorno maintained that media are inextricably entangled with structures of political-economic power. For Adorno, the culture industry manufactures and distributes its commodities to integrate the masses into capitalist-consumer society, a contention with which Innis, when focusing on contemporary media, was in full agreement. For both scholars, the exercise of political and economic power requires control of culture, which is to say control over the means of communication, a control which both writers attested is never absolute.

Adorno and Innis were both dialectical writers. One manifestation pertains to their analyses of class. Although Adorno abandoned the Marxist division between capital and labor by amalgamating the proletariat and the bourgeoisie into a "mass class," he retained the basic Marxist notion of class conflict. For Adorno, the mass class is manipulated and oppressed by the elite.[213] Innis had a similar view; he considered class in various civilizations, but in all of them there is a small elite controlling the means of communication (a priesthood in control of parchment, an industrial elite in control of radio and the newspaper, a scientific elite in charge of knowledge at Alexandria, and so on). Both Innis and Adorno, moreover, proposed a coterie of dissenters: "high" artists for Adorno who by their independence and superior insight could see society as it really is; and for Innis, groups at the margin (in former years often located in universities) contesting domination, or challenging established power by introducing new media of communication.

These writers were dialectical in other matters. Adorno saw an opposition between high art and low art, for example, but thought they were merging as both became debased by commodification. Likewise, in Innis' view, popular culture and science, the vernacular and the scholarly, although in principle vastly different, are today reinforcing one another to constitute the (space-binding) monopoly of knowledge of our time. Innis, of course, emphasized an opposition between time and space as organizing principles, but a similar dialectic can be discerned in Adorno's treatment of art: he maintained that non-commodified art, whether "high" or "low," critically appraises current conditions within a temporal (lived historical) context, whereas commodified art is narcissistic, erases problems from consciousness, and encourages audiences to live in and for the present ("present-mindedness").

Innis and Adorno were both, consequently, concerned about the waning of high art and/or critical scholarship. For Innis, space-binding media had become so prevalent that even the universities (last bastions of free expression) were becoming complicit in supporting corporate and military control. Innis bemoaned, too, the standardization of cultures once penetrated by the price system and other space-binding media of communication. He maintained that only at rare intervals did scholarship and creativity become freed from pressures for conformity. For Adorno, the high arts have been largely emptied of critical content and have essentially become status goods renowned for their exchange value. Adorno emphasized standardization and sameness in cultural artifacts once absorbed by the culture industry, while Innis likewise critically appraised mechanized media and their need to achieve economies of scale through standardization.

Adorno and Innis shared dialectical perspectives on knowledge and power. For Innis the paradox of science was that after becoming freed from the grip of time-binding control (the Church), it succumbed to space-biased interests (corporations, military). For Adorno, the irony has been that while science (instrumental reason) freed people from superstition, common people soon became enslaved by applications of instrumental knowledge. A further implication, and irony, for both writers is the collapse of meaning in an age of space-binding knowledge, commodification, mechanization, and instrumental reason. For Innis, mathematical formula and the mechanization of knowledge were even a cause of war: "The large-scale mechanization of knowledge [creates] monopolies in language which prevent understanding and hasten appeals to force."[214]

Innis distinguished between scholarly knowledge and popular culture, whereas Adorno's distinctions were among science (instrumental knowledge), high culture, and low (popular) culture. Both writers saw intellectuals as too often working at the behest of elite interests, and in that way supporting the indoctrination accomplished by popular culture. Both agreed that elite interests endeavor to control knowledge and cultural production of all types, and are generally successful in doing this. Whereas for Innis, during times of transition from one medium to another creative artists and scholars may become free for a time to pursue truth, and for Adorno high culture in the past was somewhat free to do this, both were skeptical regarding the autonomy of arts and sciences in our day.

Both Innis and Adorno were reflexive thinkers. Innis wrote: "We must all be aware of the extraordinary, perhaps insuperable, difficulty of assessing the quality of a culture of which we are a part."[215] Adorno's self-reflexivity as a scholar is manifest in his self-identification as a critical theorist, as opposed to an "Enlightenment" thinker. Adorno insisted that it is impossible for scholars to be value free. Rather than feigning objectivity or detachment, as do the "positivists," Adorno was up-front about his agenda to transform society. By making that agenda transparent, he may be understood as being much more reflexive than ostensibly objective scientific researchers. Adorno and Horkheimer went still further, insisting the Enlightenment (i.e., scientific or instrumental reason) had all but abolished reflexivity. They stated, "Enlightenment has put aside the classic requirement of thinking about thought. . . . Mathematical procedure became, so to speak, the ritual of thinking."[216]

In response to their critique of the Enlightenment, however, neither Innis nor Adorno recommended a poststructuralist path that would deny truth, deauthenticate grand theories, detach language from material conditions, and take flight into the realm of linguistic interpretation.[217] Rather, both drew upon classicism, particularly the reinstitution of dialectical thinking, as an antidote to what Innis termed present-mindedness and the mechanization of knowledge, and what Adorno saw as the totalitarian implications of the Enlightenment. For Innis, scientific, instrumental reason ought always to be counterbalanced by time-binding, moral knowledge; that would entail, for example, the reintegration of political economy and moral philosophy—a resolution of Adam Smith's previously discussed "mistake."[218] Innis also believed that local and regional histories should serve to qualify abstractions and abstract social "laws" posited by mechanized social science, a recommendation with which Adorno could agree since for him awareness of lived experience is one of the best protections against elite indoctrination. For Adorno, too, instrumental/abstract reason was to be counterbalanced by the critical arts and scholarship, by authentic popular culture, and by what Lazarsfeld termed enduring "human values." (By contrast, Lawrence Grossberg, representing poststructuralist cultural studies in the Colloquy, insisted that we must abandon dialectical thinking altogether, to instead focus on "articulations," "de-articulations," and "re-articulations." *Articulation* is addressed in chapters 2 and 3. Poststructuralist Mark Poster, who is compared with Innis in chapter 8 of this book, likewise rejects dialectical thinking).

The indebtedness of Innis and Adorno to the classics is found not only in their reflexivity (their thinking about thinking), in their dialectical mode of analysis, and in their critical understanding of knowledge *as* power and knowledge *vs.* power, but also in their literary allusions: Innis cited the flight of Minerva's owl and, of course, made detailed references to ancient civilizations; Adorno-Horkheimer made extended metaphorical reference to Odysseus steering a midcourse between Scylla and Charybdis.[219] In the present book, scholars are urged to set a course between the Scylla of an undue determinism characteristic of fundamentalist or "vulgar" political economy and the Charybdis of overextended linguistic-interpretative analyses characteristic of poststructuralism.

Both writers were at least implicitly influenced by Freud. Both saw media as entering subconscious regions of their audiences' minds to exert influence. Both authors, consequently, set about warning the public of these nefarious practices.

Finally, neither writer adopted a position of inevitable progress through technological change. Adorno wrote famously, "No universal history leads from savagery to humanity, but one indeed from the slingshot to the H-bomb; it culminates in the total threat of organized humanity against organized human beings, in the epitome of discontinuity."[220] Innis, too, toward the end of his life, became quite apocalyptic, declaring for example: "The conditions of freedom of thought are in danger of being destroyed by science, technology, and the mechanization of knowledge, and with them, Western civilization."[221]

But these unquestionably pessimistic thoughts ought not to obscure these writers' optimism. Adorno stated explicitly that his goal as an author was to shine light upon the hidden operations of the culture industry in order that people could more ably defend themselves against its machinations. A similar ambition undoubtedly directed Innis in his warnings against undue present-mindedness and space bias. Because they did not resign themselves to the seemingly inevitable, these two critical writers were in truth more idealist, more optimistic, and less cynical than the scores of their "administrative" colleagues who were then contracting with the military-industrial establishment. Such optimism, idealism, and integrity are at the very root of critical political economy.

NOTES

1. The opening paragraphs of this section draw upon chapter 2 of my book *Culture of Ecology: Reconciling Economics and Environment* (Toronto: University of Toronto Press, 2006).

2. Cf. Vincent Mosco, *The Political Economy of Communication* (Thousand Oaks, CA: SAGE Publications, 1996), 25. Also, Robert W. McChesney, "The Political Economy of Communication and the Future of the Field," *Media, Culture and Society* 22, no. 1 (2000): 110.

3. Innis, for example, regarded Adam Smith as "the Mount Everest of political economy." Harold Innis, "The Passing of Political Economy" (1938; reprint, Harold Innis, *Staples, Markets, and Cultural Change,* ed. Daniel Drache, Montreal and Kingston: McGill-Queen's University Press, 1995), 439.

4. Adam Smith, *An Inquiry into the Nature and Causes of the Wealth of Nations* (1776; reprint, ed. Edwin Cannan, New York: The Modern Library, 1937), 395.

5. Smith wrote several books, these two being, however, the most famous. See Jacob Bronowski and Bruce Mazlish, *The Western Intellectual Tradition: From Leonardo to Hegel* (New York: Harper and Row, 1960), 342.

6. Roger Backhouse, *The Ordinary Business of Life* (Princeton, NJ: Princeton University Press, 2002), 123; Warren J. Samuels, *The Classical Theory of Economic Policy* (Cleveland, OH: World Publishing Company, 1966), 21–97; D. D. Raphael and A. L. Macfie, "Introduction," in Adam Smith, *The Theory of Moral Sentiments* (Indianapolis, IN: Liberty Press, 1982), 21.

7. In Smith's Preface to the sixth edition of *Moral Sentiments* he did remark that the two volumes were intended to be part of a "tripartite system of social science covering the domains of moral rules, government and law, and market." Warren J. Samuels, personal communication, December 21, 2003. See also Backhouse, *The Ordinary Business of Life*, 123.

8. Smith wrote: "Sympathy, however, cannot, in any sense, be regarded as a selfish principle. When I sympathize with your sorrow . . . I consider what I should suffer if I was really you. . . . My grief, therefore, is entirely upon your account, and not in the least upon my own. It is not, therefore, in the least selfish." Adam Smith, *The Theory of Moral Sentiments* (1759; reprint, ed. D. D. Raphael and A. L. Macfie, Indianapolis, IN: Liberty Press, 1982), 317.

9. Raymond Williams quotes Coleridge on classical political economy's split from moral philosophy: "It is this accursed practice of ever considering *only* what is *expedient* for the occasion, disjoined from all principle or enlarged system of action, of never listening to the true and unerring impulses of our better nature, that has led the colder-hearted men to the study of political economy." Raymond Williams, *Culture and Society 1780–1950* (1958; reprint, Harmondsworth: Penguin, 1984), 73.

10. I develop these arguments more fully in Babe, *Culture of Ecology: Reconciling Economics and Environment* (Toronto: University of Toronto Press, 2006).

11. The parallels between the two theories of value are exact. Just as Marx concluded that labor being the source of value means that labor should receive that value, neoclassicism's naming consumers' preferences as the source of value implies that consumers should be "sovereign," their preferences always to be unquestioned and to be satisfied.

12. George Stigler and Gary Becker, "De Gustibus Non Est Disputandum," *American Economic Review* 67, no. 2 (1977): 76–90.

13. Tibor Scitivsky, *The Joyless Economy: The Psychology of Human Satisfaction and Consumer Dissatisfaction* (Oxford: Oxford University Press, 1976).

14. Citing Kant, Hannah Arendt remarks on the general dubiousness of the *de Gustibus* maxim: "It was because of their public relevance that he [Kant] insisted, in opposition to the commonplace adage, that taste judgments *are* open to discussion because 'we hope the same pleasure is shared by others,' that taste *can* be subject to dispute, because it 'expects agreement from everyone else.' . . . The activity of taste decides how this world . . . is to look and sound, what men will see and what they will hear." Hannah Arendt, "The Crisis in Culture," in *Between Past and Future* (1954; reprint New York: Penguin, 2006), 218–19; emphasis added.

15. William Stanley Jevons, *The Theory of Political Economy* (3rd ed., London: Macmillan and Co., 1888), 3. See also Philip Mirowski, *More Heat Than Light: Economics as Social Physics, Physics as Nature's Economics* (Cambridge: Cambridge University Press, 1989).

16. Samuels, *The Classical Theory of Economic Policy.*

17. These methods include: marginal or incremental analysis, presuming a psychological basis of value, constrained maximization, equilibrium analysis, privileging the criterion of Pareto optimality, methodological individualism, and affording supremacy to the doctrine of consumer sovereignty. A situation is said to be *Pareto optimal* if for every conceivable change, at least one person will become worse off. The doctrine is ostensibly premised on the reluctance of economists to make interpersonal utility comparisons.

18. Gary Becker, *The Economic Approach to Human Behavior* (Chicago: University of Chicago Press, 1976).

19. Ronald Coase, "The Problem of Social Cost," *Journal of Law and Economics* 31 (1960): 1–44. For a critique, see Babe, *Culture of Ecology*, 111–14.

20. Warren J. Samuels, "The Chicago School of Political Economy: A Constructive Critique," in *The Chicago School of Political Economy*, ed. Warren J. Samuels (New Brunswick, NJ: Transaction Publishers, 1993), 11.

21. Samuels, "The Chicago School of Political Economy," 12.

22. See, for example, John Kenneth Galbraith, *The New Industrial State* (Boston: Houghton Mifflin, 1967).

23. See note 17.

24. For example, Milton Friedman, *Essays in Positive Economics* (Chicago: University of Chicago Press, 1953). On Pareto optimality, see note 17 above.

25. Terry Eagleton, *Figures of Dissent* (London: Verso, 2003), 71.

26. Martin Jay, *The Dialectical Imagination: A History of the Frankfurt School and the Institute of Social Research 1923–1950* (1973; reprint, Berkley, CA: University of California Press, 1996), 21.

27. Stephen Crook, "Introduction," 9.

28. "Vulgar" Marxism is an unduly deterministic Marxism, the implication being that Marx, himself, was not unduly deterministic. See, for example, Raymond Williams, *Culture and Society 1780–1950* (Harmondsworth: Penguin, 1963), 266.

29. As noted by Samuels, the Chicago school of political economy, despite insisting that it is "positive" or value free, is actually quite "normative," as reflected in its stance toward both consumer sovereignty and Pareto optimality, and in its unyielding preference for market outcomes.

30. Paul Felix Lazarsfeld, "Administrative and Critical Communications Research" (1941; reprint, *Mass Communication and American Social Thought*, ed. John Durham Peters and Peter Simonson, Lanham, MD: Rowman and Littlefield Publishers, Inc. 2004), 169.

31. Jay, *The Dialectical Imagination*, 41.

32. Brian O'Connor, ed., *The Adorno Reader* (Oxford: Blackwell Publishers Ltd. 2000), 7.

33. Judith Stamps, *Unthinking Modernity: Innis, McLuhan and the Frankfurt School* (Montreal and Kingston: McGill-Queen's University Press, 1995), 4.

34. Jay, *The Dialectical Imagination*, 42.

35. Mosco, *Political Economy of Communication*.

36. Quoted in Wilbur Schramm, *The Beginnings of Communication Study in America: A Personal Memoir,* ed. Steven H. Chaffee and Everett M. Rogers (Thousand Oaks, CA: SAGE Publications, 1997), 109.

37. Terry Eagleton, *Figures of Dissent* (London: Verso, 2003), 74.

38. J. M. Bernstein, "Introduction" to *The Culture Industry* by Theodor W. Adorno, ed. J. M. Bernstein (London: Routledge, 1991), 4.

39. Andrew Fagan, "Theodor Adorno," *The Internet Encyclopedia of Philosophy* (2006). http://www.iep.utm.edu/a/adorno.htm (accessed Dec. 15, 2007).

40. Theodor W. Adorno, "Culture Industry Reconsidered" (1975; reprint, *The Culture Industry,* ed. J. M. Bernstein, London: Routledge, 1991), 85.

41. Deborah Cook, *The Culture Industry Revisited: Theodor W. Adorno on Mass Culture* (Lanham, MD: Rowman and Littlefield Publishers, Inc., 1996), xiii.

42. Cook, *The Culture Industry Revisited*, x.

43. Bernstein, "Introduction," 3.

44. Bernstein, "Introduction," 23.

45. Central to Adorno's thought on the culture industry, after all, is that in capitalism exchange value replaces use value; items take on value by aiding capital accumulation, as opposed to stemming from their intrinsic properties.

46. Bernstein, "Introduction," 3.

47. Crook, "Introduction," 13.

48. Alexander John Watson, *Marginal Man: The Dark Vision of Harold Innis* (Toronto: University of Toronto Press, 2006), 163.

49. Harold A. Innis, "The Work of Thorstein Veblen" (1929; reprint, *Essays in Canadian Economic History*, ed. Mary Q. Innis, Toronto: University of Toronto Press, 1956), 17–26.

50. Harold A. Innis, "A Critical Review" (1948; reprint, *The Bias of Communication*, Toronto: University of Toronto Press, 1971), 190. Citing Ian Parker, Kamilla Pietrzyk has suggested that Innisian media analysis can complement fundamentalist Marxism by bridging the chasm between economic/material *base* and the symbolic/cognitive *superstructure* through its emphasis on contending forces vying to control the means of communication/means of indoctrination. Kamilla Pietrzyk, *Exit From the Myopic Social Movement Strategy in the Age of the Internet* (M.A. Thesis, Faculty of Information and Media Studies, The University of Western Ontario, 2007), 27. See also Ian Parker, "Innis, Marx, and the Economics of Communication," *Queen's Quarterly* 84 (1977): 545–63.

51. Robert E. Babe, "Innis and the News," *Javnost–The Public* 13, no. 3 (2006): 44.

52. Paul Heyer, *Harold Innis* (Lanham, MD: Rowman and Littlefield Publishers, Inc., 2003), 52.

53. James W. Carey, "Culture, Geography, and Communications: The Work of Harold Innis in an American Context," in *Culture, Communication and Dependency: The Tradition of H. A. Innis*, ed. William H. Melody, Liora Salter, and Paul Heyer (Norwood, NJ: Ablex Publishing Corp, 1981), 80.

54. For example: David Crowley and Paul Heyer, eds., *Communication and History: Technology, Culture and Society* (5th edition, New York: Allyn and Bacon, 2007); Ian Angus, *A Border Within* (Montreal and Kingston: McGill-Queen's University Press, 1997); Ian Angus, *Primal Scenes of Communication* (New York: SUNY Press, 2000); James Beniger, *The Control Revolution: Technological and Economic Origins of the Information Society* (Cambridge, MA: Harvard University Press, 1986); James W. Carey, *Communication as Culture: Essays on Media and Society* (Boston: Unwin Hyman, 1989); Ronald J. Deibert, *Parchment, Printing, and Hypermedia: Communication in the World Order Transformation* (New York: Columbia University Press, 1997); Elizabeth Eisenstein, *The Printing Press as an Agent of Change: Communications and Cultural Transformations in Early-Modern Europe* (Cambridge: Cambridge University Press, 1980); Walter Ong, *Orality and Literacy: Technologizing the Word* (New York: Methuen, 1982); Marshall McLuhan, *The Gutenberg Galaxy* (Toronto: University of Toronto Press, 1962); Heather Menzies, *No Time: Stress and the Crisis of Modern Life* (Vancouver: Douglas and McIntyre, 2005); Vincent Di Norcia, "Communications, Power and Time: An Innisian View," *Canadian Journal of Political Science* 13, no. 2 (1990): 336–57.

55. Arthur Lower, "Harold Innis As I Remember Him," *Journal of Canadian Studies* 20, no. 4 (1986): 4.

56. Donald Creighton, *Harold Adams Innis: Portrait of a Scholar* (Toronto: University of Toronto Press, 1957), 63.

57. Jay, *The Dialectical* Imagination, 37. In defense of this, see Theodor W. Adorno, "Resignation" (1978; reprint, *The Culture Industry,* ed. J. M. Bernstein, London: Routledge, 1991): 171–75.

58. Jay, *The Dialectical Imagination*, 22.

59. Jay, *The Dialectical Imagination*, 23.

60. Jay, *The Dialectical Imagination*, 35.

61. Robert E. Babe, *Canadian Communication Thought: Ten Foundational Writers* (Toronto: University of Toronto Press, 2000), 55.

62. Thorstein Veblen, "The Intellectual Pre-eminence of Jews in Modern Europe" (1919; reprint, *The Portable Veblen,* ed. Max Lerner, New York: Viking Press, 1950), 474–75.

63. Smythe was joined at Illinois by George Gerbner in 1956 and later, albeit briefly (due to Smythe's imminent departure), by Herbert Schiller, and an American tradition in critical political economy of media was born.

64. Smythe's publications are listed in John A. Lent, *A Different Road Taken: Profiles In Critical Communication* (Boulder, CO: Westview Press, 1995), 269–79. Some of the early content analyses are excerpted in Dallas Smythe, *Counterclockwise: Perspectives on Communication,* ed. Thomas Guback (Boulder, CO: Westview Press, 1994).

65. As noted by Robin Mansell, earlier use of the term, "consciousness industry," was by H. M. Enzensberger in an article in 1970 and in his book, *The Consciousness Industry* (New York: Seabury, 1974), and by Stuart Ewen in his *Captains of Consciousness* (New York: McGraw Hill, 1976). Smythe himself was insistent on distinguishing "consciousness industry" from Adorno's "culture industry." According to Smythe, Adorno was not suitably "materialist," as in Smythe's view Adorno did not recognize that the commodity produced by the culture industry is audience. However, granted distinctions may be made, there is surely much commonality between the two theorists in this matter of culture industry and consciousness industry. See Dallas W. Smythe, "Communications: Blindspot of Western Marxism" (1977; excerpted in *Counterclockwise: Perspectives on Communication,* ed. Thomas Guback, Boulder, CO: Westview Press, 1994), 268; and Robin Mansell, "Introduction to Part II: Communication History and Policy" in Robert E. Babe, *Media, Structures and Power: The Robert E. Babe Collection,* ed. Edward Comor (Toronto: University of Toronto Press, 2009).

66. *Cf.*, J. M. Bernstein, "Introduction," 3.

67. David Held, *Introduction to Critical Theory: Horkheimer to Habermas* (Cambridge: Polity Press, 1980), 78.

68. Simon Jarvis notes that Adorno "illuminated an extraordinary range of subjects in his lifetime—from dialectical logic to newspaper astrology columns, from the authoritarian personality to sonata form, from the syntax of poetry to the Hollywood studio system." Nonetheless, Jarvis adds, Adorno addressed certain key questions

throughout: "What is the relationship between power and rationality? Can there ever be a kind of thinking which does not live off the suffering of others?" Simon Jarvis, *Adorno: A Critical Introduction* (Cambridge: Polity Press, 1998), 1–2.

69. Max Horkheimer and Theodor W. Adorno, *Dialectic of Enlightenment* (New York: Continuum, 1991), 120; (originally published in German in 1944). Statements of this sort have attracted critique. J. M. Bernstein suggests, for example, that Adorno overemphasized the culture industry's goal of homogenization. J. M. Bernstein, "Introduction," 23. See also, Douglas Kellner, "Critical Theory and the Culture Industries: A Reassessment," *Telos* 62 (1984–1985): 196–206.

70. The terms *postmodern* and *poststructural* will be used throughout this book almost interchangeably. However, while agreeing there is significant overlap, Ben Agger distinguishes between them, writing: "Poststructuralism (Derrida, the French feminists) is a theory of knowledge and language, whereas postmodernism (Foucault, Barthes, Lyotard, Baudrillard) is a theory of society, culture, and history." Agger attributes the advent of poststructuralism to Jacques Derrida and his deconstructionist claim that "language produces meaning only with reference to other meanings against which it takes on its own significance; thus, we can never establish stable meanings by attempting correspondence between language and the world addressed by language." We are destined, in other words, "to remain locked up in the prison house of language." Agger traces postmodernism, on the other hand, to Jean-François Lyotard's *The Postmodern Condition: A Report on Knowledge* (1984). There, Lyotard rejected totalizing perspectives on history and society ("grand narratives"). Lyotard maintained that "one cannot tell large stories about the world but only small stories from the heterogeneous 'subject positions' of individuals and plural social groups." See Ben Agger, "Critical Theory, Poststructuralism, Postmodernism: Their Sociological Relevance," *Annual Review of Sociology* 17 (1991) www.uta.edu/huma/illuminations/agger2.htm (accessed June 10, 2008).

71. Grant McCracken, *Culture and Consumption: New Approaches to the Symbolic Character of Consumer Goods and Activities* (Bloomington, IN: Indiana University Press, 1988).

72. Crook, "Introduction," 35.

73. Horkheimer and Adorno, *Dialectic of Enlightenment*, 126.

74. Adorno, *The Culture Industry*, 85.

75. Adorno, quoted in Cook, *The Culture Industry Revisited*, 27.

76. Robert Hughes, *The Shock of the New: Art and the Century of Change* (London: BBC, 1980), 66–80.

77. Horkheimer and Adorno, *The Dialectic of Enlightenment*, 131.

78. Adorno, *The Culture Industry*, 86.

79. Horkheimer and Adorno, *The Dialectic of Enlightenment*, 158. Horkheimer and Adorno's analyses of high art/low art are amplified and extended, under the terms culture and entertainment, by Hannah Arendt in "The Crisis in Culture," *Between Past and Future* (1954; reprint, New York: Penguin, 2006), 194–222.

80. Cook, *The Culture Industry Revisited*, 3

81. Adorno, quoted in Cook, *The Culture Industry Revisited*, 3.

82. Adorno, "On the Fetish Character in Music and the Regression of Listening" (1938; reprint, *The Culture Industry,* by Theodor Adorno, edited with an Introduction by J. M. Bernstein, London: Routledge, 1991), 26.
83. Adorno, "On the Fetish Character in Music," 28–29.
84. Adorno, "On the Fetish Character in Music," 27.
85. Adorno, "Culture Industry Reconsidered," 85.
86. Adorno, "Culture Industry Reconsidered," 85; Adorno, "On the Fetish Character in Music," 31.
87. Adorno, "Culture Industry Reconsidered," 90.
88. Adorno, "Culture Industry Reconsidered," 85; and Horkheimer and Adorno, *Dialectic of Enlightenment*, 132
89. Benjamin Ginsberg, *The Captive Public: How Mass Opinion Promotes State Power* (New York: Basic Books, 1986).
90. Theodor Adorno, "The Stars Down to Earth."
91. J. M. Bernstein, "Introduction," 12.
92. J. M. Bernstein, "Introduction," 14.
93. Horkheimer and Adorno, *Dialectic of Enlightenment*, 122.
94. Horkheimer and Adorno, *Dialectic of Enlightenment*, 121; emphasis added.
95. Horkheimer and Adorno, *Dialectic of Enlightenment*, 144.
96. Horkheimer and Adorno, *Dialectic of Enlightenment*, 126.
97. Adorno, "Free Time." 170.
98. Jean Baudrillard, *Simulations,* trans. Paul Fox, Paul Patton, and Philip Beitchman (New York: Semiotext [e], 1983), 7.
99. Although in *The Truman Show,* for example, the protagonist eventually exits his simulated world and the author of that world is identified, it is also the case that in the movie the television audience lived Truman's activities vicariously, making their situation likewise a simulation (as do the viewers of the movie). In the case of *Last Year at Marienbad*, the distinction between fact and fancy is never made clear; the movie presents contradictions all of which seem equally true. *The Purple Rose of Cairo* deals with parallel universes that temporarily merge, one of which consists of a cast of characters in a movie within the movie and the other populated by "real" people. On the other hand, as Edward Comor has pointed out to me, the film *Memento* could be understood as a critique of poststructuralism since the main character must write down everything in order to remember, and these little scraps of "memory" thereby become devoid of context, continuity, and meaning. Arguably TV news, too, helps spread this poststructuralist mindset through constant revision of previously hyped stories, such as the eventual repudiation of the tearful claim that incubator babies had been thrown onto hospital floors by Iraqi troops, the Jessica Lynch imbroglio, and of course media support and then denunciation of the deceitful "weapons of mass destruction" campaign. See, for example, Paul Rutherford, *Weapons of Mass Persuasion: Marketing the War Against Iraq* (Toronto: University of Toronto Press, 2004); John R. MacArthur, *Second Front: Censorship and Propaganda in the 1991 Gulf War,* Foreword by Ben H. Bagdikian (Berkley, CA: University of California Press, 2004); Eric Alterman, "Afterword: 'Operation Iraqi Freedom," in *What Liberal Media? The Truth About Bias and the News* (New York: Basic Books, 2003), 268–92.

100. Horkheimer and Adorno wrote: "Amusement under late capitalism is the prolongation of work. It is sought after as an escape from the mechanized work process, and to recruit strength in order to be able to cope with it again. But at the same time, mechanization has such power over a man's leisure and happiness, and so profoundly determines the manufacture of amusement goods, that his experiences are inevitably after-images of the work process itself." Horkheimer and Adorno, *Dialectic of Enlightenment*, 137.

101. Adorno, "Free Time," 168.

102. Theodor W. Adorno, "The Schema of Mass Culture," in *The Culture Industry,* by Theodor W. Adorno, edited with an Introduction by J. M. Bernstein (London: Routledge, 1991), 77; originally published in German in 1981.

103. Michael R. Real, "The Super-Bowl: Mythic Spectacle," in *Mass-Mediated Culture* (Englewood Cliffs, NJ: Prentice-Hall, 1977), 92–117; Arthur Asa Berger, *Media Analysis Techniques*, 3rd Edition (Newbury Park: SAGE Publications, 2004), 106–17; Michael Mandelbaum, *The Meaning of Sports: Why Americans Watch Baseball, Football and Basketball and What They See When They Do* (New York: Public Affairs, 2004).

104. Horkheimer and Adorno, *Dialectic of Enlightenment,* 137.

105. Theodor W. Adorno, "How to Look at Television" (1954; reprint, *The Culture Industry,* by Theodor W. Adorno, edited with an Introduction by J. M. Bernstein, London: Routledge, 1991), 138.

106. Cook, *The Culture Industry Revisited*, 61.

107. Cook, *The Culture Industry Revisited*, 7–8.

108. Adorno, "How to Look at Television," 141.

109. Adorno, "How to Look at Television," 142.

110. According to Adorno, since film, for example, accommodates various levels of response, "this would imply that the ideology provided by the industry, its officially intended models, may by no means automatically correspond to those that affect the spectators." Theodor W. Adorno, "Transparencies on Film," (1981–82; reprint, *The Culture Industry,* by Theodor W. Adorno, edited with an Introduction by J. M. Bernstein, London: Routledge, 1991), 157.

111. Adorno, "Transparencies on Film," 156.

112. Horkheimer and Adorno, *Dialectic of Enlightenment*, 123.

113. Raymond Williams, *The Year 2000* (New York: Pantheon, 1983), 118.

114. Horkheimer and Adorno, *Dialectic of Enlightenment*, 123.

115. Robert McChesney, *Rich Media, Poor Democracy* (New York: The New Press, 1999); Ben Bagdikian, *The Media Monopoly* (6th ed., Boston: Beacon Press, 2000).

116. Adorno, "Culture Industry Revisited," 89.

117. Adorno, "Culture Industry Revisited," 91, 90.

118. Adorno, "Culture Industry Revisited," 89.

119. Adorno, "Culture Industry Revisited," 91.

120. Horkheimer and Adorno, *Dialectic of Enlightenment*, 4.

121. Odysseus plugged the ears of his crew so they would not be lured by the sirens' seductive call; he had himself strapped to the mast so that he could hear their call but be rendered incapable of responding. Jarvis, interpreting Horkheimer and

Adorno, explains: "Freedom [through human rationality] from the blind compulsion of nature [here represented by the sirens' call] does not remove compulsion altogether; instead it is won at the cost of self-blinding social and psychological compulsion. Odysseus, the master, is also mastered and self-mastered. Domination over nature is paid for with the naturalization of social domination." Jarvis, *Adorno,* 27.

122. Horkheimer and Adorno, *Dialectic of Enlightenment*, 29.

123. Horkheimer and Adorno, *Dialectic of Enlightenment*, 5.

124. Horkheimer and Adorno, *Dialectic of Enlightenment*, 25. Note the parallel remarks by Harold Innis: "The extension of the mathematical device as a means of checking discussion, and bringing it to an end by an appeal to a majority vote, offers little or no relief." Harold Innis, *Innis on Russia: The Russian Diary and Other Writings*, ed. William Christian (Toronto: Harold Innis Foundation, 1981), 81.

125. Adorno, "How to Look at Television," 136.

126. Cook, *The Culture Industry Revisited*, 2.

127. Cook, *The Culture Industry Revisited*, 9.

128. Jay, *The Dialectical Imagination*, 41. In the preface to the new edition of *Dialectic of Enlightenment,* Horkheimer and Adorno declared: "The core truth is historical, rather than an unchanging constant to be set against the movement of history." Horkheimer and Adorno, *Dialectic of Enlightenment,* ix.

129. Jay, *The Dialectical Imagination*, 41.

130. Portions of this section are based on Robert E. Babe, "Harold Innis and the Paradox of Press Freedom," *Fifth Estate On-Line*, May 2007 http://www.fifth-estate-online.co.uk/criticsm/haroldinnisandtheparadox.html (accessed Dec. 15, 2007), and on Robert E. Babe, *Canadian Communication Thought: Ten Foundational Writers* (Toronto: University of Toronto Press, 2000), chapter 3.

131. Harold A. Innis, *The Cod Fisheries: The History of an International Economy* (1940; reprint, Toronto: University of Toronto Press, 1954), 388.

132. Harold A. Innis, *Empire and Communications* (1950; reprint, revised by Mary Q. Innis with a Foreword by Marshall McLuhan, Toronto: University of Toronto Press, 1972), 5–6.

133. Harold A. Innis, *The Fur Trade in Canada: An Introduction to Canadian Economic History* (1930; new edition based on the revised edition prepared by S. D. Clark and W. T. Easterbrook, with a foreword by Robin W. Winks, Toronto: University of Toronto Press, 1962), 15.

134. Innis, *The Fur Trade in Canada*, 391.

135. Vincent Di Norcia, "Communications, Power and Time: An Innisian View," *Canadian Journal of Political Science* 13, no. 2 (1990): 338.

136. Innis, *The Fur Trade in Canada*, 391.

137. Innis, *The Fur Trade in Canada*, 110.

138. As Innis put it, "The persistent and increasing demand for European commodities led to the more rapid extermination of the beaver, to increased hostilities, especially between Indian middlemen such as the Huron and Iroquois, to the westward flight of the Indians, to the spread of new cultural traits, and to further expansion of the trade. The pressure of tribes on the territory of the Indians to the interior was an additional and important cause of renewed Indian wars and destruction. Wars between

tribes, which with bows and arrows had not been strenuous, conducted with guns were disastrous." Innis, *The Fur Trade in Canada,* 20.

139. Innis, *The Fur Trade in Canada*, 388.

140. I discuss this at length in Babe, *Canadian Communication Thought*, chapter 3.

141. Watson, *Marginal Man*, 149.

142. Heyer, *Harold Innis*, 15.

143. Watson, *Marginal Man,* 216.

144. Heyer, *Harold Innis*, 30. See also Ronald J. Deibert, "Between Essentialism and Constructivism: Harold Innis and World Order Transformations," in *The Toronto School of Communication Theory,* 30–32.

145. Marshall McLuhan, "Introduction," in Harold A. Innis, *The Bias of Communication* (Toronto: University of Toronto Press, 1971), xv.

146. Robin Neill, *A New Theory of Value: The Canadian Economics of H. A. Innis* (Toronto: University of Toronto Press, 1972), 49.

147. Neill, *A New Theory of Value*, 94, 7.

148. Innis, *Empire and Communications*, 7.

149. Harold A. Innis, "The Problem of Space," in *The Bias of Communication* (1951; reprint, with an Introduction by Marshall McLuhan, Toronto: University of Toronto Press, 1971), 111.

150. Such is the charge often levelled at Innis by anti-political economy researchers, for example Everett Rogers, *A History of Communication Study: A Biographical Approach* (New York: Free Press, 1994), 484–89. Robin Neill is one of several refuting that charge, writing: "His belief in the existence of creativity as a factor in economic change eliminated any pretense of deterministic science." Neill, *A New Theory of Value,* 114.

151. Edward Comor, "Harold Innis's Dialectical Triad," *Journal of Canadian Studies* 29, no. 2 (summer, 1994): 112.

152. Comor, "Harold Innis's Dialectical Triad," 115.

153. Comor, "Harold Innis's Dialectical Triad;" also, Paul Heyer, *Communications and History: Theories of Media, Knowledge, and Civilization* (New York: Greenwood Press, 1988), 115.

154. Innis, *Empire and Communications*, xiii.

155. Harold A. Innis, *The Bias of Communication* (1951; reprint, with an Introduction by Marshall McLuhan, Toronto: University of Toronto Press, 1971), xviii.

156. Innis wrote: "Immediately [as] we venture on this inquiry we are compelled to recognize the bias of the period in which we work. An interest in the bias of other civilizations may in itself suggest bias of our own. Our knowledge of other civilizations depends in large part on the character of the media used by each civilization in so far as it is capable of being preserved or of being made accessible by discovery. . . . Writing on clay and on stone has been preserved more effectively than on papyrus. Since durable commodities emphasize time and continuity, studies of civilization such as Toynbee's tend to have a bias toward religion and to show how a neglect of problems of space, notably administration and law. The bias of modern civilization incidental to the newspaper and the radio will presume a perspective in consideration of civilizations dominated by other media. We can do little more than urge that we must

be continually alert to the implications of this bias and perhaps hope that consideration of the implications of other media to various civilizations may enable us to see more clearly the bias of our own." Innis, "The Bias of Communication," in *The Bias of Communication* (1951; reprint, with an Introduction by Marshall McLuhan, Toronto: University of Toronto Press, 1971), 33–34.

157. In his essay, "The Role of the Social Scientist," Innis quipped that "the task of attempting to become a social scientist may be regarded as beyond human endurance. He may take comfort in the argument that thought in the social sciences grows by the development and correction of bias. On the other hand, he will receive small thanks and possibly much contempt and persecution for attempting to tear the mask from innumerable biases which surround him. . . . The first duty of the social scientist is to avoid martyrdom. As a tribute to that duty the writer hereby brings to an end a list of biases which can be illustrated, or extended, or interpreted to illustrate the bias of the writer to the reader's content." See Harold A. Innis, "The Role of the Social Scientist" (1935; in *Staples, Markets and Cultural Change: Selected Essays, Harold A. Innis*, ed. Daniel Drache, Montreal and Kingston: McGill-Queen's University Press, 1995), 432.

158. As noted by Pencak, Innis admired Veblen's conscious struggle against his own biases. William Pencak, "Harold Innis, Thorstein Veblen, and In-formation," in *Semiotics and Information Science,* ed. Paul Perron, Marcel Danesi, Jean Umiker-Sebeok, and Anthony Watanabe (Toronto: LEGAS, 2000), 159.

159. Innis, *The Bias of Communication*, xvii.

160. Innis, "The Role of the Social Scientist," 430. In fact, Innis' entire staples thesis was in reaction to his dissatisfaction with his PhD thesis on the Canadian Pacific Railway. See Neill, *A New Theory of Value,* 35–36, for citations from Innis' "Autobiography."

161. Neill, *A New Theory of Value*, 100.

162. Watson, *Marginal Man*, 313ff.

163. Innis declared: "Learning tends to follow force to move to centres in which force [is] able to protect it"—as when, we might note, Jewish intellectuals like Adorno and Horkheimer fled Nazi Germany for the USA. Harold A. Innis, *The Idea File of Harold Innis,* ed. William Christian (Toronto: University of Toronto Press, 1980), 60.

164. Harold A. Innis, *Changing Concepts of Time* (1952; reprint, with Introduction by James W. Carey, Lanham, MD: Rowman and Littlefield, Publishers, Inc., 2004), xxvi.

165. Harold A. Innis, "Minerva's Owl" (1947; reprint, *The Bias of Communication*, Introduction by Marshall McLuhan, Toronto: University of Toronto Press, 1971), 30–31.

166. Innis wrote, "In the fourth century Plato attempted to save the remnants of Greek culture in the style of the Socratic dialogues which in the words of Aristotle stood half way between prose and poetry. In the seventh epistle he wrote, 'no intelligent man will ever be so bold as to put into language those things which his reason has contemplated, especially not into a form that is unalterable—which must be the

case with what is expressed in written symbols.'" Innis, "The Bias of Communication," 44.

167. Tom Sorell, "Tobacco Company Sponsorship Discredits Medical but Not all Research—Ethical Debate: Should Industry Sponsor Research?" *British Medical Journal*, 1 August, 1998, www.findarticles.com/p/articles/mi_m0999/is_n7154_v317/ai_21023727 (accessed Dec. 15, 2007).

168. James Winter, *Lies the Media Tell Us* (Montreal: Black Rose Books, 2007), 121–78.

169. Environmental Defense, "Global Warming Skeptics: A Primer" (2006), www.environmentaldefense.org/article.cfm?contentid=4870 (accessed Dec. 16, 2007). See also, Gerald Markowitz and Daniel Rosner, *Deceit and Denial: The Deadly Politics of Industrial Pollution* (Berkeley, CA: University of California Press, 2002).

170. Regarding the Kyoto Protocol and the enlistment of anti-environmental climate-change "scientists" by the American conservative movement, see Aaron M. McCright and Riley E. Dunlap, "Defeating Kyoto: The Conservative Movement's Impact on U.S. Climate Change Policy," *Social Problems* 50, no. 3 (2003): 348–73.

171. Innis, *Changing Concepts of Time*, 91.

172. Innis, "A Critical Review," 195.

173. Innis, "The Problem of Space," 129.

174. Innis, "A Critical Review," 192.

175. See, for example, George Grant, *Time as History* (Toronto: CBC, 1969).

176. Innis, "Minerva's Owl," 27; also Innis, *Innis on Russia*, 82.

177. Harold A. Innis, "Industrialism and Cultural Values" (1950; reprint, *The Bias of Communication*, Toronto: University of Toronto Press, 1971), 139.

178. Innis, "Adult Education and Universities," (1947; reprint, Harold A, Innis, *The Bias of Communication,* Introduction by Marshall McLuhan, Toronto: University of Toronto Press, 1971), 205–06.

179. Innis, "A Plea for Time" (1951; reprint, *The Bias of Communication,* with Introduction by Marshall McLuhan, Toronto: University of Toronto Press, 1971), 83.

180. Innis, "A Critical Review," 193.

181. Innis, "Adult Education and Universities," 204–05.

182. Innis, *Empire and Communications*, 138; also, Innis, "A Critical Review," 191.

183. Innis, "A Plea for Time," 86.

184. Innis, "Industrialism and Cultural Values," 139. This quest for "efficiency" in education has other deleterious consequences, according to Innis, for instance "a systematic closing of students' minds" and a weakening of initiative and independence. He continued: "Factual material, information, classification, reflect the narrowing tendencies of the mechanization of knowledge in the minds of staff and students. Professions become narrow and sterile. The teaching profession suffers perhaps most of all. A broad interest in the complex problems of society becomes almost impossible. The university graduate is illiterate as a result of the systematic poisoning of the educational system. Student and teacher are loaded down with information and prejudice." Harold A. Innis, "Adult Education and Universities," 208.

185. Innis, "Minerva's Owl," 5.

186. Innis, "The Problem of Space," 130.

187. Innis, "Industrialism and Cultural Values," 139; also Innis, "Technology and Public Opinion in the United States" (1949; reprint, *The Bias of Communication,* with Introduction by Marshall McLuhan, Toronto: University of Toronto Press, 1971), 167; also, Innis, *Changing Concepts of Time*, 11.

188. Myles Ruggles, *Automating Interaction: Formal and Information Knowledge in the Digital Network Economy*, with a Foreword by Robert E. Babe (Cresskill, NJ: Hampton Press, 2005). James Winter quotes David Radler, at the time president of Hollinger Inc., then Canada's largest newspaper chain: "I am ultimately the publisher of all these papers, and if editors disagree with us, they should disagree with us when they're no longer in our employ. The buck stops with the ownership. I am responsible for meeting the payroll; therefore, I will ultimately determine what the papers say and how they're going to be run." Winter, *Lies the Media Tell Us,* 43.

189. Innis, *Changing Concepts of Time*, 89.

190. Innis, *Changing Concepts of Time*, 89.

191. Innis, *Changing Concepts of Time*, 80–83.

192. Innis, "Technology and Public Opinion," 179.

193. Innis, "Technology and Public Opinion," 187, 186.

194. Innis, *Changing Concepts of Time*, 103.

195. Innis, "The English Publishing Trade in the Eighteenth Century" (1951; reprint, *The Bias of Communication*, Toronto: University of Toronto Press, 1971), 143.

196. Innis, *Changing Concepts of Time*, 82.

197. Innis, *Changing Concepts of Time*, 17.

198. Innis, "A Plea for Time," 77–78.

199. Innis, "Technology and Public Opinion," 187.

200. Innis, *Empire and Communications*, 170

201. Harold Innis, "The Concept of Monopoly and Civilization" (1951; reprint, *Staples, Markets and Cultural Change*, by Harold A. Innis, edited by Daniel Drache, Montreal and Kingston: McGill-Queen's University Press, 1995), 388. Edward Comor is one who has extended Innisian analysis into the age of the Internet, declaring: "The Internet's reach and speed . . . constitute its greatest weakness. While its infrastructure is predictably robust, the messages transmitted are extraordinarily perishable and overwhelmingly visual. Website content is especially transient and sensational. The lifespan of what is found on most websites ranges from hours to months." Moreover, he remarks, the point and click content presented through visual cues reinforces the "more general ahistorical, immediate gratification, sensual-over-intellectual predilections" of the space-bound consumer society. Edward Comor, *Consumption and the Globalization Project: International Hegemony and the Annihilation of Time* (New York: Palgrave Macmillan, 2008).

202. Innis, "A Plea for Time," 76.

203. Innis, "A Plea for Time," 79.

204. Innis, "The Problem of Space," 106.

205. Innis, "A Critical Review," 190; also, Harold A. Innis, "Adult Education and Universities," 203.

206. Harold A. Innis, *Political Economy in the Modern State* (Toronto: The Ryerson Press, 1946), 4.

207. Innis, "A Plea for Time," 64.

208. Innis, "A Plea for Time," 89.

209. See Philip A. Massolin, "Academic Modernization and the Decline of Higher Learning: The University Question in the Later Scholarship of Harold Innis," *Canadian Journal of Communication* 23, no. 1 (1998) www.cjc-online.ca/viewarticle.php?id=445 (accessed Dec. 15, 2007).

210. Innis, "A Plea for Time," 90.

211. Innis, "A Plea for Time," 88; emphasis added.

212. Stamps, *Unthinking Modernity*. Actually, Stamps' project was somewhat larger, linking Innis and McLuhan on the one hand with Adorno and Walter Benjamin on the other.

213. Cook, *The Culture Industry Revisited*, 12.

214. Innis, "Minerva's Owl," 29.

215. He adds, "or of assessing the quality of a culture of which we are not a part." Innis, "Industrialism and Cultural Values," 132.

216. Horkheimer and Adorno, *Dialectic of Enlightenment*, 25.

217. Innis declared: "But always the university must foster the search for truth and in its search must always question the pretentions of organized power whether in the hands of church or state. . . . It will also insist that any group which pretends to have found the truth is a fraud against civilization and that it is the search for truth and not truth which keeps civilization alive." Harold Innis, "The Canadian Situation" (1940, 1952), quoted in Robin Neill, *A New Theory of Value*, 90.

218. Kenneth Lux, *Adam Smith's Mistake: How a Moral Philosopher Invented Economics and Ended Morality* (Boston: Shambhala Publications, 1990).

219. Richard S. Ruderman, "Odysseus and the Possibility of Enlightenment," *American Journal of Political Science* 43, no. 1 (January 1999): 138–61.

220. Theodor Adorno, *Negative Dialectics* (1966), trans. Dennis Redmond, 315, www.efn.org/~dredmond/ndtrans.html (accessed Dec. 15, 2007).

221. Innis, "Industrialism and Cultural Values," 190. One seldom thinks of Raymond Williams, inaugurator of British cultural studies, as expressing apocalyptic views, but that is precisely how he ended his first book: "A knot is tied, that has come near to strangling our whole common life, in this century. We live in almost overwhelming danger, at a peak of our apparent control. We react to the danger by attempting to take control, yet still we have to unlearn, as the price of survival, the inherent dominative mode." Raymond Williams, *Culture and Society 1780–1950* (1958; reprint, Harmondsworth: Penguin, 1984), 321.

Chapter Two

Genealogy of Cultural Studies

WHAT IS CULTURAL STUDIES?

John Hartley begins his book on the history of cultural studies with the following, possibly perplexing observation: "There is little agreement about what counts as cultural studies. . . . The field is riven by fundamental disagreements about what cultural studies is for, in whose interests it is done, what theories, methods and objects of study are proper to it, and where to set its limits."[1]

Some definers of cultural studies cast their nets far and wide. The entry in *Wikipedia*, for instance, suggests that cultural studies "combines political economy, communication, sociology, social theory, literary theory, media theory, film/video studies, cultural anthropology, philosophy, museum studies and art history/criticism to study cultural phenomena in various societies."[2] Likewise, Blundell, Shepherd, and Taylor remark that among the "resources" available to cultural studies are "the disciplines of English literature, sociology, communication, anthropology, linguistics and various forms of semiology, film and television studies, and, more recently, art history and musicology." They continue: "Cultural studies takes these resources, interrogates them, adapts them to the task at hand, and interpellates them within its own continuously developing theoretical matrices."[3] Richard Johnson apparently agrees, declaring that cultural studies is both winnower and scavenger, "stealing away the more useful elements [of other disciplines] and rejecting the rest."[4] Blundell, Shepherd, and Taylor claim that writing histories of cultural studies or describing its "schools" is quite difficult, that really "the most that is possible are accounts from various practitioners, each account being informed by the practitioner's own biography and relation to cultural studies."[5] Likewise, Sardar and Van Loon declare: "Cultural studies is . . . a collective term for diverse and often contentious intellectual endeavours that address numerous questions, and consist of many different theoretical and political positions."[6] In brief, according to the foregoing, cultural studies is difficult to pin down and hence to analyze or critique.

In this book, however, I propose that cultural studies is not nearly as formless or inchoate as these excerpts indicate, that its main fissures are readily identifiable. The major fissure, I will argue, is between *cultural materialism* and *poststructuralism* (see figure 2.1).[7] Cultural materialism was how the inaugurators of British cultural studies envisaged the emerging field as they set out to understand and describe working class culture as a "full rich life," whereas poststructuralist cultural studies, particularly as it developed in the United States, focuses on the language component—to such an extent it often addresses little else. This contrast highlights a fundamental difference in ontology between these two approaches to cultural studies, a difference that might be summed up as critical realism vs. radical subjectivity/interpretative freedom[8]— a theme developed in several chapters of this book.

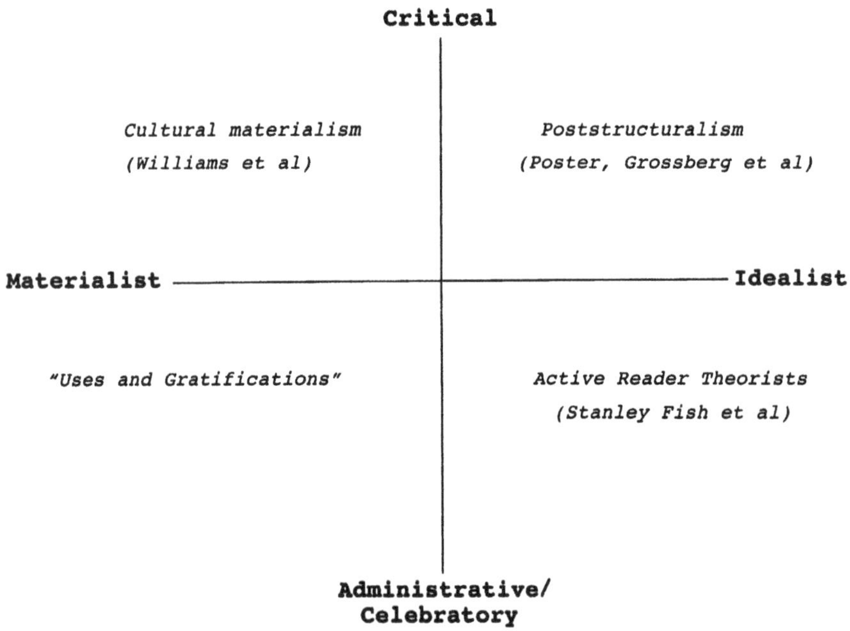

Figure 2.1. Typology of Cultural Studies. Cultural Studies ranges from the administrative/celebratory, which does not challenge existing power relations, to critical cultural studies, which presumes to identify and rectify cultural injustices. Cultural Studies also ranges from idealist to materialist, the former focusing on language and the latter on lived practices.

Related to this basic difference in ontology are other points of departure within cultural studies, for example macro vs. micro views, and long-term vs. short-term. As inaugurated by Raymond Williams and other British theorists, cultural studies was to be holistic ("macro") and take into account long-term trends.[9] By contrast, according to contemporary poststructuralists Lawrence Grossberg and Janice Radway, "cultural studies is committed to the radically contextual [i.e., micro], historically specific [i.e., short-term] character not only of cultural practices but also of the production and knowledge within cultural studies itself."[10] These terms, *radically contextual* and *historically specific*, accurately describe poststructuralist cultural studies' emphasis on specific occurrences as opposed to general or abstract structures that influence, or even determine, specificities.[11]

Again, in a more recent formulation, this time in his capacity as editor of the journal *Cultural Studies*, Grossberg declared that cultural studies is "a *radically contextual* practice of the *articulation* of knowledge and power."[12] As developed particularly in chapter 3, *articulation* is a key element in poststructuralists' arsenal of analytical tools; it denotes what is taken to be the pliable and essentially fluid nature of structures. Evidently keen, though, on establishing some continuity with the inaugural British cultural studies ("cultural materialism"), Grossberg has equated *articulation* with an expression found in Richard Hoggart's foundational book, *The Uses of Literacy*, namely "modification-with-adaptation."[13] However, Hoggart's phrase brings to mind biological, evolutionary, ecological, and systemic processes in the material (nonverbal) world, whereas "articulation" in the first instance connotes speech and language, making it consistent with the linguistic emphasis of poststructuralist cultural studies.

Finally, another major difference between cultural materialism and poststructuralism concerns the status of the dialectic. The very name, *cultural materialism* (and the title of one of Williams' books, *Problems in Materialism and Culture*), indicates dialectical interplay and tension between material conditions and (among other things) language practices. In contrast, poststructuralists insist we reject dialectical thinking; in Poster's words we must shift our attention from action in the material world to language.[14]

Another fissure is between *critical* and *celebratory* cultural studies. It was noted previously that treatment of power separates critical political economy from conservative (Chicago) political economy. Treatment of power likewise separates critical cultural studies from what may be termed conservative or celebrative cultural studies, the latter proposing essentially that message recipients make their own meanings ("active reader" thesis), or that people select cultural products from a vast array of possibilities according to which ones best satisfy their preexisting wants and needs ("uses and gratifications") or, setting theory aside, that media products are just plain fun. By contrast, within *critical* cultural studies, asymmetries and injustices in the distribution of communicatory power are front and center. Indeed, among the five characteristics of (critical) cultural studies listed by Sardar and Van Loon, three explicitly have to do with power:

> [Critical] cultural studies aims to examine its subject matter in terms of cultural practices and their relation to power. Its constant goal is to expose power relationships and examine how these relationships influence and shape cultural practices.
>
> [Critical] cultural studies' . . . objective is to understand culture in all its complex forms and to analyse the social and political context within which it manifests itself.
>
> [Critical] cultural studies is committed to moral evaluation of modern society and to a radical line of political action. . . . Cultural studies aims to understand and change the structures of dominance everywhere, but in capitalist societies in particular.[15]

At this point, however, a cautionary note must be sounded, to be amplified throughout the book. Although the upper right-hand quadrant of figure 2.1 is labeled critical-idealist, it is also the case that the more poststructuralist the writings are, the greater is the tendency to abandon certain defining properties of critical analysis, including the presumption that there are enduring criteria (or in Lazarsfeld's terms, "human values,") by which to judge events, situations, conditions, structures, and practices. As well, due to its emphasis on language, poststructuralism tends to emphasize interpretive freedom on the part of message recipients, again melding this ostensibly critical stance with "celebrative" cultural studies. In the course of this book, I will in fact propose that poststructuralist positions are in practice *faux-critical*, that they are quite status quo-affirming.[16] But we are not ready to probe quite so deeply just yet.

Today, exponents of poststructuralist cultural studies often write as if *their* presumptions and *their* modes of analysis encompass the entire cultural studies field. Notwithstanding the fragmentation of cultural studies discussed earlier, when poststructuralist cultural studies scholars denigrate political economy, they usually do so as if they were speaking for the entire field, which is far from the case. I will argue in this book that in fact the differences between poststructuralists and political economists today are no greater than they are with cultural materialists, that indeed the differences are identical! So, when poststructuralists like Lawrence Grossberg, Angela McRobbie, and others point to irreconcilable differences between cultural studies and political economy, one should always be aware that really they are representing only their particular (poststructuralist) mode of cultural studies, not the entire field.

One complaint lodged by contemporary (poststructuralist) cultural studies scholars against political economy concerns *economism*, that is, an undue economic determinism regarding culture;[17] they have maintained that political economy's purported economism and class emphasis must be "supplemented" by other considerations, particularly ones relating to race, gender, sexuality, and ethnicity. Some of these scholars also claim that since "modernity has passed into postmodernity," contemporary analyses must be "more preoccupied with the fragmentation of cultures than they are with structures of cultural production, dissemination and consumption."[18] In this view, critical political economy, as it is premised on the existence of structures of domination and oppression, is an anachronism in the postmodern age of ever-shifting, ever-fragmenting, and ever-recombining structures.

Another contentious but related issue concerns the relative importance to be accorded the production of cultural artifacts vs. their reception/interpretation. Johnson, for example, after acknowledging contributions to cultural studies by political economists, by the early Frankfurt School, and by E. P. Thompson's classic book *The Making of the English Working Class,* disparaged them all for taking "if not the viewpoint of cultural producers, at least the theoretical standpoint of production."[19] Johnson thereupon defined *productivism* as inferring the character of cultural artifacts and their social uses from their conditions of production, in other words contending that production determines culture.[20]

Economism and productivism, although frequently conflated, are separate issues. In his essay "Sociology and Psychology," for instance, Adorno proposed that "the psychological reality of repression finds its basis in the reality of economic exploitation and the domination of the exchange principle."[21] By linking economic conditions to the psychological states of message recipients, Adorno here might arguably be charged with economism, but certainly not with productivism.

The main thesis of this chapter and the next is that a momentous change occurred when poststructuralism displaced cultural materialism as the dominant cultural studies paradigm, and that this change is the source of the split between contemporary cultural studies and political economy. The present chapter explores the origins and foundations of British cultural studies and establishes the initial unity with political economy, while chapter 3 (reviewing the Colloquy) focuses on the departure of poststructuralist cultural studies from its foundations and the concomitant split with critical political economy. Chapter 4 looks at the birth of American cultural studies and places that within the historical development of mainline American media/communication studies.

To see how cultural studies was conceived at its beginnings, I propose again two major points of origin. One is Britain, where Richard Hoggart and Raymond Williams, albeit in different ways, turned from literary analyses of "great works" to critical appreciations or "readings" of everyday life, and where historian E. P. Thompson recounted the cultural histories and contributions of ordinary, working class people.[22] Stuart Hall, Lawrence Grossberg, and many others have nominated these three writers as inaugurators, certainly, of *British* cultural studies. The second point of origin is, again, the Frankfurt School, and Adorno in particular. Terry Eagleton, a former student of Raymond Williams, wrote: "It was the Frankfurt School which first turned serious attention to mass culture, and so lies at the origin of what is known today as Cultural Studies."[23] Kostas Gouliamos notes that Adorno was influenced particularly by Siegfried Kracauer of the School, who built up theories based on a series of small examples and was one of the first to treat cinema seriously.[24] However, as Adorno is the more renowned and prolific of the two, and given also his status as inaugurator of political economy approaches to media studies, I focus on Adorno.

Other points of origin, too, can be identified. Particularly compelling are the fascist prison cells where Antonio Gramsci was incarcerated from 1926 to 1937. Raymond Williams regarded Gramsci's work on hegemony as "one of the major turning points in Marxist cultural theory."[25] Today, Gramsci's term, *hegemony*, is virtually a household word. His contributions to cultural theory are undoubtedly seminal and highly significant. On the other hand, his work was not disseminated, even in Italian, until after the War—subsequent to the pioneering work of Adorno. As well, the English translation of *The Modern Prince* appeared only in 1957, while *Selections From The Prison Notebooks* and *Letters From Prison* were published in English in 1971 and 1973 respectively. While Gramsci's work is not considered further in the present book, it is clear that fuller consideration would assuredly support, not refute, the main thesis: in its beginnings cultural studies was fully integrated with, and not antithetical to, political economy. In particular, there is a great affinity between Gramsci's notion of hegemony and Innis' concept of monopolies of knowledge.

The thrust of Adorno's position is less populist than that of the British cultural theorists, but nonetheless Adorno shared many elements with them. By juxtaposing in these opening chapters the sometimes linguistically diverse and geographically disparate beginnings of cultural studies, we can derive the essentials of a critical cultural studies for today which is consistent with and supportive of critical political economy. The origin of cultural studies in the United States is addressed in chapter 4.

BRITISH CULTURAL STUDIES

In 1964, Richard Hoggart (b. 1918), then professor of modern English literature, founded the Centre for Contemporary Cultural Studies at the University of Birmingham, giving cultural studies both a name and a home. In 1968, Hoggart left the Centre to become assistant director-general at UNESCO, his replacement being Stuart Hall.[26] Hoggart's 1957 book, *The Uses of Literacy,* is by general consensus the first of three founding texts of British cultural studies, the others being *Culture and Society* by Raymond Williams and *The Making of the English Working Class* by E. P. Thompson.[27] All three books, according to Hall, proposed that culture is tied closely to changes in industry, democracy, class, and art.[28] Moreover, all three placed "the 'politics of intellectual work' squarely at the centre of Cultural Studies."[29] Furthermore, all three are interdisciplinary, combining sociological, historical, political, ethnographic, and economic analyses, going beyond textual analysis to speculate on the relations between texts and patterns of lived experience.[30] And all three focus on class. For present purposes, though, their most significant shared feature is their weaving seamlessly analyses of culture with what is now known as critical political economy of media.

Richard Hoggart

As an adult educator, Richard Hoggart taught students who, for reasons of class, income, or personal situation, had not attained normal entry into post-secondary education. It was primarily for them that *The Uses of Literacy* was written.[31] Hoggart was himself of working class origin, helping to explain his approach. In his book, Hoggart employed tools of literary criticism as used by F. R. Leavis and others in their analyses of "high culture," but applied these instead to "the full rich life" of working class communities. He maintained that through close analyses of cultural artifacts and practices, one can comprehend "the felt quality of life." He addressed popular entertainments (the pubs, the movies, the music), and related these to the social practices, language patterns, community activities, and family relations. He "read" the living culture as a text which, for Stuart Hall, was "a throughgoing departure."[32]

Hoggart was reacting to the "canonical elitism"[33] of theorists like Leavis and Matthew Arnold, and more generally to cultural domination of wage-earners by the upper class. He maintained that elite power stems partly from the legitimacy accorded *their* cultural forms and hence contended that greater political equality (democracy) must entail *cultural* struggle. Hoggart's first aim, therefore, was to elevate the stature of working class culture.

He had also a second purpose. He compared English working class culture before and after World War II, detecting a marked deterioration when commercial or mass culture gained ascendancy. Mass culture does not emerge from the lived conditions of ordinary people and hence, for Hoggart, lacks organicism and authenticity. He deemed commercial cultural products (popular music, American television, crime and romance novels, and so forth) banal, pretentious, and intrinsically phony. By displacing indigenous culture, he claimed, commercial culture "colonized" the working class.[34] To gain audience, media appealed to, but in the process distorted, many admirable working class traits. For instance, advertisers played upon working class tolerance and love of freedom, but debased these traits through exaggeration.[35] Media amplified the ideal of freedom, for example, "until it [became] the freedom "to 'be' anything at all, and certainly not to object to anything at all."[36] Here, as elsewhere in Hoggart's work, a basic Aristotelian principle (good carried to an extreme reverts to ill) is in play.

Finally, in *The Uses of Literacy,* Hoggart addressed concentrations of press ownership and aspects of the production of media texts, not merely their consumption or interpretation. Thereby Hoggart, too, helped establish critical political-economic treatments of British cultural industries.

The Uses of Literacy shares several characteristics with Adorno's work. First, Hoggart presented a nondeterministic, dialectical mode cultural analysis. On the one hand, he wrote that in the face of commercial indoctrination "working class people still possess some older and inner resistances."[37] He noted particularly the "capacity of the human spirit to resist."[38] He speculated that common people regard art and entertainment primarily "as an escape, as something enjoyed but not assumed to have much connection with the matter of daily life."[39] He proposed, too, that people are able to compartmentalize their lives, so that life at home is distinguished from life outside, and "real" life is segregated from mere entertainment.[40] On the other hand, resistance and cynicism as audiences' chief defenses against media dissimulations can themselves be detrimental, engendering the stance that nothing is worth much: "The new attitude," he lamented, "is frequently a refusal to consider any values, because all values are suspect."[41] (Support for this assessment is to be found in Michael Mann's remarks that contemporary British working class culture is characterized by inconsistencies, cynicism, and fatalism.[42]) Even though the British working class may resist the intended indoctrination, then, media may have detrimental consequences nonetheless.

Hoggart remarked, too, on the deskilling of the labor force through industrialization, which one could regard as an additional source of apathy and cynicism. He wrote: "The common man knows his job and can do it without much strain; it requires no special skill other than that long established by practice. After a time he can hardly be interested in what he does; the same dozen or so jobs recur too often for that."[43]

Like Adorno, Hoggart thought of mass media as displacing traditional class cultures, and hence weakening class consciousness. Regarding the "undiscriminating looking-in, night after night" of the television audience, for example, he declared:

> Everything and almost anything is acceptable because, as important as the intrinsic interest of any programme itself, is the sense that you are one in the big group watching the world (the world of events and personages) unroll before you. These tendencies, I think, may assist the emergence of a cultural group almost as large as the sum of all other groups. But it would be a group only in the sense that its members shared a passivity.[44]

Hoggart described the emerging *mass culture* as a "soft mass-hedonism," and as a "hedonistic-group-individualism."[45] An associated aspect of this new mass culture is the "temptation to live in a constant present"[46]—what Innis referred to as *present-mindedness*.

Over his long career Hoggart authored or edited twenty-seven volumes. *The Uses of Literacy* remains, however, by far his most influential. Once Hoggart left the Centre, "the role of the theoretical pioneer passed over to Raymond Williams."[47]

Raymond Williams

Raymond Williams (1921–1988)—a self-proclaimed "Welsh European" (as opposed to an English subject or person of British ancestry)[48]—is the second, and certainly the most renowned, of the three British founders of cultural studies. According to Graham Murdock, "Raymond Williams . . . did more than anyone else to map out the terrain that cultural studies would come to occupy."[49] For that reason, this chapter devotes the most space to Williams. Like Hoggart, Williams was born to a wage-earning family. For many years, he was a professor of drama at Cambridge. His ascent to the highest echelons of international scholarship made him, in class-riven England, one of "the awkward squad."[50] Like Hoggart, Williams had been an adult educator and he likewise believed that democracy requires that working class culture be authenticated. Williams authored over twenty scholarly books, some seven novels, several plays, and was editor or coeditor of numerous other volumes.[51] His first book, *Culture and Society 1780–1950*, published in 1958, is the second chronologically of the three founding texts of British cultural studies.

Culture and Society

Cultural and Society traces changes in the meaning of culture over a period of one hundred and seventy years, as gleaned from the writings of a succession of British authors including Burke, Shelley, Keats, Coleridge, J. S. Mill, Carlyle, Matthew Arnold, William Morris, Tawney, D. H. Lawrence, and T. S. Eliot. Williams' objective was to develop "a new general theory of culture" by interrelating all of culture's major elements[52]—*industry, democracy, class*, and *art*—to show that as these changed, so did the meaning of culture.[53] Political-economic concerns, then, are built into the very core of Williams' theory of culture. Indeed, he declared, "the development of the word *culture* is a record of a number of important and continuing reactions to these changes in our social, economic, and political life;"[54] and again: "Our meaning of culture is a response to the events which our meanings of industry and democracy most evidently define."[55]

For Williams, *culture* was "a special kind of map by means of which the nature of the changes can be explored."[56] For example, when traditionalists equate culture with elitist ("high") culture,[57] they are being antidemocratic, for the implication is that working people are inferior and hence incapable of participating wisely in political affairs. This class bias, according to Williams, infuses the schools, which he thought normally reinforce existing social relations.[58] A virtue of T. S. Eliot's famous but otherwise conservative essay, *Notes Towards the Definition of Culture* (1948), according to Williams, is its treatment of culture as "a whole way of life."[59] Eliot pronounced that "culture includes all the characteristic activities and interests of a people: Derby Day, Henley Regatta, the twelfth of August,[60] a cup final, the dog races, the pin table, the dart board, Wensleydale cheese, boiled cabbage cut into sections, beetroot in vinegar, nineteenth century Gothic churches, and the music of Elgar."[61]

This notion of culture as a whole way of life, which Williams appropriated, did not originate with Eliot, however. Williams understood that it had already become commonplace within anthropology and sociology, and that it may even be traced to such literary theorists as Coleridge (1772–1834) and Carlyle (1795–1881). Nonetheless, as compared to those literary conservatives,[62] Williams' innovation was to apply this broad conception of culture as an antidote to elitist schools of thought. It is true, Williams affirmed, that due to its historically subservient position, the working class had not (yet) contributed substantially to culture in the restricted sense of a body of imaginative and intellectual "works." But then, for him, "a culture can never be reduced to its artifacts while it is being lived."[63] What the working class *had* accomplished, however, and magnificently so, was the creation of institutions based on a collectivist view of society: trade unions, the cooperative movement, a political party. And this, too, is culture—albeit in the broader and deeper sense of "a whole way of life."[64]

Moreover, Williams noted, working class people often engage in a wide range of "skilled, intelligent, and creative activity," such as gardening, carpentry, metal working, and politics, which not only give pleasure but also improve community life. From the contemptuous eye of the highly literate, such activities are likely be scorned. But for Williams (displaying a high degree of reflexivity), the contempt of the highly literate "is a mark of the observers' limits, not those of the activities themselves."[65] Indeed, he maintained that the highly literate are "deluded" when they judge the quality of life by the standard of great literature: "The error resembles that of the narrow reformer who supposes that farm labourers and village craftsmen were once uneducated, merely because they could not read."[66]

Rather than seeking out and documenting "proletariat literature" or other working class "works," Williams proposed it would be better to focus on "alternative ideas of the nature of social relationship."[67] Whereas *individualism* is the hallmark of bourgeois social relationships, and *service* (or *noblesse oblige*) characterizes an authoritarian, aristocratic, protective stance, Williams claimed we can "properly associate" the following with the working class' conception of social relationship: communism, socialism, cooperation, community, solidarity, neighborhood. Each of these terms connotes a conception of society neither as neutral (as in the bourgeois or liberal view), nor protective (as in the paternalistic conception), but rather as "the positive means for all kinds of development, including individual development."[68]

Like Hoggart, Williams was at pains to distinguish between popular culture as transmitted by mass media, and authentic working class culture: "We cannot fairly or usefully describe the bulk of the material produced by the new means of communication as 'working class culture,'" he insisted. "For neither is it by any means produced exclusively for this class, nor, in any important degree, is it produced by them."[69] Williams and Hoggart both saw commodified entertainment, rather, as eroding authentic working class culture.

Williams dated the onset of commercialized culture, particularly the routine commodification of literary works, to the late eighteenth century. In support of this claim he cited Adam Smith, who not only noted the narrow, class-based origin of most cultural works (an observation having affinity to Innis' monopolies of knowledge), but who also may be regarded as anticipating Gramsci's notion of *hegemony*.[70] For Williams, however, Smith's remarks were most notable for depicting conditions whereby artists' work was "purchased, in the same manner as shoes or stockings.'"[71] The commodification of cultural production, Williams added, "followed inevitably from the institution of commercial publishing."[72]

For Williams, like Adorno, the commodification of cultural artifacts caused a rift in conceptions both of art and the role of the artist. "When art is a commodity," he advised, "taste is adequate, but when it is something more, a more active relationship is essential."[73] In the period of the Romantics (Blake, Shelley), genuine art was viewed as issuing from the superior imagination and as being a vehicle for the perfection of humankind, whereas art for the marketplace stems merely from "the calculating faculty."[74] From this distinction, it was not a huge leap to set "high" art (as appreciated by the elite) against "low" art (or art for the plebs). For Williams, however, that distinction bore all sorts of antidemocratic ramifications, which he set about rectifying, his method being, essentially, the recasting of the notion of *culture as art* into the axiom *culture as a whole way of life*.[75]

In support of culture as a whole way of life, Williams referred to and compared novelists Elizabeth Gaskell and Charles Dickens. Regarding Gaskell's *Mary Barton,* he remarked that what he found most impressive "is the intensity of the effort to record, in its own terms, the feel of everyday life in the working class homes . . . the carefully annotated reproduction of dialect, the carefully included details of food prices . . . the itemized description of the furniture of the Barton's living-room."[76] In contrast, Dickens's *Hard Times*, for Williams, was "an analysis of Industrialism, rather than an experience of it." He conjectured that Dickens likely had Mill's *Political Economy* (1849) in mind in making his general indictments of industrialism, adding: "In terms of general understanding of the industrial working people Dickens is obviously less successful than Mrs Gaskell."[77] For our purposes, though, what is most significant is that Williams chose to juxtapose and compare Gaskell and Dickens, the first proffering through fiction a study of working class culture, the second through narrative a critique of classical political economy.

In *Culture and Society*, and consistent with his interweaving of political economy, Williams claimed that "the dominant class can to a large extent control the transmission and distribution of the whole common inheritance." He explained:

> A tradition is always selective, and that there will always be a tendency for this process of selection to be related to and even governed by the interests of the class that is dominant. These factors make it likely that there will be qualitative changes in the traditional culture when there is a shift of class power.[78]

Williams insisted, however, that "communication is not only transmission; it is also reception and response."[79] Thereby he again proposed a unity between what are now known as cultural studies and political economy. Regarding transmission, he stated that "any governing body will seek to implant the 'right' ideas in the minds of those whom it governs," but then quickly qualified that observation by noting that interpretation by message receivers depends not only upon their skill with the language but as well on their "whole experience," adding: "Any real theory of communication is a theory of community."[80]

Williams' version of cultural studies, as inaugurated in his foundational book, differs markedly from contemporary poststructuralist cultural studies. Many poststructuralists maintain that meaning is in language, that one can never escape language to get at the "real" state of affairs, or indeed that no "real" exists beyond language. For Williams, in contrast, changes in the meanings of words (for instance, *culture, industry, art, democracy*), and the invention of new words, are responses to changes in the lived conditions. Changes in the meanings of words, for him, constituted "a record" of reactions to changes in social, economic, and political life. That record is a type of "map" guiding explorations into the nature of the changes.[81] Among the words originating in the "decisive period" from 1750 to 1850 are: "*ideology, intellectual, rationalism, scientist, humanitarian, utilitarian, romanticism, atomistic; bureaucracy, capitalism, collectivism, commercialism, communism, doctrinaire, equalitarian, liberalism, masses, medieval* and *medievalism, operative* (noun), *primitivism, proletariat* (a new word for 'mob'), *socialism, unemployment; cranks, highbrow, isms,* and *pretentious.*"[82]

According to Williams, moreover, words and concepts developed in previous times cannot be applied with equanimity or without modification to current situations. Meanings change as lived experience changes; there is interaction between language and lived conditions.[83] Williams' emphasis on language reflects his vocation as an English professor, and that orientation he certainly shared with contemporary poststructuralists. However, by insisting on a two-way interaction between language and material conditions, he was far removed from contemporary poststructuralism.

Culture and Society was first in what can now be regarded as a family of books, others including *The Long Revolution* (1961), *Keywords* (1976), *Problems in Materialism and Culture* (1980), and *The Year 2000* (1983).[84] The later tomes further clarified and extended the author's position regarding interdependencies between culture and political-economic conditions and trends. Now I will focus on matters raised but left underdeveloped in *Culture and Society* but dealt with more extensively in his later books—in particular, Williams' treatments of the "mass," the relation between base and superstructure (economic determinism), and technological determinism.

Mass and Class Consciousness

Williams used the term, *the long revolution*, to denote the drawn-out process whereby common people increasingly came to "direct their own lives, by breaking through pressures and restrictions of older forms of society, and by discovering new common institutions."[85] Begun in the late 1700s, the long revolution comprised three subsidiary revolutions, only two of which received much scholarly attention prior to Williams. One was the *democratic revolution,* whereby the franchise and other rights and freedoms—freedom of speech, freedom to assemble, freedom to be represented on juries and in Parliament, freedom to be a parliamentary representative, freedom to unionize and strike—were gained by common people through long and painful struggle. (See, for example, Thompson's *The Making of the English Working Class.*) Second was the *industrial revolution*, backed by science and capital, which gave rise to (the idea of) the working class.[86] Third was the *cultural revolution,* which Williams defined as the extension of learning, including the skills of literacy and other advanced communications, to classes other than the elite.

Victories and accomplishments attained in the long revolution continue to affect the lives of us all. For Williams, however, the long revolution had stalled. Writing in 1961, well before Thatcherism, he observed "a serious state of unbalance between provision for social and individual need. . . . It is easy to get a sense of plenty from the shop windows of contemporary Britain, but if we look at the schools, the hospitals, the roads, the libraries, we find chronic shortages far too often."[87] Also highly problematic, he noted elsewhere, are escalating environmental stresses.[88] These concerns all involve "collective goods," transcending the wants and needs of individuals.

A significant factor impeding the long revolution's continuance, according to Williams, has been popular acceptance of the concept of *the mass.* As people came increasingly to view themselves as part of the mass, their class identity weakened, and with it the collectivist desire which had motivated the long revolution. Williams asked rhetorically, "If everyone is only out for himself, why bother about social change?"[89] To be *in* the mass is to be, by definition, *outside of* community, out of neighborhood, out of solidarity.[90]

Without class consciousness, Williams continued, a new domination by elites sets in.[91] Indeed, he proposed, the idea of the mass was created by elites ("who work very hard at it, by the way") and is absolutely required for the current organization of society.[92] An elite-mass dichotomy means, essentially, that the great majority of people are expected to do little other than express "a pattern of demands and preferences."[93] They are to be observers and consumers. Their demands and preferences are gauged and assessed through polls, focus groups, and other methods of market research, and if need be are then manipulated through advertising, PR, control of news, changes to the educational curricula, and by pressures brought to bear through financing of the arts. In such circumstances, democracy amounts to little more than, to cite Chomsky, a "necessary illusion."

Contributing mightily to people's self-conception as members of the mass are, of course, the mass media. Listeners and viewers of mass media, although separated and out of communication with one another, focus their attention on the same commercial products. For Williams, capital-intensive media are, by and large, "institutions of cynicism, of denial, and of division."[94] In a 1978 essay, he enlarged on the importance to elites of controlling the media:

> Problems of social order and relationship . . . centre in issues of control of and access to the developed means of amplification or duration. Characteristically these are of direct interest to a ruling class; all kinds of control and restriction of access have been repeatedly practised.[95]

Williams understood broadcasting, in particular, to be a "powerful form of social integration and control," adding: "Many of its main uses can be seen as socially, commercially and at times politically manipulative."[96] For democracy to be more than mere illusion, he wrote, "the [communication] system must be free."[97] To move toward an effective democracy, he counseled, centralization must be redressed by applying through public policy two principles: first, *the right to transmit,* and second, *the right to receive*. In western societies, we often feel that our communication system is an instrument of democracy because the right to receive is widespread (albeit constrained by government and corporate secrecy and often by user-pay requirements). However, we tend to pay scant attention to the fact that there is little in the way of a right to transmit. Williams noted that "the proprietors of [most] media retain the right to chose who may transmit messages via their media"—a far from democratic situation, given the high concentration of media ownership. Williams died before the Internet became a reality in millions of people's lives; one suspects he would have found much to rejoice over and to despair about in contemplating this new medium.

Williams distinguished among three types of media: *amplificatory media* (for example the megaphone) extend directly the spatial reach of messages from senders; *durative media* (such as tape recordings) preserve messages over time; and *alternative* or *symbolic* media (television, radio, film, the printed page) require special skills of encoding and decoding (literacy, media literacy). Often media entail large capital investments, and hence favor centralized control.[98] That in turn means that very large audiences are required to sustain such media. For Williams, this was not necessarily a problem in itself;

the problem, rather, arose from the low esteem accorded these large audiences by message providers. When audiences are seen merely as a mass or a mob, there results a marked tendency on the part of message senders "to make a profit out of ignorance or inexperience." Williams added: "The existence, in our own [society] of powerful media of persuasion and suggestion make [the temptation to exploit audiences] virtually irresistible."[99]

Base and Superstructure (Economic Determinism)

Also germane to Williams' integrated understanding of culture and political economy are his pronouncements on *base* and *superstructure*. In an essay entitled "Literature and Sociology," he stated unambiguously: "I have always opposed the [Marxist] formula of base and superstructure," explaining,

> It was above all . . . the received formula of base and superstructure which made Marxist accounts of literature and thought often weak in practice. [According to that account] the economic base *determines* the social relations which determine consciousness which determines actual ideas and works.[100]

For Williams, the word *determines* is fraught with difficulty. On the one hand, it can denote an external cause controlling all subsequent change or activity (the hard definition); on the other, it can mean setting limits or exerting pressure or influence,[101] in which case, one might add, it recalls Innis' notion of *bias*. "Vulgar Marxism," according to Williams, routinely, but mistakenly, uses the term *determines* in the hard sense when referring to the economic base and legal/cultural superstructure.[102] In *Marxism and Literature,* Williams stated that *economism,* or hard economic determinism, "as a philosophical and political doctrine . . . is worthless."[103]

Williams gave several reasons for rejecting the notion that the economic base *determines,* in the hard sense, literature, art, and culture (the superstructure). Here I note two. First, reminiscent of Innis, Williams maintained that to presume hard determinism is tantamount to denying human agency or what he termed "active consciousness." The study of culture, he insisted, must incorporate "all the active processes of learning, imagination, creation, performance."[104] Despite that affirmation, however, Williams also proposed that meanings ascribed to cultural artifacts normally depend on the interpreter's social class, and indeed he defined *possible consciousness* as the "objective limit that can be reached by a class before it turns into another class, or is replaced."[105] Analogously, he defined *community* as people sharing "a specific general way of seeing other people and nature."[106] These arguments, in a sense, are opposite sides of the same coin and in combination urge the analyst to allow for the possibility of different interpretations (i.e., human agency) while always bearing in mind that interpretation is, to a considerable extent, class based.

Second, according to Williams, the superstructure in some ways has priority over the base. In *Communications* he remarked that "the struggle to learn, to describe, to understand, to educate is . . . not begun, at second hand, after reality has occurred; it is, in itself, a major way in which reality is continually formed and changed."[107]

In place of the formula, *base determines superstructure*, therefore, Williams recommended theorizing "the social totality," which might be paraphrased as *theorizing society as a total system*. A theory of the social totality, he continued, must present culture as comprising "relations between elements in a whole way of life."[108] And that is precisely what he meant by *cultural studies*! And that is why Williams' work so seamlessly integrates culture and the concerns of political economy.

His rejecting the base/superstructure model is not to suggest, therefore, that in Williams' mind economic factors can be safely disregarded when studying culture, at least certainly not in contemporary, capitalist society. To the contrary, economic/financial considerations predominate.[109] Consistent with general systems theory, he maintained that structures or nodes (what he referred to as "elements") wax and wane in influence. As the "totality" evolves, the strength and direction of influence among the elements change. For Williams, capitalism is the lived system giving inordinate importance to economic factors.[110] He decried, for instance, "the deepest cultural damage" that industrial capitalism had wrought by fostering our tendency to think of economic affairs as separate "from the whole network of activities, interests, and relationships,"[111] thereby making us oblivious to the deep impact economic processes have on our whole way of life. For economic elements to exert the influence they now do, Williams insisted, is not merely an imbalance, it is an aberration, if not indeed a travesty. Referring approvingly to writings of Lukács and Goldmann, he declared:

> The dominance of economic activity over all other forms of human activity, the dominance of its values over all other values, was given a precise historical explanation. . . . This dominance, this deformation, was the specific characteristic of capitalist society.[112]

In addition to falsely insisting that economic relations and activities are largely separate from other human activities, Williams declared that elite groups *reify* (render falsely objective) dominant values and meanings. Previously we noted Williams' objections to how elites encourage people to think of themselves as part of the *mass*—a reification consistent with a strategy of divide and conquer.[113] Elites also reify *value*, making value seem to be synonymous with price, all but obliterating non-market-based value. It is in regard to value and price that Williams noted one of the great paradoxes of modern media. On the one hand, the rise of commercial media competed with and in the end weakened the influence of high or elite culture, thereby also weakening distinctions between elites and the working class. On the other hand, those same new media, highjacked by commercial forces, utterly reverse that movement toward democratization, for as mass media artifacts attract working class attention, the constant indoctrination of individualist ideology pushes aside authentic (collectivist) working class culture, and value becomes synonymous with price.

Although contemporary media generally are controlled by and help buttress existing power, Williams emphasized that within the social totality there is always opposition and contradiction: "The degree of existence of these alternative and oppositional forms is itself a matter of constant historical variation in real circumstances,"[114] he declared. At the margins of society, too, are "autonomous artists and independent scholars" who, Williams pronounced gloomily, despite radical beginnings, often "slip into the prepared ideological positions: the 'mass' culture; the 'technologised world.'"[115]

Technological (Media) Determinism

Williams addressed the issue of technological change in several ways. He recognized, for example, that contestations between established and emergent cultures are often associated with the rise of new media. Although he did not fully pursue the Innisian notion that new media are introduced as a way of countering existing monopolies of knowledge, he did claim that new media are generally a response to gaps in the existing social system. For example, "the development of the [daily] press . . . was at once a response to the development of an extended social, economic and political system and a response to crisis within that system."[116] Prior to industrialization and mass production, the existing lines of communication were adequate to transmit simple orders, and traditional institutions, like the Church, were sufficient to propagate ideology. With industrialism, however, new modes of production and consumption required also a new medium to combine "news and background—the whole orienting, predictive and updating process."[117] The newspaper was also a response to heightened private mobility,[118] as was broadcasting.[119]

As well as rejecting hard *economic* determinism, Williams also dismissed hard *technological* determinism. He wrote:

> Virtually all technical study and experiment are undertaken within already existing social relations and cultural forms, typically for purposes that are already

> foreseen. Moreover, a technical invention as such has comparatively little social significance. It is only when it is selected for investment towards production, and when it is consciously developed for particular social uses—that is, when it moves from being a technical invention to what can properly be called an available *technology*—that the general significance begins.[120]

Likewise, in *Television: Technology and Cultural Form,* after providing a cursory review of the histories of electricity, telegraphy, photography, motion pictures, radio, and television, Williams insisted: "It is especially a characteristic of the [modern, technological] communications systems that all were foreseen—not in utopian but in technical ways—before the crucial components of the developed systems had been discovered and refined. In no way is this a history of communications systems creating a new society or new social conditions."[121]

More generally, according to Williams, we must reject all doctrines of technological determinism as they obscure real social, political, and economic intentions and decision-making.[122] "The reality of determination," he wrote, sounding positively Innisian, "is the setting of limits and the exertion of pressures, within which variable social practices are profoundly affected but never necessarily controlled."[123]

On the other hand, although rejecting technological determinism, certainly, Williams also insisted that we not fall into the opposite error, namely *determined technology*—the belief that all consequences of technological innovation are foreseen. For Williams, technological innovation usually gives rise to "unforeseen uses and unforeseen effects;"[124] thereby he dismissed also the contention that economic-political factors determine (in the hard sense) what also might be seen as technologically induced outcomes.

Innis and Williams

It is time now to take stock of differences and similarities between Williams' cultural studies and Innis' political economy, and in particular to establish whether and the extent to which these inaugural positions are broadly consistent, mutually supportive, and/or complementary.

To begin, Williams' tripartite demarcation of *amplificatory, durative,* and *alternative* or *symbolic* media certainly differs from the dualist schemata set forth by Innis, but the intent is the same. Williams wrote: "This typology, while still abstract, bears centrally on questions of social relationships and social order within the communicative process."[125] Innis' aim, likewise, was to relate changes in media to changes in social relationships and the social order. Both writers, therefore, were *media theorists*. Furthermore, Williams' category, amplificatory, bears on communication over space, and durative relates to communication through time. On the other hand, Williams' distinctions were premised on whether media extend (through space or over time) direct emanations of the message sender—his or her voice or image—or whether the messages are worked upon or processed (coded) prior to transmission as with writing and print, television news clips and interviews, feature films, and so forth, thereby requiring specialized encoding and decoding skills such as literacy, photography, and media literacy. This distinction related, of course, to Williams' desire to increase democratic communication in the face of centralized control. The connections with Innis in this regard are closer than they might at first seem. Innis wrote extensively on "monopolies of knowledge," aspects of which were special skills required for encoding and decoding messages. For example, in describing the biases of clay tablets and cuneiform script as used in the civilization along the Euphrates and Tigris rivers, Innis drew attention to the monopolizing consequences of special skills:

> Dependence on clay in the valleys of the Euphrates and Tigris involved a special technique in writing and a special type of instrument, the reed stylus. Cuneiform writing on clay involved an elaborate skill, intensive training, and concentration of durable records. The temples with their priesthoods became the centres of cities. A culture based on intensive training in writing rendered centralized control unstable and gave organized religion an enormous influence.[126]

A similar point is made with regard to Chinese pictographs, a highly complex symbol system consisting of tens of thousands of characters that necessitated the emergence of "a learned class" that denigrated traditional knowledge.

Moreover, Williams and Innis were agreed that popular media (Williams) and the vernacular (Innis) enable elites to connect with common people, and in our day that means spreading the ideology of individualism/consumerism (Williams) or present-mindedness (Innis). Both writers bemoaned tight concentration of control over our contemporary media—for Williams because concentration offsets the democratic potential inherent to widespread reception, and for Innis because it reinforces the neglect of time and inhibits two-way interaction.

In addition, Williams and Innis were dialectical writers. The contradiction or tension highlighted in Williams' work was democracy vs. autocracy, or some variant (such as working class culture vs. elite culture) while tensions between centralization/decentralization, and hierarchy/leveling of authority figured prominently in Innis' writings.[127] Both writers, of course, were opposed to tyranny, and both saw unmitigated market forces as tyrannical. One of the means of avoiding, or redressing, tyranny, Williams and Innis agreed, was for elites to loosen their grip over the means of communication. For Williams, that meant removing large portions of media from commercial control and the commodity form, and instituting rights for common people to access media as message senders; for Innis, all that certainly was part of the solution, but as well he called for a reinvigoration of the oral dialectic to offset mechanized, space-binding media.

For Innis and Williams (as for Adorno), true understanding of present conditions comes mainly from the margins of society. For Williams, however, artists and intellectuals, despite radical beginnings, often succumb to economic pressures and "slip into the prepared ideological positions of mass culture and the technologised world."[128] Innis agreed, claiming that it is only at rare intervals that creative artists and intellectuals are truly freed from elite control, and hence it is only at such times that a culture, even if but briefly, can truly flourish.

Certainly Innis' canvass was much grander than Williams.' Innis understood media to be implicated in the veritable rise and fall of civilizations—Egypt, Greece, Rome, Mesopotamia, the Dark and Middle Ages—as well as being paramount in contemporary western civilization. Williams' specialty, on the other hand, was England during and since the Industrial Revolution. Williams saw the control exercised by commercial forces over media as an aberration peculiar to capitalism, and as a travesty. Innis, on the other hand, with his transcivilizational view that included also the various staples economies of Canada, emphasized that monopolies of knowledge are the rule, not the exception, and these knowledge monopolies are inextricably tied to political-economic power. In our time, as it happens, it is corporate, commercial concerns that possess (and propagate) their monopolies of knowledge.

Neither Williams nor Innis was a hard economic or technological determinist, although both certainly saw economic and technological factors as being highly significant.

Most significantly, although Williams was versed in English literature and language, he was also a political economist in undertaking his cultural studies; and Innis, although trained in the social sciences and practising economics/economic history, placed culture (time and space as organizing principles, extended analyses of literacy) at the very heart of his political economy. Despite marginal differences in positions and approaches, the writings of these two seminal authors show no bifurcation of cultural studies/political economy, and considered together, both their works gives rise to an even more comprehensive and nuanced view than when they are considered separately.

E. P. Thompson

E. P. (Edward) Thompson (1924–1993) is the third of the foundational British theorists, and his landmark book, *The Making of the English Working Class*

(1963), is third of the inaugural cultural studies texts. Interestingly, like *Culture and Society* and *The Uses of Literacy, The Making of the English Working Class*, too, came out of adult teaching.[129] Poet, historian, and peace activist, Thompson was also biographer of the British socialist William Morris and of the poet William Blake.

The opening paragraphs of *The Making of the English Working Class* show both the inseparability in Thompson's mind of what are today known as political economy and cultural studies, and the inadequacy, for him, of the base/superstructure model. "Class," he declared, "is a cultural as much as an economic formation."[130] Class "happens,"

> when some men, as a result of common experiences (inherited or shared), feel and articulate the identity of their interests as between themselves, and against other men whose interests are different from (and usually opposed to) theirs. The class experience is largely determined by the productive relations into which men are born—or enter involuntarily. Class-consciousness is the way in which these experiences are handled in cultural terms: embodied in traditions, value-systems, ideas, and institutional forms. . . . Class is a relationship, and not a thing.[131]

Later, even more clearly and insistently in what may be taken as a précis of his entire book, he wrote:

> The making of the working class is a fact of political and cultural, as much as of economic, history. It was not the spontaneous generation of the factory system. Nor should we think of an external force—the "industrial revolution"—working upon some nondescript undifferentiated raw material of humanity, and turning it out at the other end as a "fresh race of beings." The changing productive relations and working conditions of the Industrial Revolution were imposed, not upon raw material, but upon the free-born Englishman—and the free-born Englishman as Paine had left him or as the Methodists had moulded him. The factory hand or stockinger was also the inheritor of Bunyan, of remembered village rights, of notions of equality before the law, of craft traditions. He was the object of massive religious indoctrination and the creator of political traditions. *The working class made itself as much as it was made*.[132]

In these excerpts, interdependencies among such key terms as culture, literature, class, productive relations, conflict, experience, traditions, religion, ideas, laws, institutional forms, and relationships are proposed with clarity and brevity. Thompson's book—over 900 pages—amplifies these connections through historical study and analysis of the period of the Industrial Revolution in England, particularly 1780 to 1832.

According to Thompson, with industrialization, the price system "penetrated" (Innis' word) the culture of the artisans, but they resisted, even if only for a time. "Customary traditions of craftsmanship," Thompson advised, "normally went together with vestigial notions of a 'fair' price and a 'just' wage." He continued, "Social and moral criteria—subsistence, self-respect, pride in certain standards of workmanship, customary rewards for different grades of skill—these are as prominent in early trade union disputes as strictly 'economic' arguments."[133]

One of the first working class organizations, illustrating the interdependence of the cultural and the political-economic spheres, was the London Corresponding Society, established in 1792 to agitate for universal suffrage but which, within the decade, was dispersed for being subversive by His Majesty's forces. Thompson described how, at the inaugural meeting in the Bell Tavern on Exeter Street, nine "sober and industrious men" first shared bread, cheese, and porter, and after supper partook of their pipes, before deliberating on the subject at hand, namely Parliamentary reform. The L.C.S. during its brief existence, Thompson remarked, typified the working class organization:

> There is the working man as Secretary. There is the low weekly subscription. There is the intermingling of economic and political themes. . . . There is the function of the meeting, both as a social occasion and as a centre for political activity. There is the realistic attention to procedural formalities. Above all, there is the determination to propagate opinions and to organize the converted, embodied in the leading rule: "That the number of our members be unlimited."[134]

Thompson placed great importance on that rule. The Society, he wrote, turned its back on property rights, ending any notion that politics was the preserve of an elite. "To throw open the doors to propaganda and agitation in this 'unlimited' way," he declared, "implied a new notion of democracy, which cast aside ancient inhibitions and trusted to self-activating and self-organizing processes among the common people." He added sardonically, "Such a revolutionary challenge was bound to lead on to the charge of high treason."[135]

At the core of the emerging working class culture of the 1790s was a belief in the "Englishman's birthright . . . the conviction that the rule of law was the distinguishing inheritance of the 'free-born Englishman.'"[136] The common Englishman at this time, Thompson summarized, actually had few affirmative rights, but did feel legally protected against arbitrary power, and claimed a constitutional right to riot to resist oppression.[137] The common person's "defensive ideology" soon nourished greater claims for "positive rights."[138]

Two works of literature—Bunyan's epic, *Pilgrim's Progress* (1678), and Paine's *The Rights of Man* (1791–92)—were foundational to the English working class movement. The former provided English youth with their "first adventure story," depicting a quest by the humble for a future far better than the present and a fate for the idle rich of eternal torment. The latter provided both "a new rhetoric of radical egalitarianism" and "a new framework" for radicalism which condemned monarchical and hereditary principles.[139] Thompson's seamless interweaving of media, culture, and political economy is bountifully illustrated by his depictions of the treatment accorded *The Rights of Man,* its author, and its readers. By the 1790s, he noted, the gentry were so distraught at the sight of miners, potters, and cutlers reading *The Rights of Man,*[140] that Paine had been driven into exile and his book banned as seditious libel.[141] "I am contending for the rights of the *living,*" Paine had written, claiming also that each generation ought not be bound by a musty Constitution but rather should define anew its rights and its form of government: "Kings succeed each other, not as rationals, but as animals. . . . It requires some talents to be a common mechanic; but to be a King, requires only the animal figure of a man—a sort of breathing automaton."[142]

Thompson summarized: "Wherever Jacobin ideas persisted, and wherever hidden copies of *Rights of Man* were cherished, men were no longer disposed to wait upon the example of a Wilkes or a Wyvill before they commenced a democratic agitation."[143]

Thompson provided a detailed analysis of the role of literacy in forming working class consciousness. "The articulate consciousness of the self-taught was above all a political consciousness,"[144] he declared. Laborers, shopkeepers and clerks alike taught themselves individually or in groups to read and write, and often the texts they used were by the radicals of the period. Workingmen thereby came to see their own situation as part of a broader political picture—"their own lives as part of a general history of conflict between the loosely defined 'industrious classes' on the one hand, and the unreformed House of Commons on the other."[145]

Initially, though, neither class consciousness nor the political culture were entirely dependent on universal literacy: "The ballad-singers and 'patterers,'" for example, "had a thriving occupation, with their pavement farces and street-corner parodies."[146] As well, illiterate workers would have political periodicals read aloud to them by their workmates. Sometimes, Thompson noted, abstract political principles were misconstrued, albeit in ways conforming to the prevailing principal of solidarity: "A 'Provisional Government' [was thought to mean] a more plentiful supply of 'provisions;' while, in one account . . . 'universal Suffrage is understood . . . to mean universal suffering. . . . If one member suffers, all must suffer.'"[147]

Radical literature, in any event, was a prominent means of fostering class consciousness and political awareness, and Thompson quoted Sherwin's *Political Register* (1817) as declaring: "If the Bible Societies, and the Sunday School societies have been attended to no other good, they have at least produced one beneficial effect; they have been the means of teaching many thousands of children to read."[148] Thompson noted it had been of some controversy in the Sunday Schools whether children should be taught to both read and write, or read only; while being able to read, it was felt, would increase working class children's exposure to "proper" literature, being able to write might equip them to agitate more effectively when they grew up. As it turned out, the working class gravitated in any event to radical literature and the "great unstamped" periodicals (*The Poor Man's Guardian, Working Man's Friend, Poor Man's Advocate*) provided foundations for "emphatically a working class press."[149] Thompson recounted that "at Barnsley as early as January 1816, a penny-a-month club of weavers was formed, for the purpose of buying Radical newspapers and periodicals."[150] He recounted, too, that by 1833, "at John Doherty's famous 'Coffee and Newsroom' attached to his Manchester bookshop, no fewer than ninety-six newspapers were taken every week, including the illegal 'unstamped,'" adding that "in the smaller towns and villages the reading-groups were less formal but no less important."[151] Thompson summarized:

> This was the culture—with its eager disputations around the booksellers' stalls, in the taverns, workshops, and coffeehouses—which Shelley saluted in his "Song to the Men of England" and within which the genius of Dickens matured. . . . The working class ideology . . . put an exceptionally high value upon the rights of the press, of speech, of meeting and of personal liberty.[152]

Thompson judged that in no other country was the battle for press freedom identified as closely with the cause of the artisans and laborers as in England,[153] making all the more ironic Hoggart's observations concerning the bemusement with which working people after World War II scanned their newspapers—but by then, of course, the commercial press predominated.[154] For Thompson, though, in writing about the early-to-mid-nineteenth century, "the rights of a 'free press' were won in a campaign extending over fifteen or more years which has no comparison for its pigheaded, bloody-minded, and indomitable audacity."[155]

Thompson insisted that "social relations" affect fundamentally the ways in which facts—events such as crop failures, floods, earthquakes, and business cycles—are worked out:

> Behind [a] trade cycle there is a structure of social relations, fostering some sorts of expropriation (rent, interest, and profit) and outlawing others (theft, feudal

> dues), legitimizing some types of conflict (competition, armed warfare) and inhibiting others (trade unionism, bread riots, popular political organization)—a structure which may appear, in the eyes of the future, to be both barbarous and ephemeral.[156]

ADORNO AND BRITISH CULTURAL STUDIES

To conclude this chapter I now compare briefly the cultural studies approach inaugurated by Adorno with that of the British theorists. At first glance they might seem to be in opposition, as Adorno is widely regarded as a cultural elitist, and hence is seemingly at odds with the populism of the British writers. In fact, there is no great divide. Certainly Adorno spent much time admiring great works of "high" culture, but equally did Williams refer continually to the great works (primarily literary) that for him constituted basic documentation for his cultural history. Moreover, Williams and Adorno shared the belief that great artists have the capacity, and duty, to stand outside their prevailing political-economic system to understand and illuminate it, even though (both writers noted) in contemporary society many talented artists and scholars are co-opted by that system.

Both Adorno and the British theorists (Hoggart, Williams) placed high value on "authentic" working class culture, defined as practices and works arising from and helping to shape their lived conditions. For Adorno, authentic popular culture (culture of the people) was both rebellious and "an expression of suffering and contradiction [whereby people attempt] to maintain a grasp on the idea of the good life."[157] For Williams, authentic working class culture entailed the struggle for human rights and democracy in the context of class consciousness, solidarity, and an ethic of cooperation and collectivity. E. P. Thompson, too, emphasized time and again working class culture as one aspiring to freedom, human rights, and group solidarity.

Both Adorno and the British theorists were greatly concerned that centrally produced and distributed commercial culture, intended to meet the exigencies of the marketplace, was replacing authentic or indigenous culture. They emphasized that although cultural artifacts are always produced and experienced within the context of some political-economic order, the prevailing (capitalist) order exerts inordinate influence. Moreover, for these writers, the economic context affected not just the production of cultural artifacts, but also the psychological state of message recipients.

Williams and Adorno had slightly different views of the innovation process. For Adorno, each innovation in media is intended to, and largely has the effect of, extending and deepening elite control. He declared: "A technological rationale *is* the rationale of domination itself."[158] Williams certainly agreed that technological innovation is undertaken with the *intent* of extending and deepening control for those with the capacity to innovate, but he also emphasized that technological innovations usually have unforeseen and unintended consequences, some of which may be to challenge existing power. He was also less pessimistic than Adorno in that he felt newer media (such as the cinema) could actually increase the creative capacity of artists. That having been said, the essential point remains that both Adorno and Williams emphasized that technological innovation often further empowers the already powerful, and hence can be quite undemocratic.

Adorno and Williams also were alike in insisting that one cannot properly understand or describe culture without affording prominence to political-economic factors. Although Williams explicitly repudiated the base/superstructure model whereby the economic system is generally held to "determine" (in the hard sense) the cultural, cognitive, or symbolic sphere, like Adorno he maintained that in *capitalist* societies the economic sphere exerts decisive control over the production of culture. Adorno, Hoggart, and Williams all maintained, however, that people do resist the "realities" presented by commercial media on account of the manifest inconsistencies with their experiences and conditions.

Like Adorno, Horkheimer, and Innis, Williams critiqued scientific (or "instrumental") reason. For Adorno, instrumental reason destroys value and meaning, results in alienation or anomie, and is a prime source of elite power. For Williams, science is false in claiming objectivity or value-neutrality and is used primarily to strengthen the elite.

Adorno, Hoggart, and Williams had much to say about the "mass." Adorno claimed that labor had essentially melded with the bourgeoisie to form a new mass class, which was in conflict with the elite class. For Williams, to the contrary, the mass was not a class at all, but merely an aggregation of self-interested individuals bereft of a sense of solidarity. Whereas Adorno saw class conflict continuing at a new level (between elite and mass), Williams saw the advent of the mass as an elite strategy to deprive common people of their group identity; elite success in this regard had stopped *the long revolution* in its tracks, and major tools in the hands of the elite to propagate the notion of the mass were the mass media. Williams undoubtedly agreed with Adorno, however, that the interests of common people are generally contrary to those of the ruling elite. Hoggart was closer to Williams than Adorno in his understanding of the mass, as he viewed the emerging mass culture as promoted particularly by commercial television as a "soft mass-hedonism" displacing class consciousness. An associated aspect of this new mass culture was the "temptation to live in a constant present."

We see, too, in the abundant similarities between cultural studies as introduced by the German-speaking Adorno and the inaugural cultural studies of the British theorists, evidence which belies James Carey's claim that "cultural studies must be ethnocentric."[159] Carey's reasoning was that "intellectual work, including both cultural studies and political economy, is always and everywhere decisively touched and shaped by the national formation (along with class, race, gender, and so forth)."[160] However, although Adorno certainly did not look into the formation of the British working class as did Thompson, nor describe their daily routines as did Hoggart, he assuredly did address the role of media in securing and perpetuating elite dominance over the cultural practices of the broader public, and that is precisely what the British theorists (and also, incidentally, the Italian-speaking Gramsci) were most concerned to do. One might say that a cultural studies bereft of political economy may incline toward ethnocentrism, but when combined with political economy it will highlight cultural commonalties of capitalist societies. Indeed, to emphasize ethnocentrism, one might argue, could be a device to deflect attention from political-economic pressures on culture.

What is most striking about the documents inaugurating critical cultural studies, whether authored by Adorno or by the British theorists (or by Gramsci, for that matter), is the seamless integration of cultural, political, and economic matters. At the beginning of media studies, then, there was no bifurcation between critical political economy and cultural studies. The inaugural cultural studies writers believed they could not adequately understand the everyday practice of culture without taking into full account the political-economic context, including that of the production of cultural artifacts, and they contended that political-economic context itself evolves in accordance with shifts in culture. Likewise Innis, inaugurator of critical political economy of media, conceived culture not just in terms of orality, literacy, and types of knowledge, but also with regard to conceptions of such basic cultural categories as conceptions of time.

NOTES

1. John Hartley, *A Short History of Cultural Studies* (London: SAGE Publications, 2003), 1.

2. *Wikipedia*, "Cultural Studies," (n.d.), http://en.wikipedia.org/wiki/Cultural_studies (accessed Dec. 15, 2007).

3. Valda Blundell, John Shepherd, and Ian Taylor, "Editor's Introduction," in *Relocating Cultural Studies: Developments in Theory and Research* (London: Routledge, 1993), 4.

4. Richard Johnson, "What Is Cultural Studies Anyway?" *Social Text* 16 (Winter 1986–1987): 38.

5. Blundell et al., "Editor's Introduction," 4.

6. Ziauddin Sardar and Borin Van Loon, *Introducing Cultural Studies* (St. Leonards: Allen and Unwin, 1998), 8.

7. Jeffrey C. Alexander, "Analytical Debates: Understanding the Relative Autonomy of Culture," in *Culture and Society: Contemporary Debates,* ed. Jeffrey C. Alexander and Steven Seidman (Cambridge: Cambridge University Press, 1990), 1–29. The distinction proposed by Stuart Hall is between "culturalism" and "structuralism." Hall associates "culturalism" with the founding British theorists (Hoggart, Williams, and Thompson), and "structuralism" with such French theorists as Levi-Strauss and Althusser. The former, according to Hall, addressed the social totality as an indeterminant system and highlighted human agency, whereas structuralists have been most concerned with detecting determinisms. In this book, however, I argue that the cultural studies of Hoggart, Williams, and Thompson, while certainly addressing the social totality and insisting on human agency, also emphasized such "structuralist" concerns as soft determinisms, disparities in wealth and power, and institutions including laws and media corporations. "Culturalism" as practised by Hoggart, Williams, and Thompson, in my view, at the very least complements "structuralism," as opposed to being antithetical to it, as Hall suggests. The real antithesis to Williams' "culturalism" (or better, his "cultural materialism"), I argue here, is "poststructuralism." Williams himself referred to his position as "cultural materialism," which he defined as "a theory of the specificities of material cultural and literary production within historical materialism." See Stuart Hall, "Cultural Studies: Two Paradigms," *Media, Culture and Society* 2 (1980): 57–72; Adam Katz, "Postmodern Cultural Studies: A Critique," *Cultural Logic* 1, no. 1 (Fall 1997): 1–16; Vincent Leitch, "Birmingham Cultural Studies: Popular Arts, Poststructuralism, Radical Critique," *Journal of the Midwest Modern Language Association* 24, no. 1 (Spring 1991): 74–86; Johnson, "What Is Cultural Studies Anyway?" and Raymond Williams, *Marxism and Literature* (Oxford: Oxford University Press, 1977), 5.

8. David Deacon, Michael Pickering, Peter Golding, and Graham Murdock, *Researching Communications: A Practical Guide to Methods in Media and Cultural Analysis* (London: Arnold, 1999).

9. David Macey, *The Penguin Dictionary of Critical Theory* (London: Penguin Books, 2000), 77.

10. Lawrence Grossberg and Janice Radway, *Cultural Studies* (1992): 111; as quoted in Lee, *Life and Times of Cultural Studies*, 2.

11. In this regard, Grossberg is fully in accord with poststructuralism's "founding texts." Adam Katz, for example, maintains that Baudrillard, Delueze, Guattari, Derrida, Foucault, Lacan, and Lyotard—poststructuralism's founding fathers—all privileged "the local and specific," and resisted "totalizing abstraction." Adam Katz, "Postmodern Cultural Studies: A Critique," 11.

12. Lawrence Grossberg, "Aims and Scope," *Cultural Studies* (2007), www.tandf.co.uk/journals/routledge/09502386.html (accessed Dec. 16, 2007). Emphasis added.

13. Lawrence Grossberg, "Rereading the Past From the Future," *International Journal of Cultural Studies* 10, no. 1 (2007): 128.

14. Mark Poster, *Cultural Theory and Poststructuralism: In Search of a Context* (Ithaca, NY: Cornell University Press, 1989), 126.

15. Sardar and Van Loon, *Introducing Cultural Studies*, 9.

16. Katz would agree with this assessment. He writes: "Postmodern philosophical and theoretical categories and presuppositions have been essential to the constitution of what I will call 'mainstream' or 'appreciative' cultural studies." Adam Katz, "Postmodern Cultural Studies: A Critique," 10.

17. Johnson, "What Is Cultural Studies Anyway?" 54–55. Also, James W. Carey, "Abolishing the Old Spirit World," *Critical Studies in Mass Communication* 12, no. 1 (1995): 83, 85.

18. Blundell, Shepherd, and Taylor, "Editor's Introduction," 8. McChesney, from the vantage point of political economy, agreed: "Cultural studies . . . often is concerned with the relationship of media 'texts' to audiences and both of them to existing class and social relations, but it is mostly uninterested in examining the structural factors that influence the production of media content. It is also uninterested, for the main part, with the broader relationship of economics to politics." Robert W. McChesney, "The Political Economy of Communication and the Future of the Field," *Media, Culture and Society* 22, no. 1 (2000): 110.

19. Johnson, "What Is Cultural Studies Anyway?" 54.

20. Johnson, "What Is Cultural Studies Anyway?" 55.

21. Quoted in Deborah Cook, *The Culture Industry Revisited: Theodor W. Adorno on Mass Culture* (Lanham, MD: Rowman and Littlefield Publishers, Inc., 1996), 11.

22. Thompson wrote, "I am seeking to rescue the poor stockinger, the Luddite cropper, the 'obsolete' hand-loom weaver, the 'utopian' artisan, and even the deluded follower of Joanna Southcott, from the enormous condescension of posterity. . . . In some of the lost causes of the people of the Industrial Revolution we may discover insights into social evils which we have yet to cure." E. P. Thompson, *The Making of the English Working Class* (1963; revised, Harmondsworth: Pelican, 1972), 13.

23. Terry Eagleton, *Figures of Dissent* (London: Verso, 2003), 74.

24. Personal correspondence, November 5, 2007. See also, Kostas Gouliamos, *Sacred Fallacies: Essays on Political Communication and Culture* (Athens: Gavrilides Publishing House, 2004).

25. Williams, *Marxism and Literature,* 108. Stuart Hall remarks that in publications following *The Long Revolution,* and as oblique response to criticisms proffered by E. P. Thompson's review of that book, Williams "appropriated" Gramsci. See Stuart Hall, "Cultural Studies: Two Paradigms," *Media, Culture and Society* 2 (1980): 62.

26. Graeme Turner, *British Cultural Studies: An Introduction* (Cambridge, MA: Unwin Hyman, 1990), 51.

27. For example, Lawrence Grossberg, "The Formation of Cultural Studies," in *Relocating Cultural Studies,* 21–66; Stuart Hall, "Cultural Studies: Two Paradigms," 57–58; Andrew Goodwin, "The Uses and Abuses of In-discipline: Introduction to the Transaction Edition," in Richard Hoggart, *The Uses of Literacy* (New Brunswick, NJ: Transaction Publishers, 1998), xv.

28. Hall, "Cultural Studies: Two Paradigms," 58.
29. Hall, "Cultural Studies: Two Paradigms," 58.
30. Goodwin, "The Uses and Abuses of In-discipline," xiv.
31. Eagleton, *Figures of Dissent*, 47.
32. Stuart Hall, "Cultural Studies: Two Paradigms," 57.
33. Sardar and Van Loon, *Introducing Cultural Studies*, 26.
34. Sardar and Van Loon, *Introducing Cultural Studies*, 28.
35. Richard Hoggart, *The Uses of Literacy* (1957; reprint, with an Introduction by Andrew Goodwin and a Postscript by John Corner, New Brunswick, NJ: Transaction Publishers, 1998), 1.
36. Hoggart, *The Uses of Literacy*, 133.
37. Hoggart, *The Uses of Literacy*, 2.
38. Hoggart, *The Uses of Literacy*, 188.
39. Hoggart, *The Uses of Literacy*, 182.
40. Hoggart, *The Uses of Literacy*, 182.
41. Hoggart, *The Uses of Literacy*, 211.
42. Michael Mann, "The Working Class Culture," *New Society*, 1976, as cited in Edward Comor, *Consumption and the Globalization Project* (New York: Palgrave Macmillan, 2008), 51.
43. Hoggart, *The Uses of Literacy*, 219.
44. Hoggart, *The Uses of Literacy*, 142–43.
45. Hoggart, *The Uses of Literacy*, 128, 129.
46. Hoggart, *The Uses of Literacy*, 145.
47. Turner, *British Cultural Studies*, 51.
48. Raymond Williams, *Keywords: A Vocabulary of Culture and Society* (1976; revised, Oxford: Oxford University Press, 1983), x.
49. Graham Murdock, "Across the Great Divide: Cultural Analysis and the Condition of Democracy," *Critical Studies in Mass Communication* 12, no. 1 (March 1995): 89.
50. Raymond Williams, *The Long Revolution* (1961; reprint, Peterborough, Canada: Broadview Press, 2001), 348.
51. Fred Inglis, *Raymond Williams* (London: Routledge, 1995), 320–22; Alan O'Connor, *Raymond Williams* (Lanham, MD: Rowman and Littlefield Publishers, Inc., 2006), 115–19.
52. Williams, *Culture and Society*, 11–12.
53. Williams, *Culture and Society*, 13, 15.
54. Williams, *Culture and Society*, 16.
55. Williams, *Culture and Society*, 285.
56. Williams, *Culture and Society*, 16.
57. For example, Allan Bloom, *The Closing of the American Mind* (New York: Simon and Schuster, 1987).
58. Williams, *Culture and Society*, 298. According to Williams, "A very large part of English middle-class education is devoted to the training of servants. This is more its characteristic than a training for leadership, as the stress on conformity and respect for authority shows" (p. 315).

59. Williams, *Culture and Society*, 229.

60. The official start of the grouse shooting season in the UK.

61. T. S. Eliot, *Notes Towards a Definition of Culture* (New York: Harcourt, Brace and Co., 1949), 31; quoted in Williams, *Culture and Society,* 230.

62. They viewed democratic culture as a moving away from an ideal. Williams, *Culture and Society,* 226.

63. Williams, *Culture and Society*, 310.

64. Williams, *Culture and Society*, 313.

65. Williams, *Culture and Society*, 297.

66. Williams, *Culture and Society*, 297.

67. Williams, *Culture and Society*, 311.

68. Williams, *Culture and Society*, 312.

69. Williams, *Culture and Society*, 307.

70. Smith wrote: "In opulent and commercial societies to think or to reason comes to be, like every other employment, a particular business, which is carried on by a very few people, who furnish the public with all the thought and reason possessed by the vast multitudes that labour." Adam Smith, draft of *The Wealth of Nations,* quoted in Williams, *Culture and Society,* 52.

71. Williams, *Culture and Society*, 52.

72. Williams, *Culture and Society*, 52.

73. Williams, *Culture and Society*, 58.

74. Williams, *Culture and Society,* 60. The quote is from Shelley's *A Defence of Poetry.*

75. Williams, *Culture and Society*, 60.

76. Williams, *Culture and Society*, 99.

77. Williams, *Culture and Society*, 99–105.

78. Williams, *Culture and Society,* 307–08.

79. Williams, *Culture and Society*, 301.

80. Williams, *Culture and Society*, 301.

81. Williams, *Culture and Society*, 16.

82. Williams, *Culture and Society*, 16; emphasis in original.

83. Williams, *Culture and Society*, 287.

84. Of *The Long Revolution,* Williams wrote: "This book has been planned and written as a continuation of the work begun in my *Culture and Society, 1780–1950.*" Williams, *The Long Revolution*, 9. Introducing the revised edition of *Keywords,* Williams noted that this book was originally intended as an appendix to *Culture and Society,* but was cut at the publisher's request to reduce length. Williams, *Keywords*, 14. In his Preface to the American edition of *The Year 2000* Williams remarked that like *Culture and Society* and *The Long Revolution,* this book, too, attempted "to probe deeply what the intellectual arguments concerning capitalism and socialism are really all about." Raymond Williams, *The Year 2000* (New York: Pantheon, 1983), xii.

85. Williams, *The Long Revolution*, 375.

86. Williams, *The Long Revolution*, 10.

87. Williams, *The Long Revolution*, 324.

88. Williams, *The Year 2000*, 243–69.

89. Williams, *The Long Revolution*, 379.

90. Hoggart made much the same point, noting that "the temptations, especially as they appear in mass-publications, are toward a gratification of the self and toward what may be called a 'hedonistic-group-individualism. . . . Contemporary society has developed with particular skill the techniques of mutual indulgence and satisfied 'ordinariness.'" Hoggart, *The Uses of Literacy,* 130–31.

91. There is also a concomitant and supportive change in the meaning of the individual. In *The Long Revolution* Williams wrote: "Slowly, and with many ambiguities . . . we have learned to think of the 'individual in his own right,' where previously to describe an individual was to give an example of the group of which he was a member, and so to offer a particular description of that group and of the relationships within it." Williams, *The Long Revolution*, 91. A *mass* may be defined as a collocation of individuals, proximate in the sense they receive common messages from a central point or points, yet who are out of touch with one another and are usually physically separated.

92. Williams, *The Long Revolution*, 379. Gabriel Tarde, in 1901, is credited as being the first to see the possibilities of elites controlling common people by segregating them even as they retain a common focus on mass media. See Stuart Ewen, *PR! A Social History of Spin* (New York: Basic Books, 1996), 68. In *Culture and Society* Williams remarked that seeing other people as part of a mass "has been capitalized for the purposes of political or cultural exploitation." Williams, *Culture and Society,* 289.

93. Williams, *The Long Revolution*, 129.

94. Williams, *Culture and Society*, 319. See also Ewen, *PR!*, 68.

95. Raymond Williams, "Means of Communication as Means of Production" (1978; reprint, *Problems in Materialism and Culture*, London: Verso, 1997), 56.

96. Raymond Williams, *Television: Technology and Cultural Form* (Glasgow: Fontana/Collins, 1974), 23.

97. Raymond Williams, *Communications* (1962; revised edition, Harmondsworth: Penguin, 1971), 116.

98. Williams, "Means of Communication as Means of Production," 56.

99. Williams, *Culture and Society*, 299.

100. Raymond Williams, "Literature and Sociology: In Memory of Lucien Goldman" (1971; reprint, *Problems in Materialism and Culture*, London: Verso, 1997), 19, 20; emphasis added. In *Culture and Society,* however, Williams denied any easy interpretation of Marx (or Engels) on the matter of base and superstructure, writing: "Either the arts are passively dependent on social reality, a proposition which I take to be that of mechanical materialism, or a vulgar misinterpretation of Marx. Or the arts, as the creators of consciousness, determine social reality, the proposition which the Romantic poets sometimes advanced. Or finally, the arts, while ultimately dependent, with everything else, on the real economic structure, operate in part to reflect this structure and its consequent reality, and in part, by affecting attitudes towards reality, to help or *hinder* the constant business of changing it." Williams then continued, "I find Marxist theories of culture confused because they seem to me, on different occasions and in different writers, to make use of all these propositions as the need serves." Williams, *Culture and Society,* 266; emphasis in original.

101. Raymond Williams, "Base and Superstructure in Marxist Cultural Theory" (1973; reprint, *Problems in Materialism and Culture,* London: Verso, 1997), 32.

102. Williams, "Base and Superstructure in Marxist Cultural Theory," 34. In *Culture and Society,* Williams had denied that Marx had actually proposed that the economic base determines the cultural superstructure. There, Williams noted that in the Preface to *Critique of Political Economy,* Marx stated, famously: "The mode of production in material life determines the general character of the social, political and spiritual processes of life. It is not the consciousness of men that determines their existence, but, on the contrary, their social existence determines their consciousness. . . . With the change of the economic foundation the entire immense superstructure is more or less rapidly transformed." Further quoting from Marx, Williams, however, immediately suggested that the relation between base and superstructure in Marx's view was not nearly as deterministic as the foregoing excerpt, in isolation, would indicate. He also quoted Engels as follows: "According to the materialist conception of history, the determining element in history is *ultimately* the production and reproduction in real life. More than this neither Marx nor I have ever asserted. If therefore somebody twists this into the statement that the economic element is the *only* determining one, he transforms it into a meaningless, abstract and absurd phrase." Williams, *Culture and Society,* 258–60.

103. Williams, *Marxism and Literature*, 86–87.

104. Williams, "Literature and Sociology," 29.

105. Williams, "Literature and Sociology," 26.

106. Williams, "Literature and Sociology," 28.

107. Williams, *Communications*, 19.

108. Williams, "Literature and Sociology," 20.

109. In the first part of his contribution to the Colloquy, Murdock gave numerous instances in which Williams afforded strong emphasis, even "deterministic" value, to the impact of economic factors on culture. Murdock, "Across the Great Divide," 90.

110. In *The Year 2000,* for instance, he remarked: "What we now have is a huge sector of capitalist-sponsored art, displayed in the polished routines of crime, fraud, intrigue, betrayal, and a glossy degradation of sexuality. Grace notes of diminishing audibility are played at its edges. . . . The sector is supported by light intellectual formulations of the ruling class ideas: 'alienation' as violent competition and impersonal appetite; 'dislocation' as arbitrariness and human disability." Williams, *The Year 2000*, 144.

111. Williams, *The Year 2000*, 16.

112. Williams, "Literature and Sociology," 21.

113. Members of a mass, although receiving common media content, are not in communication one with another.

114. Williams, "Base and Superstructure in Marxist Cultural Theory," 40.

115. Williams, *The Year 2000*, 144.

116. Williams, *Television: Technology and Cultural Form*, 21.

117. Williams, *Television: Technology and Cultural Form*, 21.

118. Williams, *Television: Technology and Cultural Form*, 22.

119. Williams, *Television: Technology and Cultural Form*, 26.

120. Williams, *The Year 2000*, 130.

121. Williams, *Television: Technology and Cultural Form*, 19.

122. For an enthusiastic recounting of the doctrine of technological determinism, see Langdon Winner, *Autonomous Technology: Technics-out-of-Control as a Theme in Political Thought* (Cambridge, MA: MIT Press, 1977).

123. Williams, *Television: Technology and Cultural Form*, 130.

124. Williams, *Television: Technology and Cultural Form*, 129.

125. Williams, "Means of Communication as Means of Production," 55

126. Harold Innis, "Minerva's Owl," in *The Bias of Communication* (1951; reprint, with an Introduction by Marshall McLuhan, Toronto: University of Toronto Press, 1971), 6.

127. Innis' views on elite vs. popular rule are in question. Prior to World War II, Innis bristled at proposals for government planning. Regarding education, he was not merely conservative, but elitist, claiming that in any community there is only "a limited number capable of sustained mental effort." Although admitting that brilliant minds are to be found "in all regions and in all strata," nonetheless he also opined that to thrive society must persistently seek out, encourage, and train the "best brains." Universality in higher education, conversely, according to Innis, meant pandering to the lowest common denominator, in which case "ideas must be ground down to a convenient size to meet the demands of large numbers." See Donald Creighton, *Harold Adams Innis: Portrait of a Scholar*, 82; Harold A. Innis, "Adult Education and Universities," in *Staples, Markets, and Cultural Change*, 474, 472; and Innis, "Government Ownership and the Canadian Scene" (1933), in *Essays in Canadian Economic History*, ed. Mary Q. Innis (Toronto: University of Toronto Press, 1956), 78–84. By the late 1940s or early 1950s, though, Innis had truly become a "Red Tory," even visiting the Soviet Union in pursuit of enlightenment.

128. Williams, *The Year 2000*, 144.

129. Richard Hoggart, "Adult Education: The Legacy and the Future," lecture in celebration of the fiftieth anniversary of the University of Glasgow's Department of Adult and Continuing Education, 18 October 2001, www.gla.ac.uk/adulteducation/latestnews/RichardHoggart.html (accessed June 9, 2008).

130. E. P. Thompson, *The Making of the English Working Class*, 13.

131. Thompson, *The Making of the English Working Class*, 9–10, 11.

132. Thompson, *The Making of the English Working Class*, 213; emphasis added.

133. Thompson, *The Making of the English Working Class*, 261.

134. Thompson, *The Making of the English Working Class*, 213.

135. Thompson, *The Making of the English Working Class*, 24.

136. Thompson, *The Making of the English Working Class*, 90.

137. Thompson, *The Making of the English Working Class*, 87.

138. Thompson, *The Making of the English Working Class*, 91.

139. Thompson, *The Making of the English Working Class*, 34–8, 103.

140. Thompson, *The Making of the English Working Class*, 61.

141. Thompson, *The Making of the English Working Class*, 95.

142. Thomas Paine, *Rights of Man*, as quoted in Thompson, *The Making of the English Working Class*, 100.

143. Thompson, *The Making of the English Working Class*, 201. On Wilkes and Wyvill, see Ian R. Christie, *Wilkes, Wyvill and Reform: The Parliamentary Reform Movement in British Politics, 1760–1785* (London: Macmillan, 1962).

144. Thompson, *The Making of the English Working Class*, 781.

145. Thompson, *The Making of the English Working Class*, 782.

146. Thompson, *The Making of the English Working Class*, 782.

147. Thompson, *The Making of the English Working Class*, 783.

148. Thompson, *The Making of the English Working Class*, 785.

149. Thompson, *The Making of the English Working Class*, 800. Thompson adds: "Perhaps 500 people were prosecuted for the production and sale of the 'unstamped.' From 1816 (indeed, from 1792,) until 1836 the contest involved, not only the editors, booksellers, and printers, but also many hundreds of newsvendors, hawkers, and voluntary agents" (p. 801).

150. Thompson, *The Making of the English Working Class*, 788.

151. Thompson, *The Making of the English Working Class*, 789.

152. Thompson, *The Making of the English Working Class*, 790, 805.

153. Thompson, *The Making of the English Working Classs*, 791.

154. Thompson, *The Making of the English Working Class*, 805.

155. Thompson, *The Making of the English Working Class*, 791.

156. Thompson, *The Making of the English Working Class*, 222–23.

157. Theodor W. Adorno, *The Culture Industry: Selected Essays on Mass Culture*, edited by J. M. Bernstein (London: Routledge, 1991), 90.

158. Max Horkheimer and Theodor W. Adorno, *Dialectic of Enlightenment* (New York: Continuum, 1991), 121; emphasis added.

159. Carey, "Abolishing the Old Spirit World," 86.

160. Carey, "Abolishing the Old Spirit World," 87.

Chapter Three

The Colloquy Revisited

THE COLLOQUY

As noted in the Introduction, the Colloquy of 1995 pitted cultural studies against political economy in a written debate involving four scholars. Nicholas Garnham and Lawrence Grossberg represented the poles of the political economy-cultural studies spectrum, while Graham Murdock (political economy) and James Carey (cultural studies) assumed hostile but somewhat intermediary positions. While representations from all four scholars are noted here, the chapter focuses particularly on the main event, namely the contestation between Garnham and Grossberg.[1]

Garnham's paper, "Political Economy and Cultural Studies: Reconciliation or Divorce?" opened the Colloquy by proposing "a narrowing of vision in cultural studies . . . a drift into an uncritical mode of interpretation."[2] One issue, then, is whether since the time of Adorno, Hoggart, Williams, and Thompson, there has in fact been a narrowing of vision within cultural studies, a lessening of critical perspectives, a drift into uncritical modes of interpretation. Although as we will see in detail below, Grossberg largely agreed with Garnham's assessment, Stuart Hall and Angela McRobbie (as cited by Garnham) certainly did not. Let us turn first to their assessments.

Both McRobbie and Hall claimed, essentially, that cultural studies had remained faithful to its critical roots. For McRobbie, British cultural studies at its beginnings was "a form of radical inquiry which went against reductionism and economism, which went against the base and superstructure metaphor, and which resisted the notion of false consciousness."[3] If correct, the implication would be that contemporary cultural studies builds on the foundations laid by the inaugural writers. Indeed, according to McRobbie, because cultural studies today remains a radical critique, because it opposes economism and disputes reductionism, and because it rejects both the base/superstructure model and the category known as false consciousness, it is consistent with its beginnings. She continued: "The return to a pre-postmodern Marxism as marked out by critics like Frederic Jameson and David Harvey [and likely, in her view, Garnham] is untenable because the terms of that return are predicated on prioritizing economic relations and economic determinations over cultural and political relations."[4] Hall, too, as cited by Garnham, claimed that inaugural British cultural studies critiqued "certain reductionism and economism, which I think is not extrinsic but intrinsic to Marxism; a contestation with the model of base and superstructure," adding that British cultural studies at its outset "was located and sited in a necessary and prolonged and as yet unending contestation with the question of false consciousness."[5]

It is apparent that the depictions cited here by McRobbie and Hall of inaugural British cultural studies differ markedly from the descriptions, citations, and analyses presented in chapter 2. Indeed, I will argue in this chapter that contemporary cultural studies, far from remaining consistent with the cultural materialism of Hoggart, Williams, and Thompson, has departed from its origins to such an extent that there is now as great an opposition between the works of contemporary poststructuralist cultural studies scholars and the founders of British cultural studies as there is with critical political economists. If this assessment is correct, the important questions become whether, in what ways, and to what extent the transformation in cultural studies—from cultural materialism to poststructuralism—is useful or benign.

In the sections to follow I identify, analyze, and assess major points of departure between cultural studies and political economy as made evident by participants in the Colloquy. Most of the differences, I will argue, are either superficial, and hence not overly problematic, or they actually constitute good reasons for reintegrating the fields. However, there is an issue (addressed toward the close of this chapter and ironically skimmed over quickly by the participants) that is so fundamental that it is likely impossible to resolve. The areas of controversy addressed in the chapter are: false consciousness, production vs. reception, base/superstructure (economic determinism), social science vs. humanities, class, and ontology. I reserve for chapter 4 the perhaps most basic issue of all, namely the political economy of scholarship.

POINTS OF DEPARTURE

False Consciousness

McRobbie, Hall, and Grossberg berated political economists for employing the category, *false consciousness*. But what exactly is *false consciousness*? I propose that the term has two distinct, albeit related meanings, and that much confusion resulted as these meanings were conflated or confused.

In his extended essay, "The Stars Down to Earth," Theodor Adorno noted that "various mass movements [have] spread all over the world in which people seem to act against their own rational interests of self-preservation and the 'pursuit of happiness.'"[6] This is as good a definition as any of the common meaning of false consciousness. "Capitalism deepens false consciousness," explains Ben Agger, by "suggesting to people that the existing social system is both inevitable and rational. . . . People 'falsely' experience their lives as products of a certain unchangeable social nature."[7] False consciousness, then, is usually understood as describing a condition whereby oppressed groups misconstrue their condition by accepting the view propagated to them by elites. In the Colloquy, Grossberg agreed that the condition usually referred to as false consciousness is prevalent and serious—*without, however, using the term*. Grossberg wrote:

> Cultural studies does assume that people live their subordination actively; that means, in one sense, that they are often complicit in their own subordination, that they accede to it, although power often works through strategies and apparatuses of which people are totally unaware. Be that as it may, cultural studies believes that if one is to challenge the existing structure of power, then one has to understand how that complicity, that participation in power, is constructed and lived, and that means not only looking at what people gain from such practices, but also at the possibilities for rearticulating such practices to escape, resist, or even oppose particular structures of power. Cultural studies refuses to assume that people are cultural dupes, that they are entirely and passively manipulated either by the media or by capitalism. But it does not deny that they are sometimes duped, that they are sometimes manipulated, and that they are lied to (and believe the lies, sometimes knowing that they are lies).[8]

Here, Grossberg is agreeing that understandings, outlooks, and interpretations proffered by media and elites are, in fact, often accepted by subordinated people—to their disadvantage. This is consistent with Raymond Williams' complaint that in turning class into mass, elites rob working people of their class consciousness. And this is indeed the most common meaning of *false consciousness*, although as just noted Grossberg refrained from using the term in this sense. What Grossberg meant by false consciousness, rather (as discussed at greater length later in this chapter), is understandings or beliefs that deviate from the objectively real; it was with that meaning in mind that he insistently denigrated political economists for using the term.

The two meanings of false consciousness overlap if, and to the extent that, one maintains that persuasion or indoctrination by elites of subjugated peoples moves the latter from knowing their objectively or manifestly real conditions or plight into a false understanding. One suspects that Raymond Williams understood the demise of class consciousness through the rise of the mass in this way. In any event, even rejecting this contention (i.e., from truth to falsity), one could still agree (as does Grossberg) that elites for their own advantage indoctrinate the masses against the interests of the masses.

Turning to Garnham, we will see he had both meanings (or rather, perhaps, the integrated meaning) in mind. One of Garnham's criticisms of contemporary cultural studies, however, was that its practitioners often fail to identify, or even recognize, "false consciousness" in the first sense, choosing instead to celebrate virtually all cultural productions as being "oppositional." Garnham declared: "The tendency of cultural studies to validate all and every popular cultural practice as resistance—in its desire to avoid being tarred with the elitist brush—is profoundly damaging to its [emancipatory] political project."[9] (As documented below, Grossberg agreed that cultural studies may very well have become unduly celebrative of cultural productions.)

If both sides had confined the term, false consciousness, to elite domination through persuasion or indoctrination (without the notion of deviation from objective truth), there would have been little or no debate over false consciousness. Unfortunately, as discussed below, disputes over false consciousness in the Colloquy were in large part a means for avoiding discussion of the real issue, differences in ontology.

Production vs. Reception

A second issue is the relative emphasis accorded production and reception. According to Garnham, cultural studies today pays scant attention to production. This contemporary imbalance, he suggested, is a marked deviation from the writings of the founders, and has two major consequences. First, it plays "politically into the hands of the Right" whose agenda includes positioning people as consumers rather than as producers. Second, the focus on consumption exaggerates the "freedoms of consumption and daily life."[10] Garnham acknowledged that people do often interpret cultural material in their own ways and for their own purposes, and that they do derive pleasures and other benefits from cultural commodities. "But," he continued, "does anyone who has produced a text or a symbolic form believe that interpretation is entirely random or that pleasure cannot be used to manipulative ends?"[11]

Surprisingly, in his rejoinder, Grossberg again gave qualified support to Garnham's pronouncements, agreeing, for example, that "perhaps cultural studies has paid too much attention to consumption," and that it may even have lost some of its critical edge by having "overemphasized the pleasure, freedom and empowerment of consumption (and reception)."[12] As a riposte to Garnham, though, Grossberg suggested that what *really* motivated Garnham in raising these points was his wish to belittle the importance of reception compared to production and to "dismiss" cultural studies,[13] charges which Garnham emphatically denied. Indeed, perhaps Garnham's central argument was precisely the opposite—namely, that production and consumption need to be integrated in our thought.

Grossberg next endeavored to justify cultural studies' relative inattention to production by invoking the scholarly division of labor:

> [Garnham asks] "Where in contemporary cultural studies are the studies of the cultural producers and the organizational sites and practices they inhabit and through which they exercise their power?" On the one hand, I am tempted to answer that they are in political economy; that is, after all, what political economists do, so why should they want cultural studies to do it? One could, after all, just as easily ask of political economy: "Where are the studies of consumption and everyday life?"[14]

Grossberg next claimed that production *is* treated by writers *not* cited by Garnham, for example by McRobbie (although clearly she was cited), by Hobson, Nixon, and Jody Berland.[15] Berland is an interesting selection here since one of her projects, in stark contrast to Grossberg, is reconciling political economy and cultural studies, so *of course* she refers to production.

Where political economy falls short, and where cultural studies is strong, in Grossberg's view, is that the former has little to say about how people come to give their consent to domination, whereas the latter has much to say.[16] In other words, in downplaying reception/consumption, political economy is inattentive to the means whereby "false consciousness" is inculcated by elites.[17] Garnham agreed with this assessment, and complimented cultural studies on its sophisticated theories of textuality and on extending the notion of domination from class to gender and to race. To agree with Grossberg on this point, however, is surely not to support the continued segregation of political economy and cultural studies, but rather to press for reconciliation.

Finally, Grossberg recalled that the inaugural British cultural theorists emphasized "the self-production of culture,"[18] whereas, he argued, political economists give undue emphasis to commercial production. What Grossberg declined to mention, however, was that Williams and Hoggart (and Adorno for that matter) fretted that in the contemporary era commercialized cultural products have largely displaced authentic, "self-produced" culture, and that both E. P. Thompson and Richard Hoggart had related the de-skilling of labor through the mechanization of industry to a "dulling" of the working class and a concomitant decline in their ability to produce their own culture. In these circumstances, the greater attention Garnham and other political economists pay to commodified cultural outputs seems warranted, although that is certainly not to say that there is no place in cultural studies and in political economy for scholars to provide analyses of "self-produced" culture. In any event, and this is the main point, rather than accusations flowing back and forth as to what one side or the other is or is not doing, it would have been far more productive to incorporate findings and analyses from both areas (production and consumption; self-produced and commercial culture) to constitute (re-constitute) an integrated field.

Base/Superstructure (Economic Determinism)

Grossberg, Hall, and McRobbie denounced political economy for its purportedly hard economic determinism, and in particular for not acknowledging that audiences have interpretive capabilities and hence are not meekly subject to dominant ideology. They charged, moreover, that political economy's allegedly hard economic determinism is a regrettable but marked departure from the position staked out by Williams and Hoggart, who they noted insistently disassociated themselves from the base/superstructure formula.

In chapter 2, I recounted in some detail Williams' stance on determinisms generally and on base/superstructure in particular. McRobbie, Hall, and Grossberg were certainly correct in noting that Williams and other founders of British cultural studies rejected the base/superstructure model as a general theory. What McRobbie and Hall neglected to mention, however, is that Williams continuously expressed disgust at the inordinate influence ("determinism," in the softer sense of guiding, directing, impacting) that economic affairs (the base) have on culture (the superstructure) in contemporary capitalist society, a disdain shared by Hoggart (and, for that matter, Adorno). These writers were univocal in contrasting the authentic working class culture as it arose and was practiced, with commercialized, centrally produced popular culture that was displacing and obliterating it.

Garnham's position on this issue is largely in agreement with that of the founders of cultural studies. Garnham acknowledged agency on the part of message recipients, but insisted that agency is exercised only within a political-economic context of concentrated power; Williams similarly emphasized that audience members exercise interpretive freedom only within the limits set by their membership in a class or community. Garnham's proposition that elites endeavor to position people as consumers, moreover, accords well with Williams' claim that elites wish people to see themselves as a class-neutered mass, as compliant and passive recipients of information.

Garnham carried over this "soft" economic determinist mode of analysis from reception/interpretation to the cultural superstructure, maintaining that while capitalism does not require any particular superstructure, it does require that the superstructure in place be consistent with the capitalist form of production.[19] Grossberg's retort was that political economy cannot account for cultural differences among, say, the USA, the UK, and Japan, all of which have similar "determining" economic bases. He charged: "Garnham is unable to consider such questions precisely because he refuses to engage the question of *articulation*, which is, of course, the principal way in which relations between production, consumption, politics, and ideology are theorized in cultural studies."[20] However, Garnham had anticipated that criticism, stating: "The capitalist mode of production does not demand, require, or determine any one form of politics. . . . It is clear from the historical record that the capitalist mode of production can grow within a variety of inherited cultural forms. All that is required is that they be compatible with the mode of production."[21] (Hence, one could argue, for example, that it is possible for U.S. and Japanese food preferences and marriage customs to differ substantially because they bear little or no necessary connection to the mode of production, whereas property relations, the price system, and commodity exchange, being central to the capitalist economy, are and must be similar in all capitalist countries).

In addition to noting that many cultural practices are irrelevant to the mode of production, and that others are necessary to and supportive of the prevailing structure of power, Garnham drew attention to other practices—for example critical scholarship—which could actually contribute to capitalism's overthrow;[22] obviously, those practices are not "determined" by the economic base, at least not in any linear (nondialectical) sense. For Garnham, the first step in critical scholarship is always to analyse the "structure of domination,"[23] an analysis which political economy routinely undertakes, but which, according to Garnham, cultural studies by itself cannot do.

Let us return again, however, to *articulation,* the term Grossberg invoked repeatedly to contrast his position with that of political economy. In cultural studies, articulation has been associated particularly with Grossberg's mentor, Stuart Hall. In an interview with Grossberg, Hall remarked that he liked using the term because of its double meaning. On the one hand, Hall noted, articulation is to utter, or speak forth, thereby connoting "language-ing." On the other, it means to join temporarily, as when a truck is connected to a trailer. "The two parts are connected to each other," Hall explained, "but through a specific linkage that can be broken."[24] As easily, and even more appropriately, however, he might have used a linguistic example, as when the letters s-c-h are brought together with other letters to spell *school*; are "de-articulated' to form such words as *secondary*, *classroom*, and *honors;* and are "re-articulated" for *schlock*. Or when a noun is articulated with an adjective and a verb to form a sentence. In any event, articulation in poststructuralist cultural studies illustrates well its linguistic bent, and is to be viewed as a major point of departure from political economy: just how representative, after all, is the truck and trailer of the ease or difficulty in the material world of forging and disassembling connections among legal, social, political, and economic structures? (And, for that matter, can a given trailer be "articulated" to all trucks, to an automobile, a bus, or a motorcycle)? I return to this topic near the end of the chapter.

In light of the preceding, the following conclusions regarding *economic determinism* in critical political economy and in inaugural cultural studies seem warranted. First, (as developed in chapter 1), Innis and Adorno, inaugurators of critical political economy in media studies, while certainly affording preeminence to economic factors, proposed a soft economic determinism. Similarly Garnham, representing contemporary critical political economy, advocates a soft economic determinism. Second, as developed in chapter 2, the founders of British cultural studies, too, can be characterized as theorizing a soft economic determinism. Third, contemporary (poststructuralist) cultural studies, represented here by McRobbie, Grossberg, and to a certain extent Hall, understate almost to the point of denial the impact on culture that the founders of British cultural studies ascribed to economic factors.[25]

Social Sciences vs. Humanities

In these first three chapters we have seen that, at the outset, media studies was a seamless whole, integrating arts/humanities (cultural studies) with social science (political economy). On the one hand, Harold Innis, the economic historian and a founder of what have become known as political economy approaches to media studies, wrote about such fundamental cultural categories as time and space, being and becoming, local vs. imperial culture, knowledge and power, the press as an instrument of culture, literacy and the vernacular, instrumental reason and the mechanization of knowledge/monopolies of knowledge. On the other hand, the musician, philosopher, and cultural theorist Theodor Adorno coined the term "the culture *industry*" to explain what he perceived to be the deterioration in both high and low culture. Moreover, textual analyses by Raymond Williams and literary approaches to the study of lived culture by Richard Hoggart constituted empirical documentation concerning the cultural life of the British working class and changes to notions of *culture* attributable to that, complementing E. P. Thompson's historical analysis; all three of the foundational British cultural theorists integrated seamlessly economic and cultural matters, which is to say political economy and cultural studies. All three emphasized cultural production, as well the consumption or interpretation of cultural artifacts.

Of course, scholars have their areas of expertise, their favored methodologies, and their foci of attention. Compared to his voluminous writings on aesthetics, for example, Adorno spent precious little time addressing the culture industry. Similarly, Innis' training in economics meant that he grounded his depictions of culture on materialist categories and spent little if any time on nuanced interpretations of texts. Of all the writers we have reviewed, Raymond Williams exhibited the greatest facility for balancing cultural, political, and economic categories to arrive at a comprehensive picture of material and symbolic structures affecting everyday life. All of these aforementioned authors, however, can be considered "models" for media scholarship today—if one believes that the integration, or re-integration, of political economy and cultural studies—of production and consumption, of causation and interpretation, of the material and symbolic realms—is a goal worth striving for.

Not everyone agrees, however, that integration or reintegration is possible or is desirable. It is sometimes noted, for instance, that political economy of media evolved from eighteenth-century social science, whereas cultural studies derives from the humanities—from literary studies, aesthetics, philosophy, art history, and so forth. Graham Murdock, for one, pointed to this as an important point of departure.[26] However, this difference, significant though it may be, is certainly not insurmountable. In the inaugural years, as Murdock pointed out, media studies seamlessly integrated political economy and the study of culture.

Class

Another point of departure, it is sometimes claimed, is "class." Garnham maintained that a fundamental difference between political economy and cultural studies concerns the importance attributed to *class*. He wrote: "Political economy sees class—namely, the structure of access to the means of production and the structure of the distribution of the economic surplus—as the key to the structure of domination, whereas cultural studies sees gender and race, along with other potential markers of difference, as alternative structures of domination in no way determined by class."[27] Grossberg took Garnham's insistence on the primacy of class as a flashpoint, remarking that "as early as 1968, the Centre for Contemporary Cultural Studies was exploring issues of the gendered relations of power, without assuming that these were merely epiphenomenal expressions of deeper, more real, bottom line economic or class relations."[28] He continued: "The fact that race and gender are *articulated* to economics (and may be articulated to class) does not say much about the appropriate ways of accounting for, or struggling against, structures of domination organized around race and gender."[29]

However, as we saw in chapter 1, in his surveys of civilizations ancient and modern, Innis bypassed the usual notion of class, and instead simply distinguished between those controlling media and knowledge, who could be a priesthood, royalty, the military, scribes, scientists, mathematicians, male or female depending on the civilization in question, and the far greater numbers of people subject to the media's influence. In no way was Innis' political economy circumscribed by or centered on Garnham and Grossberg's notion of "class." Adorno, too, another founder of political economy of media, chose not to deal with traditional conceptions of class and distinguished instead between the privileged elite and the mass. Ironically, the inaugural British *cultural* theorists were more imbued with the traditional labor-capital dichotomy than were the pioneering political economists! Undoubtedly cultural studies is well positioned to refine Adorno's distinctions between elite and mass along gendered, occupational, racial, ethnic, and other lines, but the point remains that there need be no contradiction between contemporary cultural studies and political economy concerning class. The issue Garnham raises, then, might distinguish basic Marxism from other branches of knowledge, but not necessarily critical political economy from critical cultural studies.

Ontology

None of the foregoing issues are irresolvable. Nor are all even important. Some, I would argue, even point to the desirability of closer integration between cultural studies and political economy. Finally, however, I turn to what *is* a fundamental breach between critical political economy and cultural studies, or at least the version of the latter advanced by Grossberg, Hall, McRobbie, and (as developed below) by Jean Baudrillard and Mark Poster. The issue, despite its monumental significance, was mentioned only in passing in the Colloquy, with *false consciousness* (dual in meaning) the cover or proxy diverting attention from it. Here are the pertinent passages:

> GARNHAM: *The rejection of false consciousness within cultural studies goes along with the rejection of truth as a state of the world, as opposed to the tem-*

porary effect of discourse. But without some notion of grounded truth the ideas of emancipation, resistance, and progressiveness become meaningless. Resistance to what, emancipation from what and for what, progression toward what?[30]

GROSSBERG: *Thus the category of false consciousness returns—actually it has never left political economy. According to Garnham, without such a notion (and the related notion of truth), intellectuals have no valid role. And cultural studies of course rejects such notions.*[31]

In these declarations, *false consciousness* is clearly meant to denote deviation of people's understanding from what is real or objectively true, as opposed to the more common meaning, namely acceptance of the dominators' views by those who are oppressed. Now it is easy to understand why Hall and McRobbie took such exception to the category, *false consciousness*, and why Grossberg refrained from using the term when acknowledging that people can be "duped," that they are lied to and manipulated by the suppliers of commodified enjoyments, and that they often adopt as their own a worldview foisted on them by antagonistic interests. For to accept the term, *false consciousness* (even regarding its more common definition), could perhaps be construed as giving implicit assent to the term's semantic opposite, namely "not false consciousness," or even "truth"—notions that have no place within the poststructuralist mindset. According to poststructuralists, "truth" is always, and is merely, a matter of interpretation, whether on the part of an individual or as a consensus attained through social interaction; truth is not to be discovered, but simply invented, constructed, interpreted, or agreed to—for a while.

The same poststructuralist doubts apply to "authenticity" as apply to "truth;" in a world overcome by simulations, hyperrealities, copies without originals, and radical freedom to interpret, the notion of authenticity has no place, poststructuralists maintain. There are many "truths" on every issue, according to poststructuralism, no one more valid than any other. And these "truths," moreover, are quite provisional, merely awaiting re-interpretation. Hence, regarding cultural studies itself, Grossberg declared, "the fact that cultural studies starts with a particular position cannot define its future—that is indeed one of its peculiarities and strengths."[32]

Critical political economy, we have seen, is by definition an evaluative discipline; it judges events and conditions by *values* deemed to have some philosophical, experiential, and moral grounding. It is a scholarly discipline dedicated to the pursuit of social justice. Pursuing social justice in the material world, however, becomes ludicrous if any of three poststructuralist postulates are accepted.

The first poststructuralist postulate is that there is no objective reality; there are only interpretations. Accordingly, poststructuralism maintains, one should not seek facts, merely discuss; not quest for understanding, merely persuade and interpret; not judge or assess because one cannot really know. Obviously, however, one cannot ameliorate lived conditions if it is impossible to transcend subjectivity. If *in principle* interpretation trumps facts and circumstances, and if one opinion or one interpretation is *in principle* never any better or worse than any other, individualist pursuits efface all concern for the social and the communal.

The second axiom (to be discussed more fully in chapter 8) is that there is now a rupture between language and material reality. We are trapped within language, it is contended, and hence can know nothing of our material conditions. Since we can know nothing of the material world, it would follow, we cannot pursue social justice, except perhaps through "language-ing" and linguistic "articulations."

Third, there is the proposition (again documented in chapter 8) that in the contemporary (postmodern) era of simulacra and articulations, both cause and effect (causation) and rationality (logic) are anachronistic baggage. But, if an effect has no cause or causes, there can be no (efficacious) policies, which is again tantamount to dismissing the pursuit of social justice, which is the heart of political economy. And if rationality (logic) is dead, so too must be all scholarship such as political economy which is based on reason.

RECONCILIATION OR DIVORCE?

In the form of a question, Grossberg briefly set out the terms whereby he could countenance closer collaboration with political economy. "The question," he wrote, "is whether it is possible to have a political economy theorized around *articulation* rather than strict determination or necessity."[33] (Note that Grossberg chose not to say, "theorized around interpretation rather than truth or authenticity," although that would have also represented his position equally well.) Substantial space has been afforded in this book to critiquing charges of "strict determinisms and necessities" in political economy, so it would be redundant to cover that ground again. It warrants another mention, though, that political economy *does* presume "soft determinisms," which means that life is *not* totally random, that there are patterns that *can* be detected, areas that *can* be researched, findings attained, and conclusions drawn.

Articulation, however, merits some further attention, an interesting question being the extent to which it might correspond to, or be consistent with, the soft determinisms advanced by writers such as Williams and Adorno, and with the notion of "bias" as forwarded by Innis. Grossberg defined *articulation* as "the production of identity on top of differences, of unities out of fragments, of structures across practices," adding that "articulation links this practice to that effect, this text to that meaning, this meaning to that reality, this experience to those politics; and these links are themselves articulated into larger structures, etc."[34] More briefly, according to Grossberg, articulation is "*the production of the real*."[35] Likewise, Grossberg's mentor, Stuart Hall, has described articulation as the forging of a whole or a structure out of parts, parts which "are related as much through their differences as through their similarities," adding that these parts inevitably relate to one another in terms of dominance and subordination.[36]

These declarations and definitions imply that there are few if any limitations with regard to what can be joined, few or no irreversibilities, few bonds that cannot be broken, few constraints on creating and disassembling structures. Articulation implies *enormous freedom to do.* The foregoing declarations and definitions, then, certainly do not call attention to disparities across sectors of society or among individuals in their relative capacities *to do*. Nor do they even hint at the capacity of some to prevent others from doing. Articulation is the joining of structures, but who or what does the joining, and for that matter the disassembling, and why these structures, and with what consequences? Can a merger between two companies really be equated to combining the letters *t* and *o* to form a new structure, *to*?[37] Or hooking a trailer onto a truck?

In one of his most celebrated essays, "The Rediscovery of 'Ideology': Return of the Repressed in Media Studies," Stuart Hall illustrated the workings of articulation: "In the discourses of the Black movement," he wrote, "the denigratory connotation 'black = the despised race' could be inverted into its opposite: 'black = beautiful.'"[38] This, for Hall, was an example of "an ideological struggle" whereby a signifier from one dominant or preferred meaning system was "disarticulated," and "rearticulated" within another.[39] It is understandable then why, in the Colloquy, Garnham would allude, albeit implicitly and critically, to this example; it is less understandable, at least from a scholarly standpoint, why Grossberg (a former student of Hall) would not only refrain from acknowledging the allusion, but accuse Garnham of "glibness" in bringing it forth.[40]

Regarding compatibility between articulation and the soft determinism of Williams and Adorno and with Innisian bias, I would suggest the following:

First, to the extent that the poststructuralist notion of articulation focuses on or derives from linguistic practice and hence presumes or implies that the "articulation" of material structures is about as difficult as forming a new sentence or making a new metaphor, there is a monumental discrepancy between critical political economy and poststructuralist cultural studies. Political economists view structures of domination and oppression as not only servicing concentrated political and economic power, but as being supported and defended by these centers of power, and as blocking new structures which might challenge that power. "Articulation" for political economists (should they ever choose to use the term) is closely related to restructuring political, economic, military, and cultural power. Political-economic power, these analysts insist, must be understood as lying behind and motivating "articulations" in the material world—for example, mergers and acquisitions, changes in the terms of trade, layoffs, copyright act revisions, law enforcement, taxation, war and annexations, weaponry, advertising and PR, and so on. On the other hand, Hall did mention that from a cultural studies perspective, articulations and rearticulations normally entail relations of dominance and dependence. To the extent, therefore, that these relations of dominance and dependence are given full consideration, and the "articulations" forged are themselves related back to power struggles, one could argue that political economy and poststructuralist cultural studies could begin to reconcile through a modified concept of articulation.

Second, although articulation according to Hall is a term meant to encompass both the realm of language (signs) and the material or nonverbal world, poststructuralists normally claim that these two realms are disengaged,[41] that by living inextricably in the world of language we can know little if anything of the material world. Political economists certainly recognize difficulties in connecting the symbolic realm to lived conditions: Innis' medium theory, after all, was devoted to exploring inherent biases in the media of communication! Nonetheless, neither Innis, nor Garnham, nor political economists generally, are willing to give up the effort to compensate for or neutralize the biases of media and language, and by dint of these efforts to view the nonverbal world afresh, and in light of the new awareness to help remove adverse conditions in that material realm.[42] Likewise, Raymond Williams, E. P. Thompson, and Richard Hoggart strove to align the verbal world more closely to the lived conditions of the majority population. The concern of all these writers was primarily *to improve the connectivity between media/language on the one hand, and material conditions/lived experience on the other*, whether by recognizing and then compensating for biases, by targeting political-economic-power controlling media, or by reformulating the verbal (discursive) world so as to align it more closely with lived conditions. All these writers had their eyes cast steadfastly on goals, values, and criteria which transcended mere verbal articulations and rearticulations, and which they saw as guides to social improvement. Fundamentally, however, poststructuralists deny the existence of transcendental values whereby material conditions can even be judged, and hence, arguably, we come again to the real (i.e., the ontological) source of their dispute with political economists.

In the Colloquy, Garnham maintained that in the absence of a truth somehow grounded outside of discourse, notions of "emancipation, resistance, and progressiveness become meaningless. . . . Resistance to what," he asked, "emancipation from what and for what, progression toward what?" These are, indeed, fundamental questions. For a political economist, understanding and describing what exists is the first step on the road to reform. For poststructuralists, evidently, in contending that we are trapped within language, saying ("articulating" or "re-articulating") something is the best we can do.

SUMMARY

The overall conclusions to this point, then, are these: First, taking Harold Innis and Theodor Adorno as founders of political-economic studies of media, and the British cultural theorists plus Adorno as inaugurators of critical cultural studies, there was at the beginning no inconsistency or breach between the fields. While the emphases of the two founding groups (Adorno straddling both) certainly differed, their works were largely cut from one cloth and they complement one another.

Second, in the more contemporary era, critical political economy of media, represented here by Garnham and Murdock, has remained largely consistent with its origins (Adorno, Innis), and as well with the cultural materialism of Raymond Williams, Richard Hoggart, and E. P. Thompson. However, contemporary cultural studies has split in two: there is at the margin *cultural materialism,* which persists in the vein of Williams et al, and there is the mainstream, at least in America—*poststructuralist cultural studies,* represented here by Grossberg and McRobbie, with Hall seemingly straddling the two camps. As editor of the journal *Cultural Studies,* Grossberg has been highly influential in defining the boundaries of mainstream contemporary cultural studies.

Third, the well-publicized antagonisms between critical political economists and cultural studies theorists actually stem from the bifurcation just noted within cultural studies itself, with the poststructuralist version being largely irreconcilable with contemporary cultural materialism, and hence with the founders' positions. Indeed, poststructuralist cultural studies has more in common with neoliberal, Chicago-style political economy than it does with cultural materialism.[43] The prospects, then, of reconciling critical political economy and poststructuralist cultural studies are slim indeed. On the other hand, the prospects for cooperation and integration between cultural materialism and critical political economy are very positive.

NOTES

1. Carey's remarks addressed the split between cultural studies on the one hand, and "abstract economistic Marxism" on the other. Carey was certainly no Marxist, but he was an admirer of Innis. In chapter 1, I quoted Carey as crediting Innis as being the founder of media imperialism (dependency theory). One wonders, then, why he did not even mention Innis in his treatment of critical political economy. Had he done so, it is likely his position would have changed significantly.

2. Nicholas Garnham, "Political Economy and Cultural Studies: Reconciliation or Divorce?" *Critical Studies in Mass Communication* 12, no. 1 (1995): 62. Garnham here is citing James McGuigan.

3. Angela McRobbie, "Post-marxism and Cultural Studies: A Post-script," in *Cultural Studies,* ed. L. Grossberg, C. Nelson, and P. Treichler (New York: Routledge, 1992), 719; quoted in Garnham, "Political Economy and Cultural Studies," 62.

4. McRobbie, "Post-marxism and Cultural Studies," 62.

5. Stuart Hall, "Cultural Studies and its Theoretical Legacies," in *Cultural Studies*, ed. L. Grossberg, C. Nelson, and P. Treichler (London: Routledge, 1992), 277–94; quoted in Garnham, "Political Economy and Cultural Studies," 62. Hall's position is restated in his "Two Paradigms" article: "[Williams] is arguing against the literal operations of the base/superstructure metaphor. . . . That is to say, his argument is constructed against a vulgar materialism and an economic determinism. He offers, instead, a radical interactionism: in effect, the interaction of all practices in and with one another, skirting the problem of determinacy." Stuart Hall, "Cultural Studies: Two Paradigms," *Media, Culture and Society* 2 (1980): 60. Carey, too, lauded cultural studies' break with "abstract economistic Marxism," but for that remark to be pertinent in the current context it would need to be established that inaugural political economists specializing in media were, in fact, "abstract economistic" Marxists. See note 1, above.

6. Theodor Adorno, "The Stars Down to Earth: The *Los Angeles Times* Astrology Column" (1952–1953; reprint, *The Stars Down to Earth and Other Essays on the Irrational in Culture,* by Theodor W. Adorno, edited with an Introduction by Stephen Crook, New York: Routledge, 2007), 46.

7. Ben Agger, "Critical Theory, Poststructuralism, Postmodernism: Their Sociological Relevance," *Annual Review of Sociology* 17, 1991. www.uta.edu/huma/illuminations/agger2.htm (accessed June 10, 2008).

8. Lawrence Grossberg, "Cultural Studies vs. Political Economy," *Critical Studies in Mass Communication* 12, no. 1 (1995): 75–76.

9. Garnham, "Political Economy and Cultural Studies," 69.

10. Garnham, "Political Economy and Cultural Studies," 65.

11. Garnham, "Political Economy and Cultural Studies," 65. While affirming a degree of interpretive freedom on the part of cultural "consumers," then, Garnham here claimed that elites, pursuing their own economic and political agendas, retain the power to determine "which meanings circulate and which do not, which stories are told and about what, which arguments are given prominence and what cultural resources are made available and to whom." He might well have added that from a political economy perspective elites also help determine what is considered feasible or even thinkable, and suggest or inculcate interpretive categories. Garnham concluded: "The analysis of this process is vital to an understanding of the power relationships involved in culture and their relationship to wider structures of domination" (p. 65). The writer often associated with emphasizing the pleasure aspects of cultural consumption as opposed to outside ideological domination is John Fiske. See John Fiske, *Understanding Popular Culture* (Boston: Unwin Hyman, 1989); also, Graeme Turner, *British Cultural Studies: An Introduction*. Cambridge, MA: Unwin Hyman, 1990, 221.

12. Grossberg, "Cultural Studies vs. Political Economy," 74–75.

13. Grossberg, "Cultural Studies vs. Political Economy," 77. In fact, Garnham's goal was to "reconcile" political economy and cultural studies. In Garnham's view, as noted by Murdock, "critical political economy [is] a necessary starting point for a critical analysis of contemporary culture." Graham Murdock, "Across the Great Divide: Cultural Analysis and the Condition of Democracy," *Critical Studies in Mass Communication* 12, no. 1 (1995): 90.

14. Grossberg, "Cultural Studies vs. Political Economy," 74. Interestingly, this position is supported by Carey, who wrote: "The dispute between cultural studies and political economy should largely be ignored; it reflects the increasing academization of the subject matter." Carey, "Abolishing the Old Spirit World," 84. Murdock provides a similar explanation, if not justification: "Part of the explanation [for the division] has to do with the prevailing academic division of labor. Cultural studies has found its primary institutional home within schools and faculties of humanities and has been most consistently supported by scholars migrating from literary studies, art history, and cultural anthropology. In contrast, critical political economy tends to be pursued within schools of social sciences and operate across the boundaries of economics, political science and sociology." Murdock goes on to remark, correctly I believe, that to perpetuate this "great divide," is to "break faith with the original project of cultural studies." Murdock, "Across the Great Divide," 90.

15. Grossberg, "Cultural Studies vs. Political Economy," 74.

16. Grossberg, "Cultural Studies vs. Political Economy," 76.

17. Interestingly, this was a major virtue of Adorno's coupling of Freudian categories and political economy. Adorno acknowledged, on the one hand, that "shifting responsibility from the manipulators to the manipulated is a widespread ideological problem." On the other, he understood media as playing upon audiences' background assumptions and motivations so as to strike a resonance whereby interpretations desired by the manipulator would likely take hold. Theodor Adorno, "The Stars Down to Earth," 54; and Stephen Crook, "Introduction," *The Stars Down to Earth,* by

Theodor Adorno, with Introduction by Stephen Crook (1994; reprint, New York: Routledge, 2007), 33.

18. Grossberg, "Cultural Studies vs. Political Economy," 74.

19. Garnham, "Political Economy and Cultural Studies," 66; emphasis added.

20. Grossberg, "Cultural Studies vs. Political Economy," 73.

21. Garnham, "Political Economy and Cultural Studies," 66.

22. Garnham, "Political Economy and Cultural Studies," 67.

23. Garnham, "Political Economy and Cultural Studies," 67.

24. Stuart Hall, "On Postmodernism and Articulation: An Interview with Stuart Hall" (1986; in *Stuart Hall: Critical Dialogues in Cultural Studies,* ed. David Morley and Kuan-Hsing Chen. London: Routledge, 1996), 141. See also, Tim O'Sullivan, John Hartley, Danny Saunders, Martin Montgomery and John Fiske, *Key Concepts in Communication and Cultural Studies,* 2nd edition (London: Routledge, 1994), 17–18.

25. According to Grossberg, "[Cultural studies never] bought into political economy as a model of cultural explanation. . . . Its founding figures, especially Hoggart and Williams, quite intentionally distanced themselves from any attempt to explain culture in *purely* economic terms." Grossberg, "Cultural Studies vs. Political Economy," 76; emphasis added.

26. Murdock, "Across the Great Divide," 90.

27. Garnham, "Political Economy and Cultural Studies," 70.

28. Grossberg, "Cultural Studies vs. Political Economy," 77.

29. Grossberg, "Cultural Studies vs. Political Economy," 78.

30. Garnham, "Political Economy and Cultural Studies," 69.

31. Grossberg, "Cultural Studies vs. Political Economy," 79.

32. Grossberg, "Cultural Studies vs. Political Economy," 77.

33. Grossberg, "Cultural Studies vs. Political Economy," 79; emphasis added.

34. Lawrence Grossberg, *We Gotta Get Out of this Place: Popular Conservativism and the Postmodern Culture* (New York: Routledge, 1992), 54; quoted in Jennifer Daryl Slack, "The Theory and Method of Articulation in Cultural Studies," in *Stuart Hall: Critical Dialogues in Cultural Studies,* ed. David Morley and Kuan-Hsing Chen (London: Routledge, 1996), 115.

35. Lawrence Grossberg, "The Formations of Cultural Studies: An American in Birmingham," in *Relocating Cultural Studies: Developments in Theory and Research,* ed. Valda Blundell, John Shepherd and Ian Taylor (London: Routledge, 1993), 59; emphasis added. One is reminded here of Ivy Lee's dictum, "Truth happens to an idea." Lee was founder of the U.S. public relations industry, and according to Stuart Ewen's gloss, Lee proposed that "something asserted might become a fact, regardless of its connection to actual events." Stuart Ewen, *PR! A Social History of Spin* (New York: Basic Books, 1996), 79.

36. Stuart Hall, "Encoding/Decoding," quoted in Slack, "The Theory and Method of Articulation in Cultural Studies," 115.

37. In May 2008, EnCana, Canada's largest energy company, announced it was voluntarily splitting into two—at an estimated cost of $300 million. Combining and disassembling structures, it would seem, requires time, energy, and resources. See An-

drew Willis, "EnCana's Breakup a Boon for Bay Street," *Globe and Mail,* May 13, 2008, B17.

38. Hall, "The Rediscovery of 'Ideology,'" 79.

39. Hall, "The Rediscovery of 'Ideology,'" 80.

40. Grossberg, "Cultural Studies vs. Political Economy," 77.

41. This claim lies at the heart of the poststructuralism of Mark Poster and Jean Baudrillard. See chapter 8. See also Frank Webster, *Theories of the Information Society* (London: Routledge, 1995), 163–92.

42. Here it is useful to recall the discussions regarding bias and reflexivity presented in chapter 1, and the excerpt from Innis, repeated here, in note 217: "But always the university must foster the search for truth and in its search must always question the pretentions of organized power whether in the hands of church or state. . . . It will also insist that any group which pretends to have found the truth is a fraud against civilization and that it is the search for truth and not truth which keeps civilization alive." Harold Innis, "The Canadian Situation" (1940, 1952; quoted in Robin Neill, *A New Theory of Value: The Canadian Economics of H. A. Innis*, (Toronto: University of Toronto Press, 1972), 90.

43. Graham Murdock noted that the growth in poststructuralist cultural studies "is almost exactly conterminous with neoliberalism's dominating economic and social policy." In his view, this is not mere happenstance, for poststructuralists aid and abet, whether intentionally or by inadvertence, neoliberalist "free market" ideals. They do this, Murdock explained, by "constructing a flat horizon of multiple differences in identities and life styles, [while] the stark, vertical structures of inequality . . . [are] bulldozed off this intellectual map"—yet another instance of theorizing in support of elite power, of what I term, in chapter 4, "the political economy of knowledge." See Graham Murdock, "Across the Great Divide," 91.

Chapter Four

Genealogy of Poststructuralist Cultural Studies, and the Political Economy of Media Scholarship

Although the early French proponents of postmodern/poststructural discourses may well have envisaged their project as constituting a radical break with the past,[1] and although contemporary poststructuralists often view their work as challenging existing power and as extending critical theory,[2] in practice poststructuralism can be and often is supportive of established power. Indeed, as it penetrates further into the mainstream, one should expect it to increasingly support status quo power arrangements for, as political philosopher C. B. Macpherson observed, mainstream scholarship, almost by definition, supports established power.[3] Through his concept of monopolies of knowledge, Harold Innis, too, can be regarded as forwarding that position. If Macpherson and Innis are correct (and I review here substantial evidence indicating that they are), then one should expect poststructuralist thought in the years ahead to become even more "domesticated."

The first part of this chapter reviews the century-long refusal of mainstream American media/communication/cultural studies scholars to deal with issues relating to disparities in communicatory power. This section substantiates empirically the Macpherson-Innis hypothesis concerning the political economy of mainline scholarship. The second part of the chapter focuses on contemporary poststructuralist scholarship, and proposes that it *already* fits the pattern established in the first part.

The continuous neglect of power in mainstream American media scholarship is evident despite the fact (or more accurately, one suspects, *due* to the fact) that communication and culture have long been central to American wealth generation, governance, and foreign policy. To draw attention to international asymmetries in communicatory and cultural power would be, for example, to question implicitly the legitimacy or justness of those asymmetries.

Similarly, to draw attention to domestic concentrations of media ownership and to the role of advertising in "filtering" news and other content, would be tantamount to questioning the existence or efficacy of American democracy. Nor should one lose sight of the pecuniary rewards awaiting scholars eschewing criticism of moneyed sponsors. These considerations are components of what may be termed the political economy of scholarship.

THE PAST

Over the past 100 years, mainline American media scholarship has taken many twists and turns, but there has been one constant: virtual silence regarding disparities in communicatory power. In many respects, we will see, mainline scholarship has been highly self-contradictory. But with regard to the concerns of political economy, there has been no contradiction: mainstream scholarship has steadfastly ignored or denied issues raised by disparities in the power to communicate. (And here we find an additional, and possibly the most important, explanation for Grossberg's lack of zeal for reconciling with political economy.)

Chicago School

Standard histories of American communication/media studies begin with the so-called "Chicago School" of John Dewey, Robert Park, and Charles Cooley.[4] The designation, "Chicago School," is something of a misnomer, at least in reference to these three. Cooley, after all, never strayed from the University of Michigan and Dewey's "communication" writings date almost entirely from his post-Chicago years at Harvard.[5] Park, though, at Chicago, was certainly seminal. In any event, whether misnamed or not, for many intellectual historians these "Chicago" theorists were foundational.

Dewey, Park, and Cooley were optimists and progressives. They speculated on how technological change—particularly emerging media of communication—could restore community in an urban setting, enlighten citizens, and increase democracy. Dewey, for example, forwarded a doctrine of *instrumentalism,* proposing virtually unlimited and inevitable human betterment through technological change. Technologies, he opined, are instruments to solve problems, and as the problems change, so do the instruments.

Dewey, Park, and Cooley inquired broadly from humanist perspectives into the role of media in American society. They viewed society as an organism, whose citizens are bound together through networks of transportation (likened to blood vessels) and communication (likened to nerves). According to Dewey, "the Great Society created by steam and electricity may be a society, but it is no community. . . . Communication alone can create a great community."[6]

Dewey, however, cast a blind eye toward other possibilities: in particular, domination and subordination through technological means. The chief failing of the Chicago School, according to Daniel Czitrom, was its "refusal to address the reality of social and economic conflict in the present;"[7] in other words, it neglected critical political economy.

Without Macpherson's insights, the naïve technological optimism of the Chicago theorists would be difficult to comprehend—given the uses to which media and other technologies were then being put. In 1917, for example, acting on the advice of journalist Walter Lippmann, the Wilson Administration created the Committee on Public Information (CPI) as the government's propaganda arm for the Great War. CPI produced hundreds of ads promoting the war effort and pressured newspapers into giving it free advertising space. It distributed thousands of official news releases and war-related public interest stories. It even published its own newspaper.[8] Meanwhile, the commercial press was "continually silenced by orders and prosecutions;" war critics were arrested, "often without warrants, hustled off to jail, held incommunicado without bail."[9] No enlightenment and fostering of democracy here!

Nor were the war years exceptional. Rather, they simply fulfilled a revolution in political and economic control begun prior to the turn of the century through the introduction of new media of communication[10] whereby media diffused image-based advertising of addictive and non-addictive branded products, opening up "a nether realm between truth and falsehood. . . . The world of advertisements," according to Jackson Lears, "gradually acquired an Alice-in-Wonderland quality."[11]

Dewey's former student and arch nemesis, renowned journalist Walter Lippmann, had a better grip on what was happening. Writing contemporaneously with the Chicago School, in his influential 1922 tome *Public Opinion*, Lippmann claimed that most of us, most of the time, live in a *pseudoenvironment*, defined as the "way in which the world is imagined . . . a hybrid compounded of 'human nature' and 'conditions.'"[12] For Lippmann, democracy had turned a corner (he called it "a new image of democracy"), because experts could garner popular consent for their purportedly wise and beneficent policies by skillfully manipulating mediated pseudoenvironments. The ultra conservative Lippmann saw this deception as necessary for governance in the modern age, and he thereby helped inspire, or at least "justify," the public relations/image manufacturing industries. Lippmann, then, unlike Dewey, did not ignore disparities in the capacity to communicate; however, he "justified" those disparities as being both necessary and good.[13]

The "Chicago" theorists' influence waned by the early 1930s, due not only to Lippmann's remarkable book, but also because it had become increasingly difficult to sustain a posture of inevitable progress through advancing technology in the wake of World War I devastations and the onset of the Great Depression. The U.S. government's psychological warfare activities of World War I also contributed to the rise of a less idealistic, more pragmatic paradigm in media scholarship.[14]

Empiricism

The cadre of empirical scholars who redefined mainstream American scholarship in the 1930s eschewed speculating on how media might contribute to community, democracy, enlightenment, or human betterment. They focused instead on persuasion, psychological manipulation, and marketing. One defining moment in this transition was in 1937 when a Rockefeller Foundation grant set up the Princeton Radio Project with Paul Felix Lazarsfeld as director. The Project's mandate was to study the possibilities for educational and public service programming by commercial radio stations; its charter, however, "explicitly forbade research that questioned the commercial basis of broadcasting."[15] Lazarsfeld's Office of Radio Research soon moved to Columbia University, where it was renamed the Bureau of Applied Social Research.

A second defining moment was in 1939, when the Rockefeller Foundation organized a "Communications Seminar," whose participants included Lazarsfeld, Harold Lasswell, and psychologist Hadley Cantril (whose 1935 book, *The Psychology of Radio,* perhaps inaugurated quantitative audience research). In their interim report of 1940, the Seminar participants unabashedly advocated war-related opinion management:

> We believe . . . that for leadership to secure that consent will require unprecedented knowledge of the public mind and of the means by which leadership can secure consent. . . . We believe . . . that we have available today methods of research which can reliably inform us about the public mind and how it is being, or can be, influenced in relation to public affairs.[16]

World War II was certainly a boon to the by-then dominant "media-effects" researchers, many of whom benefited from funds dispensed by the U.S. military and intelligence services. Christopher Simpson lists the following, among others, as eminent American communication/media scholars engaged in propaganda and psychological warfare research for or with the military during World War II: Harold Lasswell, Hadley Cantril, Rensis Likert, Leonard Doob, Wilbur Schramm, Leo Lowenthal, Paul Felix Lazarsfeld, Frank Stanton, George Gallup, Elmo Roper, Ithiel de Sola Pool, Daniel Lerner, Edward Shils, Carl Hovland, Louis Gutman, Robert Merton[17]—a veritable *Who's Who* of American media studies. Conservative media scholar Everett Rogers agrees—albeit *sans* Simpson's critical edge:

> An invisible college of communication scholars came together in Washington, D.C. They met in formal conferences and informally in carpools. Communication was considered crucial in informing the American public about the nation's wartime goals. . . . Communication research initially focused on studying the effects of communication. This consensus about the role of communication happened during World War II, and it happened mainly in Washington, D.C. . . . World War II thus created the conditions for the founding of communication study.[18]

Through the 1950s and into the 1960s, government-sponsored research on attitude and opinion change and on the art of propaganda continued apace as CIA and State Department money, always unacknowledged publicly and often laundered by the Carnegie and Ford foundations, poured into university think tanks. Government funding accounted for over three-quarters of the revenue at Lazarsfeld's Bureau, at Cantril's Institute for International Social Research (Princeton), at de Sola Pool's Center for International Studies (MIT), and at "similar research shops."[19]

Given their martial orientation and their scholarly fixation on persuasion, it might at first seem surprising that the sole media "law" these eminent researchers could come up with was the *law of minimal media effects*, "discovered" by Paul Felix Lazarsfeld and elaborated by many mainline researchers over succeeding decades. In his seminal study of the 1940 U.S. presidential election campaign, *The People's Choice,* Lazarsfeld declared that "conversion" (as opposed to "reinforcement" and "activation") was the sole indictor of strong media effects. Since few voters in his panel of Erie County, Ohio voters deviated from their initial voting intentions during the course of the campaign preceding the landslide Roosevelt victory, a "law" of minimal effects was declared.[20] Lazarsfeld explained the "law" partly by proposing a *two-step flow* theory of mass communication, subsequently elaborated in *Personal Influence* by Lazarsfeld and his one-time research assistant, Elihu Katz.[21]

Researcher Deborah Lubken suggests that "the first chapter of *Personal Influence* has contributed, perhaps more than any other book, to the orthodox history of mass communication research in general."[22] Likewise, Jefferson

Pooley maintains that the inaugural fifteen pages of *Personal Influence* had "more influence on the field's historical self-understanding than anything published before or since. . . . This 'powerful-to-limited effects' story line," he continued, "remains textbook boilerplate and literature review dogma fifty years later."[23]

According to Lazarsfeld and Katz, prior to publication of their book, the "potency of the media" had been undoubted: "The media of communication were looked upon as a new kind of unifying force—a simple kind of nervous system—reaching out to every eye and ear, in a society characterized by an amorphous social organization and a paucity of interpersonal relations."[24] The two-step flow, in contrast, as proposed by Lazarsfeld and Katz, insisted that people's attitudes are little affected directly by media, but rather are influenced by opinion leaders (everyday contacts). Even the title, *Personal Influence,* is indicative of the flight from, or denial of, political economy: *personal* influence is stressed, not *structures* of influence, or institutions of power.[25]

Soon the two-step flow was superceded by the *multi-step flow*, forwarded by such mainline researchers as Everett Rogers and Floyd Shoemaker.[26] They maintained that "the ultimate number of relays between the media and final receivers is variable,"[27] which is to say that general audiences are even further removed from direct media influence than had been proposed in the original model.

According to Chaffee and Hochheimer, "for four decades 'limited effects' was a major defense of owners of new media technologies, including television, from government regulation in the United States."[28] Likewise, Schramm remarked that "the two-step flow hypothesis was widely quoted and used through the 1950s and 1960s."[29] Joseph Klapper's *The Effects of Mass Communication* (1960) was perhaps "the watershed" of the doctrine;[30] at the time of the book's publication, Klapper was director of social research for CBS, of which Frank Stanton (a close colleague, coauthor, and friend of Lazarsfeld) was president.[31]

The law of minimal effects may be regarded as an umbrella term—a prophylactic—under cover of which researchers investigated ways of changing people's beliefs and perceptions. Carl Hovland's studies on persuasion, for example, among others, received funding during the war from the U.S. military and, after the peace, from funds flowing from the military through the Rockefeller Foundation. According to Lowery and DeFleur, between 1946 and 1961 Hovland's team conducted more than fifty experiments on how opinions and beliefs could be modified by persuasive communication.[32] Schramm summarized the research findings as follows: "Experimental research on opinion change showed that one-third to one-half of an audience is significantly affected by even a single exposure to a persuasive message."[33] Despite such evidence, mainline researchers (including Schramm as we will see momentarily) continued supporting the "law;" as late as 2007, Elihu Katz, for example, was still claiming that "the conclusion of 'limited effects' [was] echoed repeatedly in studies of mass persuasion."[34]

The "law," however, was also belied by practices and premises of media companies and commercial propagandists. Broadcasters sold advertising on the assumption that *activation* (getting people to act) is an important and sought-after consequence of media exposure, although in *The People's Choice* Lazarsfeld had classified activation as a "minimal effect." Hitler's "big lie theory" contended that if something is said often enough it becomes "true" for many, a principle endorsed also by such PR industry founders as Ivy Lee and Edward Bernays, but for Lazarsfeld "reinforcement" was a minimal effect.[35]

An insight into the longevity of the minimal effects doctrine, despite abundant contradictory evidence, is gleaned by noting Lazarsfeld's admission, confided to researcher Elizabeth Noelle-Neumann, that he abandoned communication research in mid-career for the safer haven of mathematical sociology because "he could no longer take the pressure that the media exerted on a communication researcher."[36] Likewise, as noted in a previous chapter, Lazarsfeld declined to undertake research projects that might rile his major clients, the commercial broadcasters. But the irony runs deeper. As Pooley remarks, "Even while 'limited effects'-style conclusions were published, in *Personal Influence* for example, research outfits like Lazarsfeld and Katz's Bureau were under federal contract to design effective propaganda campaigns overseas. . . . The Bureau was hardly concerned to show that media influence is limited, since it was in the business of making persuasion work for its commercial and government clients."[37]

Given such blatant contradictions, it is certainly understandable that an oppositional (albeit marginalized) media paradigm would arise. In 1948, at the University of Illinois, Dallas W. Smythe began teaching a course on the political economy of communication.[38] Smythe was joined at Illinois in 1956 by George Gerbner and later, albeit briefly, by Herbert Schiller. That their line of research was, and remains, "marginal" to the U.S. mainstream is warranted by the fact (among many others) that Everett Rogers' *A History of Communication Study* mentions Smythe but once and that merely in a footnote acknowledging that he was one of Wilbur Schramm's hires. Schiller's name, too, appears but once in Rogers' history: in a diagram purporting to depict critical research. And there is no reference at all to Gerbner, even though (or perhaps because) Gerbner was particularly successful in challenging the law of minimal effects on its own terms through empirically rigorous "encultura-tion" studies.[39]

When "minimal effects"—belied by methodological problems, conflicting evidence (as provided by Hovland, Lasswell, Gerbner, and many others), and its overdrawn conclusions—finally waned as mainstream doctrine by the late 1960s, another theory, namely *uses and gratifications,* promptly took its place. Actually, audience uses and gratifications had been studied by Lazarsfeld in the 1940s as a way of helping clients garner larger audiences. In the 1960s, though, it blossomed from being merely a market research tool into becoming "one of the most popular theories of mass communication."[40] Simpson attributed this remarkable renewal and ascendance to a 1959 paper by RAND Corporation researcher W. Phillips Davison.[41] In any event, by 1968, with the publication of *Television in Politics: Its Uses and Influences* by Blumler and McQuail, uses and gratifications were mainstream.

Unlike the law of minimum effects, uses and gratifications theory did not deny the possibility of profound impacts of media on audiences. What it asserted, rather, was that those consequences are anticipated and actively sought out by audiences in light of their preexisting needs and desires.[42] As formulated by its innovators, uses and gratifications can include: attaining information, gaining a sense of personal identity (as through role modeling), facilitating social interaction, and being entertained.[43] Uses and gratifications like these, however, for a political economist, raise a host of serious questions: for instance, what types of information are and are not made available to curious audiences and by whom—issues addressed with telling results by such marginalized researchers as Edward S. Herman and Noam Chomsky.[44] Explosive questions like these, however, *cannot even be thought* if and when the research paradigm is that of audience "uses and gratifications."

By the 1980s, uses and gratifications, too, had waned in influence, but only to be replaced by yet another media power-denying doctrine, namely Stanley Fish's *active reader*. As Paul Cobley summarizes:

> For [Stanley] Fish, the reader supplies everything; this is because there can be nothing that precedes interpretation. As soon as human beings apprehend an item in the world they have already embarked on a process of interpreting it. There can be no 'given' as such.[45]

As noted in chapter 3 and again in chapter 8, the "active audience" and the primacy of interpretation form a cornerstone of poststructuralist positions. The flip side of the doctrine of the active reader/active audience, of course, is denying the power of message senders, whose role is reduced, in effect, to compiling Rorschach tests for audiences to interpret as they will. Fish's position, as Anthony Easthope summarizes, is "resoundingly conservative."[46]

Again, however, real world events and practices belie mainstream posturings. Operation Desert Storm in 1991 was one notable instance of the triumph of the well-crafted, well-censored image in molding U.S. public opinion. Determined not to suffer another Vietnam by allowing uncensored stories and clips on the nightly television news, the U.S. military restricted war coverage by constraining journalists' freedom to move in the absence of military escorts: "journalists who did not accommodate themselves to the rules stated by the central command were threatened with losing their accreditations."[47] The government attained the overwhelming assent of the American public to wage the war in the first place, it may be recalled, through an untrue story told before Congress under the coaching of Hill and Knowlton, a PR firm, by the daughter of Kuwait's U.S. ambassador. She represented herself as a volunteer nurse, and claimed she had witnessed the atrocity of Iraqi troops hurling babies from hospital incubators and allowing them to die on the cold hard floor. Her story was treated as fact, without investigation, by the U.S. media and was repeated seemingly endlessly; indeed, her testimony was recounted by the U.S. president as justification for waging war in the first place. Likewise today, the phrase, "weapons of mass destruction," is sufficient to cause most people's eyes to roll, but when first used, repeatedly, by White House officials, it was sufficient to gain overwhelming support for waging a second war on Iraq. These are examples of Lippmannesque pseudoenvironments being put to the service of the U.S. military and are a far cry from the "limited effects," "uses and gratifications," and "active audience" theses of mainline media theorists.

In the opening chapter of the revised edition of his widely acclaimed textbook, *The Process and Effects of Mass Communication* (1971), Wilbur Schramm (by at least one account *the* founder of U.S. communication studies[48]) immodestly declared that he had been the first, way back in 1952, to suggest that audiences are "highly active, highly selective . . . manipulating rather than being manipulated by a message—a full partner in the communication process." Schramm added candidly that his original article, "How Communication Works," had been intended to be "a reaction against . . . the irrational fears of propaganda being expressed in the early 1950s." He continued: "The unsophisticated viewpoint was that if a person could be reached by the insidious forces of propagandas carried by the mighty power of the mass media, he could be changed and converted and controlled. So propaganda became a hate word, the media came to be regarded fearfully, and laws were passed and actions taken to protect defenseless people against 'irresistible communication.'"[49] Schramm here is as much as admitting that his research program and publications were designed to neutralize or discredit political economy treatments of media.

Schramm's position takes on a somewhat different complexion, though, when considered in the context of his wartime propaganda activities.

Schramm served as director of the education division of the Office of Facts and Figures (OFF). There he helped draft Roosevelt's "fireside chats" and other speeches. He also helped institute major propaganda campaigns for domestic and foreign consumption, and through surveys assessed the effectiveness of the campaigns.[50] Recall, too, Schramm's declaration, cited earlier, that "experimental research on opinion change showed that one-third to one-half of an audience is significantly affected by even a single exposure to a persuasive message."[51] On their own, these antithetical positions are irreconcilable; in the context of the political economy of scholarship, Schramm's contradictions, like those buzzing around the limited effects model generally, become quite comprehensible.

Much else could be addressed here, space permitting: the *media transfer model* of Schramm, Lucien Pye, Ithiel de Sola Pool, Everett Rogers, and Daniel Lerner, for instance;[52] the apolitical *social constructionism* of Peter Berger and Thomas Luckmann;[53] the agenda setting model of Maxwell McCombs;[54] and the paradox of First Amendment freedoms.[55] The conclusion, though, would be the same: obfuscation or outright denial of media power on the part of mainstream American media scholars, even as many of them were investigating means of augmenting media power through funding from the U.S. military and intelligence services. The remainder of this chapter argues that contemporary poststructuralist scholarship has much more in common with this conservative, ostensibly apolitical, status quo-affirming mainstream scholarship than it does with critical political economy—as it must (according to the Macpherson-Innis thesis) if poststructuralism is now mainstream.

POSTSTRUCTURALISM AS MAINSTREAM SCHOLARSHIP

From the beginning, through foundational texts by writers like E. P. Thompson, Raymond Williams, and Richard Hoggart, political economy was a mainstay—even the driving force—of *British* cultural studies.[56] By contrast, mainstream cultural studies in the United States, even from the outset, largely eschewed incorporating political-economic considerations. "Questions of power and politics, class and intellectual formation, so fundamental to the British exponents of cultural studies, lost their significance in the United States," reported Sardar and van Loon.[57]

Intellectual historian Richard E. Lee dates the inception of American cultural studies to a 1966 international conference at John Hopkins University entitled, "Criticism and the Sciences of Man/Les Langages Critiques et les Sciences de l'Homme."[58] It was there that Paul de Man (1919–83), newly arrived at Yale, listened intently to a paper delivered by Jacques Derrida, and the Yale School of deconstruction was born.

Yale deconstructionists, according Terry Eagleton, proposed a literary theory "notable for its belief that meaning is indeterminate, language ambiguous and unstable, the human subject a mere metaphor."[59] For de Man and the Yale poststructuralists, there were "no facts, only interpretations; no truths, only expedient fictions," and they applied their axioms not only to literature but also to the human sciences.[60] The impossibility of political economy, given these presuppositions, is readily apparent. Whereas Derrida's intention in proposing deconstruction may have been, in part, to liberate people from oppressive verbal structures, de Man's influence was "profoundly conservative."[61] Eagleton writes,

> De Man's discontinuous career . . . manifests a remarkable continuity: a resolute opposition to emancipatory politics. The early extreme right-wingism [de Man was a Nazi collaborator in World War II] mutates into a jaded liberal scepticism about the efficacy of any form of radical political action.[62]

In their emphasis on the ambiguity of texts and meanings we see a convergence between poststructuralist cultural studies and the doctrine of the active audience/active reader in communication studies. The distances separating Derrida, de Man, Fish, and Schramm (sometimes) are not large.

There is, then, a dialectic to postmodernist/poststructuralist thought. On the one hand, postmodernist discourses undermine the Enlightenment project, perhaps more thoroughly than any other critique. Here, "reality" is merely a product of language, ever-shifting in meanings, particularly as new digitized signs refer to one another with little, if any, correspondence to the "real world." Thus categories that realists have taken for granted—capital and labor, progress, gender, ethnicity, intelligence, sanity, and on and on—categories that in their seeming givenness have often "justified" outcomes like those bemoaned by writers like Marx, Durkheim, and Thoreau, are here seen to be the result merely of linguistic conventions, which are themselves not unrelated to the distribution of power. By this understanding of poststructuralism, there could be an alignment with political economy, as language and culture become recognized as sites of struggle.

On the other hand, though, the seeds of the destruction of the poststructuralists' radical bent are clearly evident. First, if "reality" is indeed merely a fabrication of language, then one might conclude that the concerns raised by Marx, Durkheim, Thoreau, and their successors are likewise mere fabrications, mere phantasmagoria, bearing no necessary relation at all to material existence. Indeed, the very criteria whereby social arrangements are to be judged (equity, human dignity, environmental health, peace) become mere linguistic constructs. It is hard indeed to do political economy in these circumstances. Moreover, postmodernist thought, if bereft of political-economic considerations regarding power centers structuring language, controlling and censoring messages, and directing culture, in effect takes the position that pseudoenvironments (or, in Jean Baudrillard's terms, *simulacra*) are all there is. Lippmann, one senses, would be delighted. The PR agencies and other spinners and weavers become absolved not only of the intent to deceive, but of deception, too. There can be no deception if all is merely interpretation, if there is no reality.

This dialectic of postmodern thought is well illustrated by comparing the early and late writings of Jean Baudrillard (1929–2007). According to Mark Poster (Baudrillard's editor in North America) Baudrillard was initially a materialist grounded in the Marxist tradition, albeit one endeavoring to extend that tradition to encompass the consumer society, but ended up a poststructuralist for whom materialist explanations are impotent.[63] Interestingly, Poster also claims that poststructuralism "is a uniquely American practice," that the writings of such seminal French theorists as Baudrillard, Derrida, Lyotard, and Foucault "have far greater currency in the United States than in France."[64] Poster's declaration makes Baudrillard's writings highly relevant to the present discussion. I reserve for chapter 8 an analysis of Poster's own work.

In "The System of Objects," first published in French in 1968, Baudrillard insisted on maintaining a constant awareness of the materiality within which signs circulate. For example, he related advertiser-induced meanings for products to social standing and power relations and maintained that this was the distinguishing feature of our consumer society compared to all others.[65] Moreover, he proclaimed that behind this "code of social standing," as manifested by owned and displayed commodities, are "illegible" but nonetheless "real structures of production and social relations."[66] We may think we understand social relations by "reading" commodities, Baudrillard claimed, but remaining invisible are the real relations of production and social existence. Designer footwear, one might say, indicates wealth and creates status for the wearer, but remaining invisible behind these signs are the Third World factories, the near slave labor used in shoe manufacture, and the unjust terms of trade existing between the rich North and the "developing" South.[67]

In "For a Critique of the Political Economy of the Sign," originally published in French in 1972, Baudrillard mapped connections among four types of value: *use value*, based on utility; *exchange value*, based on equivalence; *sign value*, based on difference (as in fashion); and *symbolic value* as in a wedding ring.[68] While in one sense Baudrillard here may be thought of as still grounding his analysis in materialism, this article actually presages his flight from materialism and from political economy by giving equal weight to use value/exchange value on the one hand, and the immaterial sign and symbolic values on the other. His equation is as follows: "Sign value is to symbolic exchange what exchange value (economic) is to use value."[69]

Baudrillard's materialist proclivities vanished utterly by the time he published his perhaps most notorious work, *Simulations*, and with them the very possibility of critiquing power and advocating social justice. In *Simulations* he maintained that in a world of circulating signs, our perceived reality is more one of simulation than it is of representation, which is to say that signs point to one another—more so than, or instead of, to material reality. He declared: "Disneyland is *presented* as imaginary in order to make us believe that the rest is real, when in fact all of Los Angeles and the America surrounding it are no longer real, but of the order of the hyperreal and of simulation."[70]

If the real and the fictitious, the objective and subjective, become merely "entangled orders of simulation . . . a play of illusions and phantasms,"[71] as he claimed, there is little possibility for political economy. Baudrillard himself recognized this, writing: "Power, too, for some time now produces nothing but signs of its resemblance. . . . Power is no longer present except to conceal that there is none."[72] He continued:

> Is any given bombing in Italy the work of leftist extremists, or of extreme right-wing provocation, or staged by centrists to bring terror into disrepute and to shore up its own failing power, or again is it a police-inspired scenario in order to appeal to public security? All this is equally true, and the search for proof, indeed the objectivity of the fact does not check this *vertigo of interpretation*. We are in a logic of simulation which has nothing to do with a logic of facts and an order of reasons.[73]

If the reality principle is in its death throes, and if the "vertigo of interpretation" now dwarfs facts, how can one possibly pursue justice? It would make much more sense simply to luxuriate in the consumer society and forge whimsical interpretations of media-concocted phantasms—a common poststructuralist recommendation, according to Frank Webster.[74]

We have seen already that Paul de Man at Yale was inspired by French poststructuralist Jacques Derrida. From chapter 8 it will be evident that poststructuralist Mark Poster is equally indebted to Baudrillard. And, by Lawrence Grossberg's account, poststructuralism defines American cultural studies.

Baudrillard's notion of simulacra is Walter Lippmann's dream come true. For if nonmaterialists, like Baudrillard, can convince the general public that simulacra is all there is, then Lippmann's experts will have even fuller reign. In the end, whatever he may himself have thought about his own purportedly critical stance, Baudrillard and like-minded poststructuralists play into the hands of authoritarianism and despots, proving the aptness of Macpherson's warning for our present era.

NOTES

1. For example, O'Donnell claims that Jacques Derrida introduced deconstruction as a way of opening texts up to new understandings, not just to dominant interpretations. Kevin O'Donnell, *Poststructuralism* (Oxford: Oxford University Press, 2003), 56.

2. See chapter 8.

3. C. B. Macpherson, *Property: Mainstream and Critical Positions* (Toronto: University of Toronto Press, 1978), 11–12.

4. See James W. Carey, "The Chicago School of Communication Research," in *James Carey: A Critical Reader*, ed. Eve Munson and Catherine Warren (Minneapolis: University of Minnesota Press, 1996), 14–33; Daniel Czitrom, *Media and the American Mind: From Morse to McLuhan* (Chapel Hill: University of North Carolina Press, 1982); Jesse Delia, "Communication Research: A History," in *Handbook of Communication Science*, ed. Charles R. Berger and Steven Chaffee (Newbury Park, CA: SAGE Publications, 1987), 20–98; Hanno Hardt, *Critical Communication Studies: Communication, History and Theory in America* (London: Routledge, 1992); Everett M. Rogers, *A History of Communication Study: A Biographical Approach* (New York: The Free Press, 1994); Wilbur Schramm, *The Beginnings of Communication Study in America: A Personal Memoir* (Thousand Oaks, CA: SAGE Publications, 1997).

5. See John Durham Peters, "Introduction," *Mass Communication and American Social Thought: Key Texts 1919–1968*, ed. John Durham Peters and Peter Simonson (Lanham, MD: Rowman and Littlefield Publishers, Inc., 2004).

6. John Dewey, *The Public and Its Problems* (Chicago: Swallow Press, 1927), 98, 141.

7. Czitrom, *Media and the American Mind*, 112.

8. Stuart Ewen, *PR! A Social History of Spin* (New York: Basic Books, 1996), 111–13.

9. Charles A. Beard and Mary Beard, *The Rise of American Civilization* (New York, Macmillan, 1930), 640.

10. James Beniger, *The Control Revolution: Technological and Economic Origins of the Information Society* (Cambridge, MA: Harvard University Press, 1986).

11. T. J. Jackson Lears, "From Salvation to Self-Realization: Advertising and the Therapeutic Roots of the Consumer Culture 1880–1930," in *The Culture of Consumption*, ed. Richard Wightman Fox and T. J. Jackson Lears (New York: Pantheon, 1983), 21.

12. Walter Lippmann, *Public Opinion* (1922; reprint, New York: Free Press, 1965), 17.

13. For a devastating critique of Lippmann's doctrine, see Edward S. Herman and Noam Chomsky, *Manufacturing Consent: The Political Economy of the Media,* 1988; revised, New York: Pantheon, 2002). For a debate on this and other matters between Chomsky-Herman and the Langs, see: Kurt Lang and Gladys Engel Lang, "Noam Chomsky and the Manufacture of Consent for American Foreign Policy," *Political Communication* 21 (2004): 93–101; Edward S. Herman and Noam Chomsky, "Reply to Kurt and Gladys Engel Lang," *Political Communication* 21 (2004): 103–07; and Lang and Lang, "Response to Herman and Chomsky," *Political Communication* 21 (2004): 109–11. Another effort at rehabilitating Lippmann is by Sue Curry Jansen, "Walter Lippmann, Straw Man of Communication Research," in *The History of Media and Communication Research: Contested Memories,* ed. David W. Park and Jefferson Pooley (New York: Peter Lang, 2008), 71–112.

14. Christopher Simpson, *Science of Coercion: Communication Research and Psychological Warfare 1945–1960* (Oxford: Oxford University Press, 1994), 16.

15. Jefferson Pooley, "The New History of Mass Communication Research," in *The History of Media and Communication Research: Contested Memories,* ed. David W. Park and Jefferson Pooley (New York: Peter Lang, 2008), 51.

16. Quoted in Pooley, "The New History of Mass Communication Research," 53.

17. Simpson, *Science of Coercion*, 26–29.

18. Everett M. Rogers, *A History of Communication Study*, 10–11. Rogers notes further that Lasswell's communication model of "*Who* says *what,* to *whom* via *what channel,* with *what effect*" was first published in a report of the Rockefeller Foundation Communication Seminars (November 1, 1940). "[It] argued that the federal government should utilize communication research in the emergency situation of approaching war and detailed various types of research needed on communication. . . . Lasswell's communication model provided the framework for the Rockefeller report, and thus for the wartime research in Washington, focusing on media effects" (p. 12).

19. Pooley, "The New History of Mass Communication Research," 56.

20. Paul F. Lazarsfeld, Bernard Berelson, and Hazel Gaudet, *The People's Choice* (New York: Duell, Sloan and Pearce, 1944).

21. Elihu Katz and Paul Lazarsfeld, *Personal Influence: The Part Played By People in the Flow of Mass Communication* (1955; reprint, New York: Free Press, 1964). See also Elihu Katz, Jay Blumler, and Michael Gurevitch, "Uses of Mass Communication by the Individual," in *Mass Communication Research: Major Issues and Future Directions,* ed. W. P. Davidson and F. Yu (New York: Praeger, 1974): 11–35. The exalted place of *Personal Influence* in the annals of American media/communication scholarship is affirmed, *inter alia*, by the production of a commemorative video, *The Long Road to Decatur,* released in 2008, celebrating the inception and fiftieth anniversary of the Katz-Lazarsfeld book; the video was sponsored by the Annenberg School for Communication (University of Pennsylvania), the Institute for Social and Economic Research and Policy (Columbia University), and the Department of Sociology of Columbia University.

22. Deborah Lubken, "Remembering The Straw Man: The Travels and Adventures of *Hypodermic*," in *The History of Media and Communication Research,* ed. David W. Park and Jefferson Pooley (New York: Peter Lang, 2008), 25.

23. Jefferson Pooley, "Fifteen Pages That Shook the Field: *Personal Influence,* Edward Shils, and the Remembered History of Mass Communication Research," *The Annals of the American Academy of Political and Social Science* 608 (November, 2006): 130.

24. Katz and Lazarsfeld, *Personal Influence,* 17, 16.

25. Robert Hackett, *News and Dissent: The Press and the Politics of Peace in Canada* (Norwood, NJ: Ablex Publishing Corporation, 1991), 52–60.

26. Everett M. Rogers and Floyd Shoemaker, *Communication of Innovations: A Cross Cultural Approach* (New York: Free Press, 1971).

27. Stephen Littlejohn, *Theories of Human Communication* (4th ed., Belmont, CA: Wadsworth, 1992), 351.

28. Steven H. Chaffee and John L. Hochheimer, "The Beginnings of Political Communication Research in the United States: Origins of the 'Limited Effects' Model," in *Mass Communication Review Yearbook* 5, ed. Michael Gurevitch and Mark R. Levy (Beverly Hills, CA: SAGE Publications, 1985), 75.

29. Wilbur Schramm, *The Beginnings of Communication Study*, 61.

30. Chaffee and Hochheimer, "The Beginnings of Political Communication Research," 95.

31. Schramm, *The Beginnings of Communication Study in America*, 61.

32. Shearon A. Lowery and Melvin DeFleur, *Milestones in Mass Communication Research* (2nd ed., White Plains, NY: Longmans, 1983), 138.

33. Schramm, *The Beginnings of Communication Study in America*, 101.

34. Elihu Katz, "Foreword: The Toronto School and Communication Research," in *The Toronto School of Communication Theory: Interpretations, Extensions, Applications,* ed. Rita Watson and Menahem Blondheim (Toronto and Jerusalem: University of Toronto Press and The Hebrew University Magnes Press, 2007), 1.

35. Schramm, referring to Klapper's book, described *reinforcement* in terms of audiences selectively seeking out content that strengthens their preexisting beliefs and perceptions, as opposed to media indoctrinating audiences through endless repetition. Schramm, *The Beginnings of Communication Study in America,* 61.

36. Schramm, *The Beginnings of Communication Study in America*, 109.

37. Pooley, "The New History of Mass Communication Research," 56.

38. Robert E. Babe, *Canadian Communication Thought: Ten Foundational Writers* (Toronto: University of Toronto Press, 2000), chapter 5.

39. Gerbner maintained that in contemporary society people no longer attain their identities primarily from their families, schools, churches, and communities, but rather from "a handful of conglomerates who have something to sell." He claimed further that people who watch large amounts of television are more likely to believe that the world is mean and violent, and he backed up these contentions with prodigious analyses of media content and comparisons in outlooks between light and heavy television viewers. See George Gerbner, *Against the Mainstream: The Selected Works of George Gerbner,* ed. Michael Morgan (New York: Peter Lang, 2002). In Congressional testimony of 1981 he summarized: "Fearful people are more dependent, more easily manipulated and controlled, more susceptible to deceptively simple, strong, tough measures and hard-line postures. They may accept and even welcome repression if it promises to relieve their insecurities. That is the deeper problem of violence-

laden television." Associated Press, "George Gerbner, Studied TV Culture," *Washington Post*, 2 January, 2006, B4. In the era of the "War on Terror," Gerbner sounds so prophetic.

40. Littlejohn, *Theories of Human Communication*, 364.

41. Simpson, *Science of Coercion*, 91.

42. See Katz and Gurevitch, "Uses of Mass Communication," 12; also Jay Blumler and Elihu Katz, eds., *The Uses of Mass Communication* (Beverly Hills, CA: SAGE Publications, 1974).

43. Daniel Chandler, "Why Do People Watch Television?" (1994), www.aber.ac.uk/media/Documents/short/usegrat.html (accessed Dec. 15, 2007).

44. Edward S. Herman and Noam Chomsky, *Manufacturing Consent: The Political Economy of the Media* (1988; revised, New York: Pantheon, 2002). Regarding the marginalization of Chomsky-Herman see Andy Mullen, "Twenty Years at the Margins: The Herman-Chomsky Propaganda Model, 1988–2008," *Fifth Estate-Online,* January 2008, www.fifth-estate-online.co.uk/comment/twentyyears.html (accessed Jan. 16, 2008).

45. Paul Cobley, "Interpretation, Ideation and the Reading Process," in *The Communication Theory Reader,* ed. Paul Cobley (London: Routledge, 1996), 405, 406.

46. Anthony Easthope, *Literary Into Cultural Studies* (London: Routledge, 1991), 48.

47. Stig A. Nohrestedt, "Ruling by Pooling," in *Triumph of the Image: The Media's War in the Persian Gulf—A Global Perspective,* ed. Hamid Mowlana, George Gerbner, and Herbert I. Schiller (Boulder, CO: Westview Press, 1992), 119–20.

48. Rogers, *A History of Communication Study*, 29, 446.

49. Wilbur Schramm, "The Nature of Communication Between Humans," in *The Process and Effects of Mass Communication,* ed. Wilbur Schramm and Donald F. Roberts (revised, Urbana, IL: University of Illinois Press, 1971), 3, 8.

50. Rogers, *A History of Communication Study,* 14–15.

51. Schramm, *The Beginnings of Communication Study in America*, 101.

52. MIT's de Sola Pool, for example, insisted that "where radio goes, there modernization attitudes come." Radio audiences in Third World countries, according to Pool, after being continually exposed to western media, will wish to imitate modern (i.e., western) attitudes and behavior and to cast off obsolete indigenous customs that inhibit economic expansion. The loss of customs and traditions that this entails is much to be desired, in the view of the media transfer scholars. Alienation and dislocation, loss of referents, social and cultural upheaval, loss of sovereignty and extension of American influence are concomitants largely unmentioned by the media transfer theorists. See Ithiel de Sola Pool, "Communication and Development," in *Modernization: The Dynamics of Growth*, ed. M. Weiner (Washington, DC: Voice of America, 1966), 106–10; Daniel Lerner, *The Passing of Traditional Society: Modernizing the Middle East* (New York: Free Press, 1958); and Everett Rogers and Floyd Shoemaker, *Communication of Innovations: A Cross Cultural Approach* (New York: Free Press, 1971). For a critique, see Gerald Sussman and John Lent, "Introduction: Critical Perspectives on Communication and Third World Development," in *Transnational Communications: Wiring the Third World*, ed. Gerald Sussman and John A. Lent (Newbury Park, CA: SAGE Publications, 1991), 5–6.

53. I have made these extensions in Robert E. Babe, "The Political Economy of Knowledge: Neglecting Political Economy in the Age of Fast Capitalism (As Before)," *Fast Capitalism* 2, no. 1 (2006), www.uta.edu/huma/agger/fastcapitalism/2_1/index.html (accessed Dec. 15, 2007).

54. Maxwell McCombs and Donald Shaw, "The Agenda-setting Function of Mass Media," *Public Opinion Quarterly* 36 (1971): 176-87. Here the thesis is that media, at most, affect the priority with which the public views issues, as opposed to, say, indoctrinating the public into accepting certain perspectives.

55. See chapter 2 on Innis' assessment of the First Amendment.

56. Ziauddin Sardar and Borin Van Loon, *Introducing Cultural Studies* (St. Leonards: Allen and Unwin, 1998), 58; Graeme Turner, *British Cultural Studies: An Introduction* (Cambridge, MA: Unwin Hyman, 1990), 41–84.

57. Sardar and Van Loon. *Introducing Cultural Studies*, 58.

58. Richard E. Lee, *Life and Times of Cultural Studies: The Politics and Transformation of the Structures of Knowledge* (Durham, NC: Duke University Press, 2003), 153.

59. Terry Eagleton, *Figures of Dissent* (London: Verso, 2003), 152.

60. Lee, *Life and Times of Cultural Studies*, 154.

61. Lee, *Life and Times of Cultural Studies*, 156.

62. Eagleton, *Figures of Dissent*, 156.

63. Mark Poster, "Introduction," in *Jean Baudrillard: Selected Writings*, ed. Mark Poster (2nd ed., Stanford, CA: Stanford University Press, 2001), 1.

64. Mark Poster, *Cultural Theory and Poststructuralism: In Search of a Context* (Ithaca, NY: Cornell University Press, 1989), 6.

65. Jean Baudrillard, "The System of Objects" (1968; reprint, *Jean Baudrillard: Selected Writings*, ed. Mark Poster, Stanford, CA: Stanford University Press, 2001), 24.

66. Jean Baudrillard, "The System of Objects," 24.

67. Kevin Bales, *Disposable People: New Slavery in the Global Economy* (Berkley, CA: University of California Press, 1999).

68. Jean Baudrillard, "For a Critique of the Political Economy of the Sign" (1972; reprint, *Jean Baudrillard: Selected Writings*, ed. Mark Poster, Stanford, CA: Stanford University Press, 2001), 60.

69. Baudrillard, "For a Critique of the Political Economy of the Sign," 63.

70. Jean Baudrillard, *Simulations*, trans. Paul Foss, Paul Patton, and Philip Beitchman (New York: Semiotext[e], 1983), 25. Earlier Baudrillard defined the hyperreal as "the generation by models of a real without origin or reality" (p. 2).

71. Baudrillard, *Simulations*, 23.

72. Baudrillard, *Simulations*, 45, 46.

73. Baudrillard, *Simulations*, 31; emphasis added.

74. Frank Webster, *Theories of the Information Society* (London: Routledge, 1995), 167–68.

Part Two

PORTALS FOR DIALOGUE

Introduction to Part II

Part II consists of four essays, all appearing originally in *Topia: Canadian Journal of Cultural Studies,* and all revised and given new titles for publication here. (Revision of a fifth *Topia* essay appears as chapter 4). The chapters of part II focus in greater depth on topics or issues introduced in part I. Moreover, three of these chapters propose *portals for dialogue* between political economy and cultural studies—means whereby the two scholarly fields, political economy and cultural studies, might resume productive dialogue.

Chapter 5, "Environment and Pecuniary Culture," is (in part) a gloss on McLuhan's maxim, "culture is our business," which opened the book. Conceiving money as a space-biased medium of communication, the chapter amplifies previous treatments of Innis' medium theory. Innis was wary of what he termed the "penetrative powers of the price system," and he regarded money as a space-biased medium *nonpareil.* This chapter, however, develops aspects of money's impact well beyond those suggested by Innis. Treating money as a culturally biased medium of communication is not only an excellent way of reopening dialogue between cultural studies and political economy, it also enables deepened understanding of ecological/environmental consequences of pecuniary culture and the price system.

Chapter 6, "Time and Space," shows how two otherwise disparate authors, namely philosopher/essayist John Ralston Saul and geneticist/ecologist David Suzuki, independently developed variants of Innis' time-space dialectic to achieve an integrated understanding of culture and media power. By "triangulating" Innis, Saul, and Suzuki, the power of the time-space dialectic as a "portal for dialogue" between cultural studies and political economy becomes even more apparent. Moreover, the chapter fills a gap in Innis' writings regarding the nature of oral culture, and it extends the media/environmental analysis of chapter 5.

Chapter 7, "Semiotics and the Dialectic of Information," addresses the common poststructuralist contention that language/discourse is now segregated from material reality, a topic raised initially at the close of chapter 3. Chapter 7 notes that in the contemporary digital age there has been a marked tendency to etherealize information, a tendency that can be traced back to the semiotics of Ferdinand de Saussure at the start of the twentieth century (if not, indeed, to Plato), and which has been pursued by such other eminent scholars as Kenneth Boulding and Norbert Wiener, as well as by contemporary poststructuralists. However, *the dialectic of information* (namely, matter-in-form), as proposed here, avoids the pitfalls of both an undue materialism (i.e., economism or hard determinism), and an overextended idealism (flight from material reality). Put more positively, by helping integrate considerations of matter, form, and interpretation, the dialectic of information is a third "portal for dialogue" between cultural studies and political economy. The chapter concludes by integrating the medium theories of Innis and McLuhan.

Each of these aforementioned chapters, focusing respectively on the cultural biases of money, time/space as organizing principles, and the dialectic of information, explores means whereby political economy and cultural studies can be brought into closer alignment. Notably, the key in all three cases is dialectical treatment. Chapter 8, the final chapter of part II, alas, is less optimistic. It revisits differences in ontology between poststructuralist cultural studies and political economy, as raised initially in chapter 3. In particular, the chapter discusses significant and likely irresolvable contradictions between the inaugural political economist, Harold Innis, and the contemporary poststructuralist, Mark Poster. Poster may be thought of as representing a school of thought that would close the "portals for dialogue," for example, by his insistence that we turn "from action to language" and by his recommendation that we abandon dialectical thinking. This chapter, moreover, forms the template of a future volume to be published by Lexington Books, entitled *Meet Harold Innis.* There, I introduce Innis' thought to such other eminent media scholars, past and present, as Ferdinand de Saussure, Walter Lippmann, Wilbur Schramm, Ithiel de Sola Pool, Daniel Bell, Marshall McLuhan, David Harvey, and Michel Foucault.

Chapter Five

Environment and Pecuniary Culture

To further amplify aspects of the political economy of culture, and cultural aspects of the political economy,[1] this chapter addresses in Innisian fashion the perhaps central issue—*money as a medium of communication*. Innis, of course, is renowned for proposing that at any time and in every place the predominant medium of communication affects significantly the organization of society. Here I address money as a medium of communication and some of its cultural and organizational biases, and in that context draw out implications for environmental well-being.

MONEY AS A MEDIUM AND MONEY AS A MESSAGE

Money is probably as old as human community. It preceded writing by millennia. Seeds, shells, cattle, coffee beans, tobacco and other naturally occurring utilitarian objects served both as a store of value and as a medium of exchange—the primary uses of money. Precious metals, too—particularly gold and silver—even in antiquity, were used as currency. Often metal fragments were "marked" or stamped to testify as to their weight and composition.[2] The modern era of money began with the printing press, which enabled the publication of identical copies of bank notes. Today, electronic currency has to a degree replaced coins and paper, allowing money, like other electronic texts, to travel at the speed of light.[3]

Money, when displayed (or even hinted at), is a text or message. The size of one's bank account constitutes a persuasive statement to bank managers of a customer's status in the community. A wad of cash is sure to attract attention in almost every setting. Pressing the hand with coin is an unambiguous way of saying, "Well done." To be known (or believed) to lack money makes one worthless in the eyes of some, and inhibits further interaction. "Money talks," and in our culture those without money are often all but silenced.

However, money is not just a message, or an assemblage of messages (texts); it is also a medium of communication. Economists define money as a "*medium* of exchange." Money mediates exchanges, easing the task of sellers to dispose of articles of which they have a superfluity and to attain items they want. Money opens communication among otherwise disinterested parties, but in so doing the subsequent interactions, if any, may generally retain a pecuniary bias.

Since a great portion of human interaction today takes the form of commodity exchange—i.e., since money mediates a preponderance of human interactions—money should be regarded as our preeminent medium of communication. Indeed, much of the mass media routinely studied by media scholars (newspapers, books, film, radio, TV, Internet) would scarcely exist were it not for the prior existence and circulation of money. Money may not be as fundamental to social life as air—the medium of oral communication—but it is certainly more basic than the aforementioned media. In this light it is surprising that money has received scant attention from communication/media scholars. Money as medium of communication is at the heart of the political economy of culture, and of the culture of the political economy.

BIASES OF MONEY

It was the prescient thesis of Harold Innis that every medium of communication is "biased." By bias, Innis meant that no medium transmits messages transparently; every medium, rather, has effects over and beyond those attributable to the delivery of the ostensible messages. He wrote:

> We may perhaps assume that the use of a medium of communication over a long period will to some extent determine the character of knowledge to be communicated and suggest that its pervasive influence will eventually create a civilization in which life and flexibility will become exceedingly difficult to maintain and that the advantages of a new medium will become such as to lead to the emergence of a new civilization.[4]

For Innis, various means of inscription could be arrayed along a continuum of time/space bias. Stone, papyrus, clay tablets, paper, and the printing press all tend to reinforce perspectives allied either with time (continuity, hierarchy, community, ritual, religiosity, sense of meaning or purpose), or with space (speed, efficiency, empire, change, discontinuity, territorial expansion, materialism, individualism, and denigration of the sacred). Innis also insisted that the predominant medium of communication in a society or culture is normally controlled by the group or class that is most powerful in society. He summarized this position with the phrase, "monopolies of knowledge," roughly equivalent today to "the political economy of information and communication." Innis maintained further that in nonrevolutionary times, culture and political/economic power are, and must be, aligned, as otherwise the disequilibrium or tension between the two will result in change—either cultural, political-economic, or both. Normally, this equilibrium or consistency between culture and the political-economic is maintained through control of the predominant medium of communication. Only when Minerva's owl takes flight (a metaphor for cultural and political instability) are political-economic power and the system of culture inconsistent, and this instability, according to Innis, is usually accompanied by the rise to predominance of a new medium of communication controlled by a hitherto marginalized group.

Let us then turn, in Innisian fashion, to the "biases" of money in its role as a medium of communication. By *biases* I mean the systematic emphasis accorded some types of information and the downplaying or excluding of other types, and as well the mind-set inculcated almost subliminally by continual use of money. Three "biases" unobtrusively propagated by the money medium are the normality of exponential growth, present-mindedness, and the naturalness of individualism/*quid pro quo*. Here I treat each briefly; elsewhere I discuss these and other biases at greater length.[5]

Exponential Growth

The medium of money induces expectations of limitless growth, as opposed to satisfaction with current affairs or, more technically, with a *steady state*.[6] Through "the magic of compound interest," any principal, say one thousand dollars, invested at a positive rate of return increases annually by ever-increasing amounts.

Money is an abstraction. It is a *symbol,* or better a *symbolic system*, which we use to represent real wealth. Because it is a symbol, money can, in principle, grow without constraint; it can, indeed, increase exponentially, forever—or at least for as long as there are human beings to create and use it. Expectations today are normally that if one invests money, it will grow exponentially, forever; this implies that the material wealth represented by money likewise should grow exponentially, forever; otherwise, there is merely "inflation."

Certain of the world's economies have had bitter experiences from exponential increases in the money supply over brief periods of time. In Germany following World War I, for example, inflation was such that by 1923 an egg cost 4 billion marks, an amount that a decade before had represented the value of all the houses in greater Berlin! This is an instance of a disjuncture between sign and what it purports to signify, between our monetary symbol and the material world. By living *within the discourse of money*, which contains its own assumptions and logic, and by continually viewing the material world in money terms, we can easily misconstrue the natural world as being able to grow forever, just like the money supply. Ecologists maintain, however, that our culture's insistence on exponential economic growth will, unless checked, endanger human survival.[7]

There are other cultural consequences, albeit more prosaic, spilling out from the "common sense" assumption of ubiquitous exponential growth. Corporations merge or take over rivals to fulfill growth ambitions, thereby increasing monopoly or oligopoly power. Governments merge municipalities since "larger" is thought to be more efficient than smaller, reducing thereby local self-governance and, some would say, democracy. Food portions increase, with concomitant accretions to the waistline[8] and deleterious repercussions to health. Stockpiles of weapons forever grow in quantity and deadliness, for not to grow is to decline. Sometimes we notice seemingly opposite trends, such as niche marketing, but even there the governing principle is growth in profits—through multiplication of niches.

Time

Money as a medium of communication is inherently biased with regard to *time*. In Harold Innis' terms, money makes us *present-minded*. Money and prices, briefly, denigrate the past and make us neglectful of the future.

With regard to *the past*, it is axiomatic for the price system that "bygones are forever bygones."[9] The past, not being variable (except, of course, in its retelling!), cannot affect the *marginal conditions* which mainstream (or neoclassical) economists insist are the bases upon which maximizing individuals make decisions. True, firms and individuals in the present can be encumbered with debts arising from past activities, even forcing some into bankruptcy, meaning that the past in a sense lingers into the present. Likewise, others may have become rich, giving them a much larger array of options from which to choose. But these considerations are more a matter of the distribution of wealth (important though that is!) than they are factors affecting the profitability or utility of choices in the present—according to mainstream economists. A bankrupt company, for example, can be taken over by new owners/managers, be refinanced with the debt obligations altered if not wiped out altogether, and decisions made in light of present understanding of the future flows of costs and revenues. More generally, and this is the main point, it is difficult to summon up memories, loyalties, traditions, or a sense of belonging when one's mode of expression consists primarily of relative prices.

As well, the price system trivializes *the future.* Assuming a 10 percent rate of interest (or discount rate), $1,000 payable thirty years from now are worth only $57.31 today! (This is the obverse of the "magic of compound interest": $57.31 invested today at 10 percent is worth $1000 thirty years hence.) A lower discount rate would raise the *present value* of the $1000 somewhat, but even so note that the time period of thirty years, considered in ecological terms, is extremely short. The more remote the benefit (or cost), the more trivial it is to present-day decision-makers.

High interest rates, if attributable to conscious monetary policy, are an attempt by monetary authorities to make present consumption and borrowing less attractive compared to saving and investment; expressed differently, in setting higher interest rates monetary authorities recognize that the future has become so trivialized that the reward for saving/investing must be increased to encourage this activity over present consumption/borrowing.

One might argue, of course, that it is not money as the predominant medium of communication that *causes* present-mindedness, but rather that interest or discount rates simply *represent* or *reflect* the preferences of people for the present as opposed to the future. Any time one decides to consume today rather than to save/invest, one is perforce making a decision with respect to the present vs. the future. Interest rates, it can be argued, specify quantitatively the collective preferences (or the will of governments) in this regard, just as prices for commodities are claimed to represent the valuation in relative terms of the ensemble of goods and services offered for sale. Except in a laboratory, of course, the direction of causation is difficult to establish. What can be said with assurance, however, is that as the price system "penetrates" more and more aspects of people's lives, those aspects necessarily become understood through the logic of the price system, including such notions as things of the past being forever bygones and the presumption that the present and future are exchangeable at the going rate of interest.

Prioritizing the present over the past and the future, one might propose, is a trait found universally in the animal kingdom. Indeed, many species may have little or no conception of the future,[10] in which case the attention/value afforded the future by the price system, albeit truncated, could be interpreted as a marked advance over "natural" ways of cognition. To argue thus, however, is to ignore the importance of past and future to some, if not most, nonpecuniary cultures. The concept of "stewardship," for example, permeated ancient Hebrew thought. Likewise, when taking certain decisions, Native

Americans endeavor to take into account "seven generations" of both ancestors and descendents. In the words of Chief Oren Lyons:

> We are looking ahead, as is one of the first mandates given to us chiefs, to make sure and to make every decision that we make relate to the welfare and well-being of the seventh generation to come, and that is the basis by which we make decisions in council. We consider: will this be to the benefit of the seventh generation? That is a guideline.[11]

Recall also the proscriptions against usury in Greek, Hebrew, and medieval moral/legal codes. To completely ban interest payments is, in effect, to set a zero rate of interest, in which case there is no discounting of the future at all. Present and future, in that circumstance, are valued equally—ecologically speaking a condition far superior to our present mode of valuation. The tragedy of human history, from an ecological point of view, is that nonpecuniary societies succumbed time and again to the present-mindedness of pecuniary cultures.

In this light one must question whether activities with long-term, often irreversible consequences—global warming, ozone depletion, the extinction of species, the exhaustion of resources, the buildup of nuclear stockpiles with half-lives of thousands of years, and so on—should continue to be based principally on monetary criteria. The price system, even when operating "smoothly," is an abysmally poor guide for making decisions concerning long-term survival.

There are other cultural consequences, too, stemming from the "bias" of money as a medium of communication. Present-mindedness means that educators and governments funding educational systems favor "mechanized knowledge" (Innis' term) over history, the classics, and other of the humanities. Moreover, the bias of present-mindedness inherent to the price system may well be a factor in the demise of the extended family and the propensity of people in pecuniary cultures to move every few years in accordance with job opportunities. Trivializing the future could go a long way toward explaining remarkable increases since World War II in personal and household debt. Habitual and continuous tobacco and drug use, as opposed to ceremonial usage, is certainly consistent with "present-mindedness."

Harold Innis, of course, made "a plea for time." He wrote: "The modern obsession with present-mindedness . . . suggests that the balance between time and space has been seriously disturbed with disastrous consequences to Western civilization."[12] Innis' "plea for time" is consistent with a call in our day for renewed environmentalism, and our response, in part at least, must entail a reduction in the predominance of money as a mode of communicating.

Individualism and *Quid pro quo*

Two further cultural characteristics stemming from the logic or biases of money and prices are *quid pro quo* and *individualism.* The terms are closely related, but provide different emphases. *Quid pro quo* means there will be no "communication" unless there is an exchange of equivalences: "What I give to you must be worth at least what you give to me." A society functioning exclusively by *quid pro quo* will engage solely in commodity exchange relations.[13] Individualism, in turn, highlights the self-centeredness of interactions. Innis, citing Mirabeau, pronounced that money "is the common language of self-interest;"[14] oral discussion, on the other hand, "inherently involves personal contact and a consideration for the feelings of others."[15] A pecuniary society, it would seem to follow, will be based on self-interest with its individualistic actors caring little for their neighbors.

It was the misguided genius of Adam Smith to propose that a society comprised of hedonistic, egoistic individuals would organize spontaneously and cohere through the "invisible hand" of markets. Ever since Smith's day, apologists for markets have insisted that the "invisible hand" transforms "private vices" (greed, selfishness) into "public virtues"—that individuals pursuing their own self-interest contribute to the *common good* because in market-governed societies the only way a person can maximize her wealth is by offering goods or services that others want. Smith viewed the invisible hand of the price system as comprising "an obvious and simple system of natural liberty" as "every man, as long as he does not violate the laws of justice, is left perfectly free to pursue his own interest his own way."[16]

Other cultures, however, reject the rugged individualism associated with pecuniary culture. Ecologist David Suzuki, for instance, has characterized the mindset of First Nations and other aboriginal people in the following terms:

> It tends to reveal a profound sense of empathy and kinship with other forms of life, rather than a sense of separateness from them or superiority over them. . . . It tends to view the proper human relationship with nature as a continuous dialogue (that is, a two-way, horizontal, communication between Homo Sapiens and other elements of the cosmos) rather than as a monologue (a one-way, vertical imperative). . . . It looks upon the totality of patterns and relationships at play in the universe as utterly precious, irreplaceable, and worthy of the most profound human veneration. . . . Native notions [are] of a vast, spiritually charged cosmic continuum, in which human society, biosphere, and the whole universe are seamlessly rolled into one.[17]

To be sure, western (neoclassical) economists have recognized that there are indirect repercussions of monetary transactions; these they have termed *externalities*, or third-party effects, which they nonetheless maintain are exceptions, not the rule. They believe, furthermore, that to improve economic efficiency, externalities should be enfolded into the logic of the price system, which is to say into the logic of individualism and *quid pro quo*. From an ecological perspective, however, internalizing externalities, and thereby giving the price system even further sway is, to say the least, counterproductive. It is to force-fit the logic of money onto a rich array of ecosystem interactions, further endangering the vitality of ecosystems.

There are many other implications of the logics of *quid pro quo* and individualism. Consider, for example, the rise of homelessness. At one time, human life was thought to have intrinsic value, and there was very little homelessness in our society. Given an ethic of *quid pro quo* and rugged individualism, however, as poor people have nothing or little to exchange, they are valued accordingly. The same logic transfers to the old, the ill, the handicapped, and we see it worked out through decreased funding of social programs and tax cuts for the rich. Culture is very much a part of the political economy, and money as a medium of communication is a transmitter of culture and affects culture.

Furthermore, the logic of *quid pro quo* instills in people's minds the idea that everything of value has a price, a position fundamentally at odds with such vital concepts as uniqueness, sacredness, and intrinsic value. Uniqueness and sacredness, of course, imply an incapacity for, or inappropriateness of, substitutions, which is to say an absence or inappropriateness of price. But the absence of price, according to the logic of the market, means an absence of value. The pressure is always, for example, to "develop" land hitherto residing outside the bounds of commodity exchange, irrespective of the intrinsic value some may accord it, as when the Aborigines in the Kakadu Conservation Zone in Australia were asked how much they would require for the use of their burial grounds for mineral exploration, or, in the case of the Mohawks near Oka, Quebec, to permit construction of a golf course.[18]

Furthermore, money is unable to carry information concerning the common good: money mediates exchanges between *individuals*, including corporate bodies as fictitious individuals, and in commodity trade no one is expected to consider the good of others. Hence, as John Kenneth Galbraith noted, the bias in money-mediated societies is toward those goods and services consumed privately. Galbraith concluded that in market-driven economies there is inevitably an undersupply of collective goods (parks, education, aesthetically pleasing architecture) because there is no market for these public goods.[19]

Ecosystems, of course, are rife with "public goods": the beauty of a verdant hillside and of a pristine lake, the glory of a sunset, the uplifting song of birds. Biodiversity, too, is a public good. Although biodiversity is vital to our existence, there can be no market for biodiversity because all markets exist within, and are maintained by, interactions among all living beings; there is simply nothing to exchange for biodiversity, nor can anyone "own" it. Since markets are unable to account for biodiversity, it is omitted from the value calculations of maximizing individuals, which is to say that in monetary terms biodiversity is worthless.

Julian Simon, an apostle of private exchange as the preferred mode of economic governance, completely missed the boat when he remarked with satisfaction that over the course of human history the trend has been to make the Earth "ever more livable for human beings."[20] Simon failed to mention that in "civilizing the wilderness," massive extinctions of plant and animal species ensued,[21] and this loss of biodiversity ultimately serves to make the planet less livable for human beings.

We would expect societies driven by the logic of money to be "leaders" in species extinctions; to experience escalating contamination of water, air, and soil; to foster detrimental climate and weather changes; and to be instrumental in ozone depletion. Money does not carry information concerning the value of such collective goods and services, and so they are not considered in the maximizing calculations of individual buyers and sellers. Nor are they imputed into calculations of Gross National Product. Through taxes and subsidies it is often suggested that prices can be made more reflective of ecological realities, but this is a delusion since the price system, whether adjusted by taxes and subsidies or not, is still and will always be premised on individualism and *quid pro quo*, as opposed to radical interdependence, ecosystem, and the common good.

MONEY AND MONOPOLIES OF KNOWLEDGE

Money has its own internal logic, which in turn has significant cultural implications. Here I have hinted at some ecological aspects of money use, and as well at existential, democratic, and community concerns that arise from the predominance of money as medium of communication in our society. Marshall McLuhan was one of the few media/communication writers to have addressed money as a mode of communication. But in the context of the foregoing concerns, McLuhan's analyses are quite trivial.[22]

Perhaps critical political economy can help us understand why there is such a paucity of critical treatments of the cultural consequences of money as a medium of communication. While on the one hand the increasing predominance of money as it further penetrates the interstices of our society is devastating in terms of democracy, community, and indeed prospects of survival.[23]

On the other hand, however, a critique of money would strike at the very heart of the current power system—at the present-day "monopoly of knowledge." To critique money as a medium of communication is to risk the ire of moneyed interests, and damage the career of the author.

The thrust of this chapter has certainly been negative in the sense of critiquing the biases of money as a medium of communication. However, to end on a more positive note: money is potentially a major portal for dialogue between cultural studies and political economy. Certainly, the bearing money has on the concerns of political economy are apparent enough. Perhaps less obvious are the cultural consequences of money, which this chapter has addressed. By considering money both as a medium of exchange/store of value, and as a space-biased medium of communication, political economy and cultural studies can be reintegrated into a coherent discipline of media studies.

NOTES

1. See chapter 1.
2. Adam Smith, *An Inquiry Into the Nature and Causes of the Wealth of Nations* (1776; reprint, edited by Edwin Cannan with an Introduction by Max Lerner, New York: The Modern Library, 1937), book 1, chapter 4.
3. Jack Weatherford, *The History of Money: From Sandstone to Cyberspace* (New York: Crown Publishers, Inc., 1997).
4. Harold A. Innis, "The Bias of Communication" (1949; reprint, *The Bias of Communication* by Harold Innis, with an Introduction by Marshall McLuhan, Toronto: University of Toronto Press, 1971), 34.
5. Robert E. Babe, *Culture of Ecology: Reconciling Economics and Environment* (Toronto: University of Toronto Press, 2006).
6. Herman E. Daly, *Steady State Economics,* 2nd ed. (Washington, DC: Island Press, 1991).
7. Anita Gordon and David Suzuki, *It's A Matter of Survival* (Toronto: Stoddart, 1990), 3.
8. André Picard, "Blue-plate Specials Indeed a Swell Deal: It's Now Official: Those Food Portions Are Getting Larger, But We're Heaping It On at Home Too," *Globe and Mail*, 25 January 2006, A6
9. William Stanley Jevons, *The Theory of Political Economy*, 3rd ed. (London: Macmillan and Co., 1888), 164.
10. Melissa Bateson and Alex Kacelnik, "Risk-Sensitive Foraging: Decision-Making in Variable Environments," in *Cognitive Ecology: The Evolutionary Ecology of Information Processing and Decision Making*, ed. Reuven Dukas (Chicago: University of Chicago Press, 1998), 316.
11. Oren Lyons, "An Iroquois Perspective," in *American Indian Environment: Ecological Issues in Native American History*, ed. C. Vecsey and R. Venables (Syracuse,

NY: Syracuse University Press, 1980); excerpted in Lisa M. Benton and John Rennie Short, eds., *Environmental Discourse and Practice* (London: Blackwell, 2000), 15.

12. Harold A. Innis, "A Plea for Time" (1951; reprint, *The Bias of Communication*, with an Introduction by Marshall McLuhan, Toronto: University of Toronto Press, 1971), 76.

13. See Kenneth E. Boulding, *A Primer on Social Dynamics: History as Dialectics and Development* (New York: The Free Press, Collier-Macmillan, 1970), 27.

14. Harold A. Innis, "Minerva's Owl (1947; reprint, *The Bias of Communication,* Toronto: University of Toronto Press, 1971), 8.

15. Harold A. Innis, "A Critical Review," (1948; reprint, *The Bias of Communication,* Toronto: University of Toronto Press, 1971), 191.

16. Smith, *Wealth of Nations*, 651.

17. Peter Knudstson and David Suzuki, *Wisdom of the Elders* (Toronto: Stoddart, 1992), 15–17.

18. John O'Neill, "Value Pluralism: Incommensurability and Institutions," in *Valuing Nature: Economics, Ethics and Environment*, ed. John Foster (London: Routledge, 1997), 79.

19. John Kenneth Galbraith, *The New Industrial State* (Boston: Houghton Mifflin, 1967).

20. Julian Simon, "The Grand Theory." Chapter 4 of *The Ultimate Resource II: People, Materials, and Environment* (Princeton, NJ: Princeton University Press, 1998). www.juliansimon.com/writings/Ultimate_Resource/TCHAR04B.txt (accessed August 22, 2008).

21. Andrew Goudie, *The Human Impact On the Natural Environment*, 5th ed. (Cambridge, MA: MIT Press, 2000), 152.

22. Marshall McLuhan, *Understanding Media: The Extensions of Man* (New York: Mentor, 1964), 123–34; also Marshall McLuhan and Eric McLuhan, *Laws of the Media: The New Science* (Toronto: University of Toronto Press, 1988), 106–07.

23. Interestingly, contentions are starting to be made that money may become less of a factor in the years to come. Chris Anderson of *Wired* magazine predicts that online costs of bandwidth, storage, and processing are already so low (and decreasing every year), that it is often no longer economical to meter usage, and hence "free" becomes inevitable. Jennifer Wells, "In the New Economy, 'Free Becomes Inevitable,'" *Globe and Mail,* May 5, 2008, B1, B4. Also, Chris Anderson, *The Long Tail* (New York: Hyperion, 2006). Unfortunately, seers projecting digital utopias often omit hidden costs. Computer components, for example, "require the use of an array of high-grade minerals that can be obtained only through major mining operations and energy-transformation processes." See Wolfgang Sachs, *Planet Dialectics: Explorations in Environment and Development* (New York: Zed Books, 1999), 192.

Chapter Six

Time and Space

The previous chapter depicted money as a medium of communication that, in the Innisian sense, helps form a mind-set and structure social relations. In this chapter I enlarge on Innis' more general *medium thesis* concerning time-space bias and its potential for reintegrating critical political economy and cultural studies. I do this by turning to two contemporary authors, political philosopher John Ralston Saul and ecologist David Suzuki, both of whom mesh cultural studies and political economy in ways reminiscent of Innis.

JOHN RALSTON SAUL

John Ralston Saul (b. 1947) is a distinguished essayist, award-winning novelist, and political philosopher. He has ruminated for many years on epistemology, the nature of the Canadian state, the Enlightenment, and other matters. He is one of *Utne Reader*'s 100 leading thinkers. Although there are but few allusions to Harold Innis in Saul's writings, he is certainly an admirer, describing the renowned economic historian and media theorist as "the first and still the most piercing philosopher of communications."[1]

While this section highlights similarities in the thought of these two giants of Canadian scholarship, there are differences. Innis was always the social scientist, seeking explanations through material causes; he maintained that human culture, organization, and even ideas/knowledge are strongly affected by the natural and human-constructed material environments. By contrast Saul, a man of letters, has insisted that freedom and indeterminacy are fundamental to the human condition; to propose determinants, Saul maintains, is tantamount to false consciousness. He goes further, quoting with approval

William Pitt: "Necessity is the plea for every infringement of human freedom; it is the argument of tyrants; it is the creed of slaves."[2] Innis was no "determinist" either, but one senses a difference in emphasis here, with Innis searching out key forces and influences, and Saul tending to dismiss the same. Although Innis (like Saul) railed against mainstream economics as a system of thought, for example, and in particular against its purported universality, Innis nonetheless set about constructing a "system" of his own, even making allusion in the process to Toynbee, Spengler, Sorokin, Marx, and other system builders.[3] Saul, in contrast, seemingly objects in principle to theoretical systems, and in this we see an affinity with poststructuralism's rejection of "grand narratives."

On the other hand, and this is of course the central point, striking similarities in the approaches of these two scholars abound. Consider the following: Like Innis, Saul contrasts societies with memory ("time-bound" in Innis' terms) with our own present-mindedness (again, Innis' term). Indeed, Saul makes an Innisian plea for time, declaring: "If you cannot remember, then there is no reality,"[4] and again: "We are faced by a crisis of memory, the loss of our humanist foundation."[5] He sympathetically quotes Cicero: "He who does not know history is destined to remain a child."[6]

What has destroyed memory in our time, Saul maintains, is technocratic insistence on applying abstract models (he calls them "structures," "systems," and "ideologies") to real life situations. These systems, structures, and models, Saul claims, are essentially ahistorical, proposing fixed relations among key variables. Innis likewise referred to formulaic, abstract knowledge, using the derogatory phrase, "monopolies of knowledge," maintaining such knowledge erodes memory and understanding of time as duration.

For Saul, each verbal structure (whether mainstream economics, accounting, political science, Marxist theory, even fascism) is an inflexible frame of reference which selects/bends/creates facts to fit its internal logic. He attributes amorality on the part of today's elites ("technocrats") to an absence of memory, explaining that memory "is always the enemy of structure;"[7] this is because memory brings forth the details and the feelings that confound the strict logic that structures impose. These comments and declarations seem to accord well with Innis' plea for time (memory), and his distress at the growing ties between the universities and the military.

Regarding the history of modern, western civilization, Saul proposed a "great divide" between 1530 and 1620.[8] At that point, he wrote, "Reason began, abruptly, to separate itself from and to outdistance the other more or less recognized human characteristics—spirit, appetite, faith and emotion, but also intuition, will and, most important, experience."[9] Although the Age of Reason was promoted by Voltaire, Diderot, and others to challenge the existing monopoly of knowledge based on superstition and arbitrary power, in the end, according to Saul, a new and equally if not more insidious monopoly of knowledge arose, one based on reason unmodified by humanist (or, in Innis' terms, "time-binding") values. And this monopoly still dominates. As Saul declared:

> The twentieth century, which has seen the final victory of pure reason in power, has also seen unprecedented unleashings of violence and of power deformed. It is hard, for example, to avoid noticing that the murder of six million Jews was a perfectly rational act [given the "structure" within which the perpetrators acted]. . . . Reason is no more than structure.[10]

In making these remarks Saul is endorsed, to a limited extent, by Nietzsche. Philosopher George Grant, interpreting Nietzsche, noted that instrumental reason in support of ill-defined ends is really irrationality.[11] But, on the other hand, Saul's invoking the period of German fascism to support his point is really over-the-top. As noted by Paul Heyer, "it was the unreasoning, anti-Enlightenment dream, steeped in romantic nationalism, which gave birth to the Third Reich, a historical development that would have made cringe the Enlightenment philosophes that Saul sees as unwitting culprits in the promulgation of what we now call instrumental rationality. For Voltaire, Diderot, Condorcet, and Co, one of reason's first principles is tolerance."[12]

Like Innis, Saul maintained that elites purposefully confuse illusion and reality. Innis compared modern-day media presentations to a shell-and-pea game at a county fair. He was most concerned, of course, that contemporary media distort the life situation in the name of profit by neglecting time. For Saul, similarly, elites propagate misconceptions. For one thing, the world is presented, according to Saul's account, not with the doubtful, skeptical mind of a Socrates, but through the template of unduly rigid, taken-for-granted models. He declared: "Today's power uses as its primary justification for doing wrong the knowledge possessed by experts."[13] Probably the most important falsity spread by elites today, in Saul's view, is denial of the existence of a public good (a time-binding, communal concept in Innis' terms). Elites do this on the one hand by largely disregarding (neglecting to mention) the public or common good; it is seldom incorporated in their systems and models. On the other hand, elites continually promote its opposite—self-interest. Nowhere is the citizenry encouraged to adopt a "disinterested" (i.e., selfless) perspective from which to contemplate the larger well-being of society.[14]

Saul and Innis, then, both focused on monopolies of knowledge as a key to understanding governance in society. Saul wrote: "Power in our civilization is repeatedly tied to the pursuit of all-inclusive truths and utopias," which is to say "systems" or "ideologies."[15] And again, "The possession, use, and control of knowledge have become [the elite's] central theme," adding: "However, their power depends not on the effect with which they use that knowledge but on the effectiveness with which they control its use."[16] In Saul's view, like that of Innis, knowledge systems empower "experts" versed in their application. Knowledge systems for Saul, however, do not provide answers to society's pressing problems; rather, they give rise to the most perplexing problems confronting us. Who could deny, for example, that applied science (technology) has contributed to today's environmental woes?

Like Innis, Saul sees communication media as linking elites and their monopolies of knowledge to the rest of society. However, whereas Innis proposed that various modes of inscription and electronic media forge these links, Saul emphasized language and the wordsmiths. "Language," he wrote, "provides legitimacy. . . . So long as military, political, religious or financial systems do not control language, the public's imagination can move freely about with its own ideas."[17] However, people in positions of responsibility "are rewarded for controlling language."[18] Today, Saul sees two languages in currency. One is *public language*—"enormous, rich, varied and more or less powerless;"[19] this is the language of democratic wordsmiths (presumably Saul is one, but also others featured in this book, like Williams and Hoggart). They are devoted to clarity and understanding. The other is *corporatist*, the language of technocrats in business and government—and, I would, suggest, much of academe; their language is "purposefully impenetrable to the non-expert;"[20] it is *intended* to obscure.[21] In truly Innisian style, Saul proclaims: "The language attached to power is designed to prevent communication."[22]

Monopolies of knowledge for Saul, as for Innis, do not go uncontested. Whereas Innis maintained that groups marginalized by lack of control or influence over a society's predominant medium may contest power by introducing rival media, Saul maintains that there is a continuing dialectic between those who, through specialized vocabularies and mathematical complexities, would use language to obscure vs. democratic forces using language to enlighten.

Saul also re-presents Innis' dialectic between the oral and written word. Innis maintained that democracy flourished in Greece when the oral dialectic and the written word were in healthy tension. That was because, Innis contended, the written word on its own stifles thought and freedom as readers are led step by step to the authors' preconceived conclusions. Saul presented a similar dialectic in his contrast of Socrates versus Plato: the former, "oral, questioner, obsessed by ethics, searching for truth without expecting to find it, democrat, believer in the qualities of the citizen;" the latter, "written, answerer of questions, obsessed by power, in possession of the truth, antidemocratic, contemptuous of the citizen."[23] Whether or not one accepts fully Saul's depictions of Socrates and Plato—Innis, an admirer of Plato, would have been unlikely to have done so—his general position on orality and writing is quite in accord with Innis.

However, Innis remained an Enlightenment scholar. Despite his trenchant critiques of monopolies of knowledge, of the mechanization of knowledge, and of space bias, he never abandoned the quest for large-scale truth. However, Innis also was a "classicist," as he urged that scientific/instrumental knowledge systems be countervailed, challenged, and ultimately directed by moral, intuitive, religious, and historical knowledge. Like the ancient Greeks, moreover, Innis maintained that the researcher should always be reflexive, striving to take into account and compensate for her own biases. Saul, in contrast, criticized the Enlightenment on grounds that it pushed all other ways of knowing to the sidelines. Saul seems to believe that no continuing dialectic is possible as scientific/instrumental reason overpowers and destroys moral/time-biased knowledge, and as they share (in his view) no common ground. Rather than suggest we steer a mid-course between time-binding and space-binding knowledge, as did Innis, Saul seems more poststructuralist, suggesting there are many knowledges, none necessarily consistent with the others, but all useful.

Saul, then, is rather unique as a theorist insofar as his writings contain more than mere traces of poststructuralism, yet nonetheless he is able to incorporate astutely elements of political economy and makes an Innisian plea for time. He does this by elaborating a version of the dialectic of time vs. space, by linking knowledge to power, by focusing on media (the means of communication) as a key site in the struggle for power, and by insisting that without memory we are lost.

DAVID SUZUKI

Even more congruent with Innis' communication thesis are the media writings of broadcaster, author, geneticist, and environmentalist David Suzuki. Suzuki holds a PhD in genetics from the University of Chicago and was formerly professor at the University of British Columbia. While likely unaware of Innis as an intellectual forebear, Suzuki nonetheless has consistently applied the Innisian time-space media dialectic in addressing people's relations with the environment. Whereas Innis illustrated the time-space media dialectic through myriad examples culled from world history, Suzuki does this by contrasting the mind-sets of indigenous peoples with the modern west. Like Innis, Suzuki draws connections between differences in culture (differences in conceptions of time and of space) on the one hand, and predominance of different media of communication and patterns of their control (monopolies of knowledge) on the other. Let us begin by describing Suzuki's depiction of cultures in terms of conceptions of time.

Suzuki judges a society's conception of time to be "one of the pillars of its worldview, its shared ideas and images that grant order and meaning to the universe."[24] He repeatedly contrasts two disparate notions of time. One, termed "the pre-scientific conception," is similar to Innisian "time-bias." According to Suzuki, the "pre-scientific mind," which was widespread in Europe before Copernicus and still characterizes the mind-set of many indigenous peoples about the globe, affirms the importance of continuity and in particular the dependence of succeeding generations on the actions of their forebears. Some variants of the prescientific mind-set endow humans with responsibility even for keeping the stars on their courses.[25] The prescientific mind also pays close attention to recurrent natural rhythms. Some of nature's cycles are held to be sacred and steeped in signs and significance, and people participate symbolically in these recurrences through rituals.

The media of communication that imbue prescientific peoples with mythic notions of time, Suzuki observed, have traditionally been songs, ceremonies, and stories.[26] For the Gitksan of central British Columbia, for example, each household is the proud heir of an *ada'ox*—the "body of orally transmitted songs and stories that acts as the house's sacred archives and as its living, millennia-long memory of important events of the past"—an "irreplaceable verbal repository of knowledge." It consists in part of sacred songs believed to have arisen "from the breaths of ancestors." According to Suzuki and coauthor Peter Knudtson: "These songs serve as vital time-traversing vehicles. They can transport members across the immense reaches of space and time into the dim mythic past of Gitksan creation by the very quality of their music and the emotions they convey."[27]

Cyclical time, Suzuki continues, bestows the notion that we are all parts of a seamless web of interconnectivity and interdependence through time and space—that we live in future generations and they in us.

The opposite conception of time, according to Suzuki, is the western scientific tradition of "time's arrow"—the idea that time is linear, sequential, and unidirectional.[28] This resembles Innis' depiction of time for space-biased societies. Suzuki writes that although science recognizes natural cycles and rhythms—the solar seasons, fluctuations of predator and prey populations, replication cycles of DNA—these expressions of cyclical time are conceived to exist only within the grander framework of linear time—for example, the relentless increase in entropy and linear chains of cause and effect.[29] Western notions of linear time, by marginalizing cyclical or mythic time, have helped demolish "the intellectual and moral order of the Western world" as nothing is thought to remain the same;[30] thereby they have helped initiate the severe environmental problems we experience today.

For Suzuki, we in the west are beset by what Innis called present-mindedness. We think little of the past and have few concerns over what may transpire in the distant future. Rather, he writes, the "bottom line is often a weekly paycheque or an annual return on investment. Political reality is dictated by a horizon measured in months or a few years." Indeed, "linear time underlies our most cherished notions of 'progress'—our collective faith in the inexorable, incremental refinement of human society, technology, and thought."[31] This explains why it is difficult to mesh economic and political deadlines with nature's time needs.

Not only are David Suzuki's pronouncements on time consistent with Innis' media thesis, they fill a gap in Innis' work. Although Innis certainly was familiar with North American indigenous cultures, as evidenced by his book on the fur trade, his analysis of the biases of oral communication, in the opinion of Paul Heyer, "ultimately suffers from the exclusivity of constructing a model based on one source: the ancient Greeks." Heyer explains that Innis' work "evidences no discussion of the phenomenon as evidenced in the prestate societies of sub-Saharan Africa, South Asia, and the New World."[32] Suzuki, therefore, can be regarded as, in a sense, completing or fulfilling this aspect of Innis' work.

Suzuki is also Innisian when he assesses the time bias inherent to modern media. When Suzuki first became a broadcast journalist, he hoped that through his craft he would enable viewers to experience nature in a way that would inspire them to love it. Later he understood that this could not be so: "Now I realize that my programs, too, are a creation, not a reflection of reality. . . . Back in the editing room, hours of this hard-earned film are boiled down to sequences of sensational shot after sensational shot."[33] He continues, "What's missing in the filmed version of nature is *time.* Nature must have time, but television cannot tolerate it. So we create a virtual reality, a collage of images that conveys a distorted sense of what a real wilderness is like."[34]

For Suzuki, the "time distortion" of modern media is not trivial. By instilling an impression that nature can move quickly, media cause people to harbor unrealistic expectations: "Fish, trees or soil microorganisms don't grow fast enough for our speedy timeframe. But if the programs we create give an impression of a hopped-up nature, we might expect it to be able to meet our ever-faster needs."[35] Suzuki suggests that although our rates of extracting resources—trees, fish, top soil, clean water—are harmonious with the speed of our information technologies and the economy, they are certainly "not in synch with the reproductive rates of natural systems." He concludes: "More and more our sources of information are no longer connected to the natural world and its limits."[36]

Like Innis, who pleaded for "balance" between time and space in order that society would neither become stagnant nor fall into chaos, Suzuki insists that we need to integrate these rival ways of understanding time. By conceiving time as a spiral, rather than as a circle or as a straight line, we could synthesize the cyclical or mythic with the linear, scientific notions, making us more aware than at present of the "simultaneous spin of nature's seasons within time's trajectory," a necessity, he concludes, if we are to survive.[37]

Suzuki, like Innis, connects control of media to culture as manifested in conceptions of time. According to Suzuki, media are purposefully propagandistic in imparting a worldview consistent with the short-term interests of their controllers. He explains:

> In our view, the media pour out stories that are full of assumptions and values in the guise of objective value-free reporting. Most programming on television simply takes for granted our right to exploit nature as we see fit, to dominate the planet, to increase our consumption, to create more economic growth, to dump our wastes into the environment. Few object to these assumptions because they are so deeply set in our culture that they are accepted as obvious truths. However, they are biases nevertheless. Yet the minute a natural history film takes a strong environmental position that questions these beliefs, it is immediately criticized and bombarded with the demand to present "the other side."[38]

The foregoing account, albeit brief, may nonetheless suffice to show that the contemporary writings of David Suzuki and John Ralston Saul are largely congruent with the mode of analysis inaugurated by Innis. Saul viewed languages as possible monopolies of knowledge and as culturally biased media. Suzuki, too, described cultural biases of media, both old and new, and extended Innis' analysis of oral culture to contemporary tribal cultures. The "triangulation" presented here—Innis, Saul, Suzuki—affirms the possibility of the Innisian medium dialectic of time-space being an important portal for dialogue between cultural studies and political economy.

NOTES

1. John Ralston Saul, *Voltaire's Bastards: The Dictatorship of Reason in the West* (Toronto: Penguin, 1992), 53.
2. John Ralston Saul, *The Unconscious Civilization* (Toronto: Anansi, 1995), 111.
3. Harold A. Innis, *Empire and Communications* (1950; reprint, with Foreword by Marshall McLuhan, Toronto: University of Toronto Press, 1972), viii.
4. Saul, *Unconscious Civilization*, 5.

5. Saul, *Unconscious Civilization*, 70.
6. Saul, *Unconscious Civilization*, 5.
7. Saul, *Voltaire's Bastards*, 14.
8. He writes: "If one is looking for an individual father of the Age of Reason, Niccolo Machiavelli (1469–1527) is probably the right candidate." Saul, *Voltaire's Bastards*, 42.
9. Saul, *Voltaire's Bastards*, 15.
10. Saul, *Voltaire's Bastards*, 16.
11. George Grant, *Time as History* (1969; reprint, edited with an Introduction by William Christian, Toronto: University of Toronto Press, 1995), 37.
12. See Paul Heyer's introduction to part III, in *Media, Structures and Power: The Robert E. Babe Collection,* ed. Edward Comor (Toronto: University of Toronto Press, 2009).
13. Saul, *Unconscious Civilization*, 43.
14. Saul, *Unconscious Civilization*, 99.
15. Saul, *Unconscious Civilization*, 18.
16. Saul, *Voltaire's Bastards*, 8.
17. Saul, *Voltaire's Bastards*, 8–9.
18. Saul, *Unconscious Civilization*, 42.
19. Saul, *Unconscious Civilization*, 46.
20. Saul, *Unconscious Civilization*, 47. Note, for example, how Ben Agger describes much of the critical, postmodernist, and poststructuralist writings: "They are incredibly, extravagantly convoluted—to the point of disastrous absurdity one would think. . . . One cannot help but wonder why these theorists do not write more clearly and in ways that show the empirical (political, cultural, existential) relevance of their work more directly." Ben Agger, "Critical Theory, Poststructuralism, Postmodernism: Their Sociological Relevance," *Annual Review of Sociology* 17 (1991): 105. www.uta.edu/huma/illuminations/agger2.htm (accessed June 10, 2008).
21. Saul, *Voltaire's Bastards*, 8–9.
22. Saul, *Unconscious Civilization*, 54.
23. Saul, *Unconscious Civilization*, 55–56.
24. Peter Knudtson and David Suzuki, *Wisdom of the Elders* (Toronto: Stoddart, 1992), 142.
25. David Suzuki and Amanda McConnell, *The Sacred Balance: Rediscovering Our Place in Nature* (Vancouver: David Suzuki Foundation and Greystone Books, 1997), 11.
26. Knudtson and Suzuki, *Wisdom of the Elders*, 145.
27. Knudtson and Suzuki, *Wisdom of the Elders*, 128.
28. Knudtson and Suzuki, *Wisdom of the Elders*, 143.
29. Knudtson and Suzuki, *Wisdom of the Elders*, 143.
30. Suzuki and McConnell, *The Sacred Balance*, 13.
31. Knudtson and Suzuki, *Wisdom of the Elders*, 143.
32. Paul Heyer, *Harold Innis*, 71.
33. David Suzuki and Holly Dressel, *From Naked Ape to Superspecies: A Personal Perspective on Humanity and the Global Eco-Crisis* (Toronto: Stoddart, 1999), 79.

34. Suzuki and Dressel, *From Naked Ape to Superspecies*, 79.

35. Suzuki and Dressel, *From Naked Ape to Superspecies*, 79.

36. Suzuki and Dressel, *From Naked Ape to Superspecies*, 79. Interestingly, Innis made the same point: "An advance in the state of industrialism reflected in the speed of the newspaper press and the radio meant a decline in the importance of biological time determined by agriculture." Innis, "A Plea for Time," 74.

37. Knudtson and Suzuki, *Wisdom of the Elders*, 145. In his staples writings Innis also observed that the demand for fur hats was out of synch with the breeding cycle of beavers, that "the length of time required for [these animals] to arrive at maturity was an important factor in the destruction of the supply of fur." Harold A. Innis, *The Fur Trade in Canada: An Introduction to Canadian Economic History* (1930; revised, with Foreword by Robin W. Winks, Toronto: University of Toronto Press, 1967), 5.

38. David Suzuki, *Metamorphosis: Stages in Life* (Toronto: Stoddart, 1987), 263.

Chapter Seven

Semiotics and the Dialectic of Information

The two previous chapters proposed money and the dialectic of time/space as being possible *portals for dialogue* between cultural studies and critical political economy. The present chapter addresses a third such portal—information. Like money and time/space, information, too, however, must be viewed dialectically if dialogue is to begin. Unfortunately, particularly in the age of digitization, many analysts conceive information as disembodied form, quite removed from material reality; hence, a source of the disjuncture between language and nonverbal reality as posited by poststructuralism. But equally detrimental, focusing exclusively on the material element of information can give rise to an undue determinism ("economism"). After surveying both of these reductionist errors, the chapter affirms the *dialectic of information,* that is, information as matter-in-form.

CONCEIVING INFORMATION

The term, *information*, is polysemous, and in much media/communication scholarship it is defined imprecisely, if defined at all.[1] A starting point for greater precision is the seminal work of German physicist Carl Friedrich von Weizsäcker (1912–2007). Recollecting Aristotle, von Weizsäcker proposed that information is the form, structure, shape, or pattern *of matter* (or of energy), detectable by the senses, to which meanings are imputed or ascribed. He explained:

> This "form" can refer to the form of all kinds of objects or events perceptible to the senses and capable of being shaped by man: the form of the printer's ink or

ink on paper, of chalk on the blackboard, of sound waves in air, of current flow in a wire, etc.[2]

Von Weizsäcker's conception of information has affinity with the *sign* as developed by the Swiss linguist and founder of semiology Ferdinand de Saussure (1857–1913), and it certainly is worthwhile drawing connections between the two. De Saussure maintained that signs are dual, that they comprise both a sound presence (or, in the case of written language, a visual form) which he termed the *signifier,* and a mental image (the *signified*) that is experienced by those recognizing the signifier.[3] One hears the word C-O-W, for instance, and the mind thereupon pictures an image ("concept") that it associates with that sound. For de Saussure, both signifier and signified (i.e., both sound-image and concept, or sound and thought) are *form*, not *substance*. De Saussure's linguistic sign, in other words, is "wholly immaterial."[4]

In effect, von Weizsäcker corrected, or at least extended, de Saussure's analysis by recognizing that a sound or a visual shape needs to be carried or embodied by a material substrate, such as air, or ink on paper. Matter and form, von Weizsäcker noted, are conceptual complements: "In the realm of the concrete, no form exists without matter; nor can there be matter without form."[5] (See figure 7.1.)

Regrettably, neither de Saussure nor von Weizsäcker had much to say about the formation of *codes*—that is, about how forms come to mean. De Saussure did insist, however, that signifieds (the mental images, or "concepts") are joined with signifiers (the forms or sounds) by social convention. C-O-W and V-A-C-H-E have similar meanings ("signifieds"), albeit to different language groups, but neither of these two signifiers bears an intrinsic relation (such as resemblance) to either the signified or to the referent (object or class of objects in the material world).

Although de Saussure's semiology was entirely *synchronic,* which is to say he sought to explain language as a system as it exists at a given moment, irrespective of its history and abstracting from external factors that may have impinged upon it, in his *preliminary* remarks he indeed acknowledged that language interacts recursively with the external (nonverbal) world. As his comments in this regard are seldom recounted, it is worthwhile reproducing them here:

> Linguistics borders on ethnology, all the relations that link the history of a language and the history of a race or civilization. . . . The culture of a nation exerts an influence on its language, and the language, on the other hand, is largely responsible for the nation. Second come the relations between language and political history. Great historical events like the Roman conquest have an incalculable influence on a host of linguistic facts. Colonization, which is only one

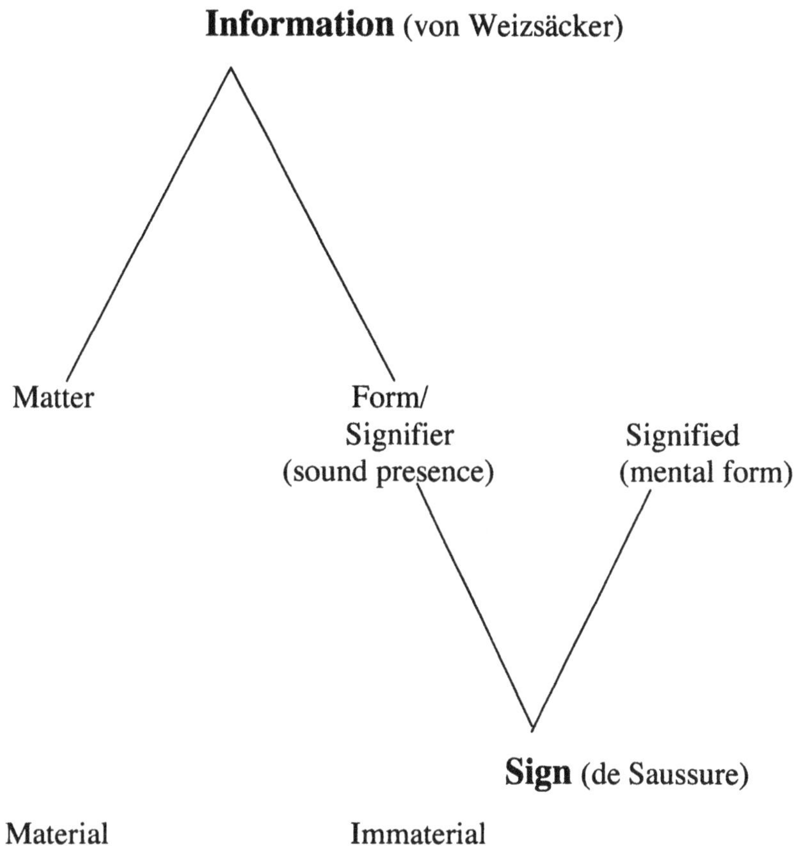

Figure 7.1. Relation of Signs and Information. Von Weizsäcker's notion of information adds the material dimension that de Saussure's idealist or immaterial semiotics lacks.

> form that conquest may take, brings about changes in an idiom by transporting it into different surroundings. All kinds of facts could be cited as substantiating evidence. . . . Here we come to the third point: the relations between language and all sorts of institutions (the Church, the school, etc.). All these institutions in turn are closely tied to the literary development of a language, a general phenomenon that is all the more inseparable from political history. . . . Finally, everything that relates to the geographical spreading of languages and dialectical splitting belongs to external linguistics.[6]

How un-de Saussurian these statements seem! They are significant, nonetheless, for at least two reasons. First, they indicate that de Saussure was aware of the limitations of his method. Second, he may be contrasted with many contemporary poststructuralists, who have embraced de Saussure's basic synchronic and immaterialist positions, but who fail to acknowledge (or perhaps even be aware of) the limitations.

What then *was* de Saussure's method? "My definition of language," he wrote, "presupposes the exclusion of everything that is outside its organism or system—in a word, of everything known as 'external linguistics.'"[7] He justified this approach by claiming that it facilitated the investigation of language as a structure or as a system. He compared language to chess, arguing that one need not understand the history of the game or account for external influences upon it in order to comprehend how chess works:

> In chess, what is external can be separated relatively easily from what is internal. The fact that the game passed from Persia to Europe is external; against that, everything having to do with its system and rules is internal. If I use ivory chessmen instead of wooden ones, the change has no effect on the system, but if I decrease or increase the number of chessmen, this change has a profound effect on the "grammar" of the game. One must always distinguish between what is internal and what is external. In each instance one can determine the nature of the phenomenon by applying this rule: everything that changes the system in any way is internal.[8]

Arguably, however, de Saussure's chess analogy is far from apt: the rules of chess (including the number of pieces) have remained static for centuries, whereas language undergoes continuous change and those changes are, arguably, in response to *external factors*. De Saussure bypassed the problem of linguistic change (and thereby the relation of language to the external world), moreover, by insisting he would only study language synchronically.

Returning now to von Weizsäcker, we can see from his declarations that *information* (and, by implication, *signs*) require: (1) an object such as ink on paper (or vocal chords, or some other vibrating object) that is, by definition, both form and substance; (2) a medium or carrier (air, water, light waves, electric current, etc.) which is altered ("re-formed") through contact with the object and which then through that patterning carries certain of the object's properties (as when white light reflects from an object); (3) a message recipient whose sensory apparatus is sufficiently acute to detect the patterned medium; and (4) a code or codes whereby the representation of the object as carried by the medium is interpreted by the recipient (a "signified" is produced). The absence of any of these components means there is no *information*, no *in-forming*. Typically, when cultural studies and political economy are set against one another, either *(a)* one or more of the requisite components of information is marginalized, attention being focused only on matter *or* on form, or *(b)* the rival paradigms adopt one or other of the dual approaches to language highlighted by de Saussure, namely internal *or* external linguistics.

In this chapter as well as chapter 8 and the Conclusion, I turn (implicitly) to internal vs. external linguistics. For the remainder of this chapter, I emphasize the de-linking of matter and form.

UNDULY EMPHASIZING SHAPE OR FORM

Many analysts, not just de Saussure, emphasize the shape or form of information while slighting the material element. Cyberneticist Norbert Wiener, for instance, viewed the human body as a "text" and rhapsodized how, over time, the body discards and replaces all of its *matter* while retaining the *pattern*: "To describe an organism," he explained, "we do not try to specify each molecule in it, and catalogue it bit by bit, but rather to answer certain questions about it which reveal its pattern." He continued:

> Life . . . is the pattern maintained by this homeostasis which is the touchstone of our personal identity. Our tissues change as we live: the food we eat and the air we breathe become flesh of our flesh and bone of our bone, and the momentary elements of our flesh and bone pass out of our body every day with our excreta. We are but whirlpools in a river of ever-flowing water. We are not stuff that abides, but patterns that perpetuate themselves.[9]

Economist Kenneth Boulding went even further. He declared that information not merely defies the first and second laws of thermodynamics, but actually counters them. Regarding the first law, namely the Law of Conservation of Matter-Energy, he wrote:

> The through-put of information in an organization involves a "teaching" or structuring process which does not follow any strict law of conservation even though there may be limitations imposed upon it. When a teacher instructs a class, at the end of the hour presumably the students know more and the teacher does not know any less. In this sense the teaching process is utterly unlike the process of exchange which is the basis of the law of conservation. In exchange, what one gives up another acquires; what one gains another loses. In teaching this is not so. What the student gains the teacher does not lose. Indeed, in the teaching process, as every teacher knows, the teacher gains as well as the student. In this phenomenon we find the key to the mystery of life.[10]

Regarding the Second Law of Thermodynamics, also known as the Law of Entropy, Boulding noted that in the absence of energy entering a system from outside, there is an ineluctable tendency over time for matter and energy within the system to become less ordered, less concentrated, less differentiated; the end of the universe, according to the Law of Entropy, is but a "thin soup without form."[11] Boulding then went on to claim, however, that information counteracts entropy through "the Law of Evolution," which he defined as the capacity/propensity of the universe or portions thereof to *increase* in complexity, organization, differentiation, and structure.[12] He saw, then, two opposing forces: the law of entropy and the law of evolution, the key to the latter being "information" which opposes (and hence is not itself subject to) entropy.

The position taken in the present chapter, however, is that in the absence of matter or energy—both of which, Boulding agrees, *are* subject to entropy—there is and can be no "information,"—nor "signs," either, for that matter. Information is (in part) the form or pattern which matter or energy assumes. Boulding's declaration is really a tautology that comes down to this: increasing order (i.e., greater complexity of form) counters decreasing order or declining complexity of form. Expressed a bit differently, information counters declines in information. Boulding's shortcoming, if I may be so bold, was to consider information as existing without the matter/energy component—that is, as pure form. But only in the problematic realms of angels and parapsychology can such be the case. Actually, entropy *means* the lessening of pattern or form on the part of matter and/or energy, that is increased randomization, a loss of information.

Cultural theorist Katherine Hayles has attributed the tendency of writers, like Boulding and Wiener, to de-materialize information—or as she put it, to view information as "an entity distinct from the substrates [or media] carrying it"[13]—to the influence of Shannon and Weaver's *mathematical theory of communication* (1948). Shannon and Weaver theorized digital communication, foreshadowing today's *convergence*.[14] With convergence, information may seem to be disembodied—as existing in a world of patterned electrons flitting about the globe via radio waves or nestled temporarily on a computer hard drive—in much the same way that Wiener emphasized the static pattern of the human body while downplaying the necessary presence of its ever-shifting materials. However, simply because patterns of electrons can be embedded onto new carriers with apparent ease does not deny that there must always be a carrier *and* that work must be done (i.e., energy expended) to execute the transferal. All this is precisely what advocates of a de-materialized notion of information omit or forget. Boulding, for example, in remarking how both he and his students were enriched by his classes, neglected to recall that students, too, are *material carriers* of information (their bodies "embody" Wiener's patterns; their brains "carry" Boulding's lectures); that energy is expended as these living organisms acquire and process the knowledge (new patterns and forms); and that energy is expended through metabolism as his students simply maintain their existence.

Stated otherwise, theorists like Boulding, Wiener, de Saussure, and Grossberg focus on but one side of the dialectic of information, namely on the form or pattern. They neglect or dismiss the matter/energy that necessarily embodies or carries these shapes or patterns.[15] Hence Grossberg, in forwarding *articulation* as a principal poststructuralist category, lost sight of the energy that must be expended to construct new forms and to disassemble other ones.

An immaterialist conception of information is at least implicit also in the work of poststructuralist Jean Baudrillard, who wrote famously about the *hyperreal,* defined as "the generation by models of a real without origin or reality." For Baudrillard, "the territory no longer precedes the map, nor survives it. Henceforth, it is the map that precedes the territory—PRECESSION OF SIMULACRA—it is the map that engenders the territory."[16]

Less pointed than the foregoing, but still in keeping with the "de-materialization" thesis—namely that shape or form counts for much more than mere matter—is the position advanced early in his career by Northrop Frye. In *Anatomy of Criticism,* Frye broke the connection (dialectic) between verbal structures/discourses on the one hand and the objects or worlds to which they ostensibly refer on the other. He claimed that literature is largely independent of outside factors.[17] "Nothing is prior in significance to literature itself," Frye announced. Rather, works of literature reflect and refer primarily to one another, through their conventions, genres, images, archetypes, and so forth. Literature is an "order of words," a seamless structure: "The new poem, like the new baby, is born into an already existing order and is typical of the structure of poetry, which is ready to receive it."[18] Frye even extended these sentiments to the sciences, which he saw also as being fundamentally "an order of words."[19]

Drawing attention from material reality and toward the symbolic world of language, discourse, and simulacra (i.e., "forms"), as the aforementioned cultural theorists do, subverts the possibility of political economy. For political economy is certainly concerned with the material world. At its best, political economy asks, among other things, how power selects certain "forms" and rejects others, and how it influences or even sets the meanings people attach to the forms that circulate. Political economy, therefore, can be understood as encompassing what de Saussure called *external linguistics.*

Critical political economy is concerned, first and foremost, with exposing injustice, particularly with regard to the distribution of wealth and income, but in other matters as well—environmental injustice, for instance. To rule out political economy by focusing mainly on language itself as opposed to what language refers to in the material world, or to the interests propagating discourses, is to debilitate the quest for justice.

UNDULY EMPHASIZING MATTER AND MEDIUM

If form is associated with fluidity, interpretation, freedom, subjectivity, radical indeterminacy, and "articulation," then matter is linked with physical laws and hard determinisms. Presumably, were a critical political economist to break the dialectic of information and treat media and communication solely from a materialist perspective,[20] the ensuing analysis would be filled with the hard determinisms which Lawrence Grossberg and other poststructuralist scholars routinely complain about. Philip Mirowski, indeed, has argued convincingly that mainstream economics took classical physics as its exemplar,[21] and the mathematical, deterministic nature of the modern, mainstream discipline was the result.

While grievous harm (loss of material bearings) follows from conceptually *de*-materializing information, the opposite error—namely, regarding information as matter alone—is equally harmful. B. F. Skinner, albeit writing outside the realms of economics and political economy, is a case in point. He adopted a totally materialist ("positivist") view of information and communication. The title of his perhaps most famous book, *Beyond Freedom and Dignity,* indicates concisely the price to be paid. In a world of total determinisms (operant conditioning), there is, of course, no freedom, but consequently as well no dignity; for surely, dignity is contingent upon the proper and wise exercise of freedom. In a world of complete determinisms, one must be fatalistic, as the future has been caused already.

Jeremy Bentham, the nineteenth-century British philosopher and political economist, was another advocate of a completely materialist view of information. Although Bentham is usually regarded as a libertarian, that designation is quite problematic, for Bentham (like Skinner) recognized no human volition in the face of the two "sovereign masters," pleasure and pain:

> Nature has placed mankind under the governance of two sovereign masters, pain and pleasure. It is for them alone to point out what we might do, as well as to determine what we shall do. On the one hand the standard of right and wrong, on the other the chain of causes and effects are fastened to their throne.[22]

Both a poststructuralist cultural studies focused only on form (or on Sausseurian signs), and a reductionist political economy focused only on matter, then, are partial and harmful. A means of reintegrating cultural studies and political economy is to introduce into the analysis the *dialectic of information*, thereby avoiding the harms and deficiencies attributable to both an undue idealism and an undue materialism.

MAINTAINING THE DIALECTIC OF INFORMATION

We have seen that the dialectic of matter and form, which I here refer to as the *dialectic of information*, has been broken by some of the most respected scholars of our time. In previous chapters, however, we noted that this dialectic figured prominently in the writings of the founding writers of media studies. Innis, Adorno, Williams, Hoggart, and Thompson all espoused a "soft determinism," which in the present context is akin to proposing a dialectic of freedom and control, of interpretation and determinism, of language and action, of form and matter, of medium and message.

To illustrate, I turn briefly again to Innis, but now also to his "disciple," Marshall McLuhan. Innis, as we have seen, provided an immensely original and heuristic way of integrating what are today called cultural studies and critical political economy of media. In his media thesis, Innis focused on the dialectic of medium and message. Far from presuming, as do theorists of dematerialized information, that the medium is of little or no consequence, Innis proposed interactivity between medium and message, which is to say between matter and form. Depending on the physical properties of any given medium of communication—its durability, lightness, ease or difficulty in being encoded, its capacity to carry messages—it is predisposed to transmit either time-binding or space-binding messages, thereby supporting elites whose power is based on the particular monopoly of knowledge made conducive by the prevailing medium. Messages, though, act recursively on media, as in choice of medium made by those with messages to send. Although some commentators[23] have accused Innis of being a technological or media determinist, enough has been said in previous chapters and elsewhere[24] to lay that charge to rest.

However, Innis neglected (but not entirely![25]) reception and interpretation, and it is in this regard that Marshall McLuhan may be understood as filling a gap in Innis' work. Like Innis, McLuhan was a medium theorist who drew attention to the interplay of medium and message, between matter and form. McLuhan, however, proposed connections between the material means of encoding messages and "biases" in interpreting them by receivers or audiences. McLuhan maintained that media, being extensions or amplifications of either the eye or ear, affect interpretation/perception in broadly predictable ways.[26] For example, he attributed the predominance of either linear logic or of analogic reasoning to the preponderance in any given culture of media extending (or amplifying the power of) the eye or ear respectively. Linear logic, according to McLuhan, derives from the (illusion of) connectedness in visual space, whereas analogy, due to gaps inherent to audile/tactile space, is more common in cultures emphasizing the ear. It is from gaps or intervals, not connections, that knowledge of proportions, and hence analogies stem. It is worth quoting McLuhan on this important insight:

> Perhaps the most precious possession of man is his abiding awareness of the analogy of proper proportionality, the key to all metaphysical insight and perhaps the very condition of consciousness itself. This analogical awareness is constituted of a perpetual play of ratios: A is to B what C is to D, which is to say that the ratio between A and B is proportioned to the ratio between C and D, there being a ratio between these ratios as well. This lively awareness of the most exquisite delicacy depends upon there being no connection whatever between the components. If A were linked to B, or C to D, mere logic would take the place of analogical perception.[27]

In important ways, however, McLuhan departed from Innis. From his perspective as literary critic, McLuhan viewed media technologies as manifesting in the material world the same operations as those in the linguistic world described by the rhetorical term, *chiasmus*. McLuhan proposed that at high intensity, there is a reversal in a medium's effects. Innis, to the contrary, never argued that a space-binding medium pushed to the limit becomes time-binding!

McLuhan claimed that other rhetorical operations, too (metaphor, cliché, and archetype) have wide applicability in the nonverbal world.[28] His justification for adopting this literary approach to media analysis was that language is a technology (i.e., an applied artifact), and hence it can properly be compared to other artifacts or technologies. "Anything that can be observed about the behavior of linguistic cliché or archetype," he wrote, "can be found plentifully in the nonlinguistic world."[29] McLuhan was fond of invoking the following lines by the poet William Butler Yeats, to emphasize that poets and inventors (wordsmiths and technologists) are alike in recycling refuse to forge new creations:

> *Those masterful images because complete*
> *Grew in pure mind, but out of what began?*
> *A mound of refuse or the sweepings of a street,*
> *Old kettles, old bottles, and a broken can,*
> *Old iron, old bones, old rags, that raving slut*
> *Who keeps the till. Now that my ladder's gone,*
> *I must lie down where all the ladders start,*
> *In the foul rag-and-bone shop of the heart.*[30]

Here, McLuhan's position would seem to be not all that different from the poststructuralist notion of *articulation*. Hence, some might regard McLuhan as potentially a bridge between Innis and poststructuralism. To make that case, however, one would really need to elaborate the connections within McLuhan's own thought between, on the one hand, his medium theory of eye-ear bias, and on the other his treatment of media as manifestations of rhetorical tropes. To my knowledge, these connections have yet to be made.

This chapter has explored the "dialectic of information" as a means of reconciling political economy and cultural studies. *Both* an extreme idealism/immaterialism (as exemplified by de Saussure, Boulding, Baudrillard, and Grossberg) and an undue materialism (Skinner, Bentham, and the "vulgar Marxists") are in grievous error on account of reductionism. Only the "dialectic of information" can avoid their grievous errors.

Exemplary in this regard are both McLuhan and Innis—the first a literary critic with an expertise in symbolist poetry, the second a "dirt economist." Considered separately, both are highly heuristic. Juxtaposed and interrelated, they provide new richness of insight, and constitute a bulwark against post-structuralist dematerializations and undue economistic determinisms. This feat both theorists accomplish through their singular, distinct, but related affirmations of the dialectic of information.

NOTES

1. Robert E. Babe, "Information Industries and Economic Analysis: Policy-Makers Beware," in *Communication and the Transformation of Economics* (Boulder, CO: Westview Press, 1995), 9–20.
2. Carl Friedrich von Weizsäcker, *The Unity of Nature* (New York: Farrar, Straus and Giroux, 1980), 38–39.
3. He wrote: "In language, one can neither divide sound from thought nor thought from sound. . . . Linguistics then works in the borderland where the elements of sound and thought combine; *their combination produces a form, not a substance.*" And again: "The linguistic sign unites, not a thing and a name, but a concept and a sound-image. The latter is not the material sound, a purely physical thing, but the psychological imprint of the sound, the impression that it makes on our senses. The sound-image is sensory, and if I happen to call it 'material,' it is only in that sense, and by way of opposing it to the other term of the association, the concept, which is generally more abstract." De Saussure treated written language phonetically, that is as standing for (signifying) a sound image. Ferdinand de Saussure, *Course in General Linguistics,* ed. Charles Bally and Albert Sechehaye (New York: McGraw-Hill, 1915), 113, 66; emphasis in original. www2.sims.berkeley.edu/courses/is296a-3/s06/Saussure .pdf (accessed Dec. 16, 2007).
4. Daniel Chandler, "Signs: Semiotics for Beginners," April 2006, www.aber.ac.uk /media/Documents/S4B/sem02.html (accessed Dec. 15, 2007).
5. Weizsäcker, *The Unity of Nature*, 274.
6. De Saussure, *Course in General Linguistics*, 20–21.

7. De Saussure, *Course in General Linguistics*, 20.

8. De Saussure, *Course in General Linguistics*, 22–23.

9. Norbert Wiener, *The Human Use of Human Beings: Cybernetics and Society* (1950; reprint, New York: Avon Books, 1967), 129, 130.

10. Kenneth Boulding, *The Image: Knowledge and Life in Society* (Ann Arbor, MI: University of Michigan Press, 1956), 35.

11. Kenneth Boulding, *Ecodynamics: A New Theory of Societal Evolution* (Beverly Hills, CA: SAGE Publications, 1978), 10.

12. Boulding, *Ecodynamics*, 10.

13. N. Katherine Hayles, *How We Became Posthuman: Virtual Bodies in Cybernetics, Literature, and Informatics* (Chicago: University of Chicago Press, 1999), xi.

14. With convergence, voice, image, video, text, and indeed combinations thereof, are stored and transmitted via phone lines, cables, satellite circuits, hard drives, and floppy disks through a series of on-off electrostatic charges or pulses.

15. To acknowledge the dialectic of information is also to controvert Boulding's contention that information is not subject to the law of conservation. Of course, the planet we inhabit is not a closed system, as energy in the form of sunlight continually enters the planetary system and heat is radiated into space.

16. Jean Baudrillard, *Simulations*, trans. Paul Foss, Paul Patton, and Philip Beitchman (New York: Semioltext(e), 1983), 2; emphasis in original.

17. Northrop Frye, *Anatomy of Criticism: Four Essays* (1957; reprint, Princeton, NJ: Princeton University Press, 1971), 17.

18. Northrop Frye, "The Language of Poetry," in *Explorations in Communication*, ed. Edmund Carpenter and Marshall McLuhan (Boston: Beacon Press, 1960), 44.

19. In subsequent work, Frye backed off from this extreme and nondialectical position to affirm what I call here *the dialectic of information*. In *The Critical Path*, for example, he saw the autonomy of literature and of criticism as constituting but one pole of an overarching dialectic, namely that of "literature as a coherent structure, historically conditioned but shaping its own history, responding to but not determined in its form by an external historical process." Northrop Frye, *The Critical Path: An Essay on the Social Context of Literary Criticism* (Bloomington, IN: Indiana University Press, 1971), 24.

20. This is what mainstream "information economists" try to do, with little success. See Robert E. Babe, "The Place of Information in Economics," in *Information and Communication in Economics*, ed. Robert E. Babe (Boston: Kluwer Academic Publishers, 1994), 41–67.

21. Philip Mirowski, *More Heat Than Light: Economics as Social Physics, Physics as Nature's Economics* (Cambridge: Cambridge University Press, 1989).

22. Jeremy Bentham, *An Introduction to the Principles of Morals and Legislation*. 1781. www.utilitarianism.com/jeremy-bentham/index.html (accessed August 22, 2008).

23. Everett Rogers, *A History of Communication Study: A Biographical Approach* (New York: The Free Press, 1994), 499; Daniel Czitrom, *Media and the American Mind* (Chapel Hill: University of North Carolina Press, 1982), 148.

24. Judith Stamps, *Unthinking Modernity: Innis, McLuhan and the Frankfurt School* (Montreal and Kingston: McGill-Queen's University Press, 1995); Edward Comor, "Harold Innis's Dialectical Triad," *Journal of Canadian Studies* 29, no. 22 (summer, 1994): 111–27; Paul Heyer, *Harold Innis* (Lanham, MD: Rowman and Littlefield Publishers, Inc., 2003).

25. Hence the reason for McLuhan stating that his book *The Gutenberg Galaxy* is but a footnote to the observations of Innis.

26. Marshall McLuhan, *The Gutenberg Galaxy: The Making of Typographic Man* (Toronto: University of Toronto Press, 1962).

27. Marshall McLuhan and Harley Parker, *Through the Vanishing Point: Space in Poetry and Painting* (New York: Harper and Row, 1968), 240; emphasis added.

28. Robert E. Babe, "McLuhan and the Electronic Archives" (Ottawa: Library and Archives Canada, 2007) www.collectionscanada.gc.ca/innis-mcluhan/002033-4010-e.html (accessed Dec. 15, 2007).

29. Marshall McLuhan with Wilfred Watson, *From Cliché to Archetype* (New York: Pocket Books, 1971), 20.

30. William Butler Yeats, "The Circus Animals' Desertion" as quoted in McLuhan with Watson, *From Cliché to Archetype*, 20.

Chapter Eight

Keeping the Portals Open: Poster vs. Innis[1]

Several years ago in England, a doctoral student suggested to one of us that the work of Mark Poster is strongly correlated with that of Harold Innis. Indeed, at a surface level, similarities do abound.

The contention here, however, is that this veneer of similarity masks deep-seated differences and significant contradictions. Moreover, as Poster is one of the more "materialist" of the poststructuralists, the incompatibility of his framework with that of political economy is of broader applicability.

Interestingly, Poster claims that poststructuralism "is a uniquely American practice," and that the writings of such seminal French theorists as Derrida, Baudrillard, Lyotard, and Foucault "have far greater currency in the United States than in France."[2] This contention, if accurate, adds support to the argument of chapter 4 regarding the marked proclivity of scholars in the United States to marginalize political economy.

MARK POSTER

At the core of Mark Poster's work are the concepts of the mode of information, language, and poststructuralism. We begin the chapter by looking at, and commenting upon, these three terms.

Language and the Mode of Information

For Mark Poster, each medium of communication (whether cave paintings, clay tablets, computer databases, or communication satellites) "profoundly intervenes in the network of relations that constitute a society."[3] Being a poststructuralist, Poster's focus is on language, and so he is concerned primarily with how changes in the medium of communication affect language, and how these changes in turn affect the network of social relations. As the means of communication change, he wrote, "the relation of language and society, idea and action, self and other," changes also.[4] Poster coined the term, *the mode of information,* to designate the nature of a medium's "interventions," particularly with regard to language.[5]

Poster proposed three stages in the mode of information, each corresponding to a particular impact on language by the means of communication. In the first stage, occurring in oral societies, *symbolical correspondences* predominate because communicators converse principally about objects in their immediate environs, or as Poster put it, "the self is constituted as a position of enunciation through its embeddedness in a totality of face-to-face relations."[6] In the second stage, where exchanges are predominantly mediated by print, the *representational property of language* comes to the fore. In this stage, the "self is constructed as an agent in rational/imaginary autonomy."[7] Presumably this is due to the private nature of reading/writing and the concern for depicting through language remote objects and events, as well as completely imaginary ones. The third stage is that of electronics, and Poster places such great emphasis on it that he often uses the term, *mode of information*, to refer solely to it, declaring, for instance, that the mode of information "designates social relations mediated by electronic communication systems,"[8] and again: "The mode of information designates social relations mediated by electronic communication systems, which constitute new patterns of language."[9]

Although language is significant in structuring human relations and configuring individual identities in all three stages,[10] according to Poster it is of most significance in the era of electronics. He claims that communication analysts (the "grand theorists") in the ages of writing and of face-to-face could with equanimity focus on *actions* or *activities* and neglect language, whereas social theorists in the electronics era *must turn from action to language*.[11] It is this focus on language, as opposed to action, that defines Poster as a poststructuralist,[12] and divorces him from political economy.[13]

In this third stage, the era of electronics, words (or more generally signs) cease to represent the outside/nonlinguistic world and refer instead chiefly to themselves (*the self-referentiality of language*). Electronic media, according to Poster (drawing particularly on Jean Baudrillard), allow or cause signifiers to float freely, attaching to and detaching from referents without rhyme or reason, and in the process transforming the linguistic context within which people function. He writes:

> In TV ads, where the new mode of signification is most clearly seen, floating signifiers are attached to commodities. . . . Each TV ad replicates in its structure the ultimate facility of language: language is remade, new connections are established in the TV ad through which new meanings emerge. . . . Floating signifiers, which have no relation to the product, are set in play; images and words that convey desirable or undesirable states of being are portrayed in a manner that optimizes the viewer's attention without arousing critical awareness.[14]

"Floating signifiers" attaching to products corresponds well to what Lawrence Grossberg referred to as *articulation* (see chapter 3). Regarding an ad for floor wax, Poster writes:

> The [television] ad takes a signifier, a word that has no traditional relation with the object being promoted, and attaches it to that object. . . . Johnson's floor wax now equals romantic rescue. The commodity has been given a semiotic value that is distinct from, indeed out of phase with, its use value and its exchange value. . . . The ad shapes a new language, a new set of meanings (floor wax/romance) which everyone speaks or better which speaks everyone. Baudrillard calls the collective language of commodity ads "the code." . . . The code may be understood as a language or sign system unique to the mode of information, to electronically mediated communication systems.[15]

We shall return later to Poster's analysis of the particular floor wax commercial. First, though, consider Poster's general claim that "representation comes to grief when words lose their connection with things and come to stand in the place of things, in short, when language represents itself."[16] This purported loss of referentiality in language is magnified by electronics, Poster continues, bringing about new patterns of human relations, creating new processes of establishing self-identities, and altering our very conception of truth, the authentic, and the real. Let us look more closely at these three purported consequences of linguistic change resulting from the predominance of electronic media.

Regarding patterns of human relations, Poster proposes that electronics change the time and space relations among communicators. He writes: "The exchange of symbols between human beings is now far less subject to constraints of space and time."[17] He explains that electronics give rise to "vast, massive, and profound upheavals" because the social world has "become constituted in part by . . . a simultaneity of event and record of the event, by an instantaneity of act and observation, by an immediacy and copresence of electronically mediated meanings to a large extent self-referentially."[18] While acknowledging that writing and print in previous eras distanced message senders and receivers, Poster claims that electronics magnifies that effect to such a degree as to bring about qualitative changes in the nature of human relations.[19] (For instance, one might note, on the Internet communicators can retain anonymity and can even assume and change their ostensible or assumed identities at a whim.)

Second, linguistic change in the electronics era, he claims, affects the construction of self-identities: "The self is [now] decentered, dispersed, and multiplied in continuous instability."[20] He continues: "In this world the subject has no anchor, no fixed place, no point of perspective, no discreet center, no clear boundary."[21] In part, this is an outcome (as noted above) of the exaggerated separation in time and/or space of message receivers and message senders. But television advertisements, too, are a factor in this regard, according to Poster, because they mold viewers into consumer-subjects, imprinting their minds "with floating signifiers attached to commodities not by any intrinsic relation to them but by the logic of unfulfilled desire."[22]

Third, and most importantly, language disconnects from material reality. Poster claims that as language loses its capacity for representation, "'reality' comes to be constituted in the 'unreal' dimension of the media."[23] Indeed, he declares, "it becomes increasingly difficult, or even pointless, for the subject to distinguish a 'real' existing 'behind' the flow of signifiers."[24] He writes: "The tendency in poststructuralism is therefore to regard truth as a multiplicity, to exult in the play of diverse meanings, in the continual process of reinterpretation, in the contention of opposing claims."[25] And again: "Social life in part becomes a practice of positioning subjects to receive and interpret messages."[26]

For Poster, the loss of referentiality in language is not something to be bemoaned, but celebrated. For him, every discourse or knowledge system claiming to contain or represent universal truth buttresses structures of power and hence oppresses the disadvantaged.[27] Regarding power, Poster is in accord not only with Derrida but also with Adorno and Horkheimer's critique of the Enlightenment, and is not far removed from Innis' objections to monopolies of knowledge, or from Williams/Hoggart's understanding of elite culture. Poster's solution, though, following Derrida, de Man, and other deconstructionists, is not to reapply systems of knowledge so that they might benefit more of humankind, or to seek to balance instrumental knowledge with other types of knowledge (aesthetic, moral, intuitive, or personal, for example), or to authenticate hitherto marginalized or disregarded knowledge systems (indigenous knowledge systems, for example, or working class culture), but rather to de-authenticate knowledge through the claim that language is now self-referential and can no longer represent external reality.

For Poster, poststructuralism is the latest advance in critical theory, which he characterizes as an approach seeking "to assist the movement of revolution by providing a counter-ideology that delegitimizes the ruling class."[28] Of course, as Poster recognizes, critical theory by this definition existed long before the arrival of poststructuralism: Marx's writings, for example, countered mainstream or hegemonic thought in the industrial age, as had Enlightenment writings in the age of faith. For our era, though, Poster maintains, there needs to be a new critical theory. This is because, he declares, with electronics discourse supercedes property as the primary site of domination, thereby obsolescing Marxism. Poststructuralism contributes to the new critical theory, he claims, by "raising the question of language."[29] In the postmodern era, the task of critical theorists must be to reveal language-based patterns of domination, and then to subvert them. Hence, the mode of information must replace the mode of production as the fulcrum for contemporary critical thought and strategy.[30] He explains:

> The focuses of protest in the 1970s were feminism, gay liberation, antipsychiatry, prison reform—the groups addressed by Foucault's writings—as well as other challenges to capitalism which were equally at the margins of the theory of the mode of production (racial, ethnic, and regional protest; antinuclear movements; ecologists; and so forth). Thus poststructuralism argues for a plurality of radical critiques, placing in question the centering of critical theory in its proletarian site."[31]

It is now apparent how one could think of Poster as covering much the same ground as Innis. Poster's mode of information seems at first glance to conform to Innis' biases of communication. Innis, after all, investigated the time/space biases of orality, various modes of writing, and electronics (primarily radio), and speculated on their implications for structuring human relations and individual consciousness. Similarly Poster distinguishes the same three "eras" of media, and proposes that they have had profoundly different consequences regarding the structuring of human relations and human consciousness. Innis saw the various media as working their effects through the types of messages they were predisposed to carry, and Poster views them as working their effects through transformations in language. Like Innis, Poster claims that the three types of media help establish different time and space relations among communicators. Both Innis and Poster expressed concern regarding what Innis termed "monopolies of knowledge," although for Poster attention is focused not on control of media *per se*, but rather on the power implications of the discourses, theories, or "grand narratives" mistakenly taken to be universally true knowledge. Neither Poster nor Innis is Marxist, either in his delineation of the stages of history or in his account of class structure. Innis attributed power to those in control of the predominant media of communication as opposed to distinguishing between capital and labor, whereas Poster attributes power to those in charge of discourses and expresses concern regarding ways in which marginalized groups (ethnic, racial, and sexual groups) are "represented" and discussed.

Despite such commonalities, however, important distinctions between Poster and Innis are manifest. First, Poster is far more interested than Innis in the "constitution" or the "structuring" of *individuals* through various modes of information. Innis' main interest was the role of various media in organizing societies along the existential dimensions of time and space.

Second, Poster contrasts language and action, writing that in the electronics era social theorists must turn their attention from action to language.[32] In the era of the electronic mode of information, he explains, control of language replaces control of capital as the locus of power, for the only "reality" we now know is of the order of language. This is a far cry from Innis' political economy. Innis would never reduce reality to language, although he certainly emphasized the bidirectional impact between language practices (messages) and material conditions, and he accorded particular emphasis to control over media of communication.

Third, whereas Poster proposes that the major consequence of media evolution from orality to print to electronics has been to transform language from symbolic correspondence to representation and finally to self-referentiality, for Innis the major consequence has been to alter the balance or tension between the existential categories of continuity and change, freedom and control, time and space.

Fourth, Innis retained a dialectical interaction between medium and message: on the one hand, media are predisposed to carry messages with either a time-bias or a space bias, while on the other hand messages act recursively on media; in space-biased societies media favoring time will shrink in relative importance and may adapt to some extent to the exigencies of space (books addressing contemporary fashion and current affairs, for instance, or scholarly tomes expounding poststructuralism). Poster, in contrast, saw causation as strictly one-way—as media affecting, indeed determining, language. In the electronics era, according to Poster, when language becomes self-referential because of the mode of communication, it detaches from material reality. Here we see clearly, I would argue, one of several inconsistencies, or flaws, in Poster's work. (More on this below).

Finally, in terms of remedies, the two writers are also far apart. Innis made a "plea for time," by which he meant that time-binding media (particularly oral debate, but also all other media emphasizing continuity and duration) should be promoted in order to help countervail the prevailing bias of space and contemporary present-mindedness. In contrast, Poster essentially wishes to de-authenticate all knowledge systems, and his way of doing this is by claiming repeatedly, in book after book, that with electronics language loses any and all connection with material reality, an eventuality not to be regretted, according to the author, but celebrated.[33]

Critique

Undoubtedly Poster is correct that some communication in oral cultures corresponds to the immediate circumstances of the interlocutors. But it is also true that much oral communication in tribal societies is/was devoted to recounting histories and myths which set the ontological framework of everyday life. Homer's poetry depicting the intervention in human affairs of the gods of Mount Olympus, for example, did not correspond (we now think) directly to the material circumstances of daily life in ancient Greece. The Old Testament, likewise, was inscribed from oral transmissions, but its mysticism did not correspond to the warp and woof of everyday existence. In animistic societies, too, each blade of grass is deemed to be host to a spirit or deity, making dubious the validity of Poster's assertion that "symbolic correspondence" characterizes oral society. One might even suggest that, due to the importance of legends, myths, superstitions and sacred stories, the self-referential ("floating signifiers") property of language was *greater* in tribal (oral) society than it is today in our largely secularized society.

Consider next Poster's claims regarding changes to language wrought by the shift to electronics from writing. As noted in chapter 7, in *Anatomy of Criticism* Northrop Frye insisted that *writing* is predominantly self-referential,[34] that "nothing is prior in significance to literature itself.'[35] For Frye, works of literature reflect and refer primarily to one another through their conventions, genres, images, archetypes and so forth. Even science, Frye contended, is largely an "order of words." Frye subsequently backed away from that firm (one might say, extreme) position, proposing instead that the self-referential properties of language/discourse are moderated by influences of the material world.[36] Frye, in other words, became dialectical with regard to his understanding of language and material reality.

Science philosopher Thomas Kuhn similarly posited a strong self-referential aspect to scientific literatures, arguing that science is in part a socio-cultural activity practiced by like-minded investigators who observe phenomena through the lens of the presuppositions and the prior expectations of their disciplines, i.e. through their *literatures*. Like Frye, though, Kuhn recognized that material reality impinges upon these discourses, bringing about, in his terms, "scientific revolutions."[37] In the end, therefore, both Frye and Kuhn are to be distinguished from contemporary poststructuralists due to the bidirectional interactivity they understood to exist between language/discourse on the one hand and material/nonverbal reality on the other. Contentions like those of Frye and Kuhn, moreover, challenge Poster's assertion that electronics ushered in a radically new era because it is with electronics that language loses its representational character and becomes merely self-referential.

To be sure, Poster qualified his argument by noting that "this [self-referential] feature of language is always present in its use," but he then added quickly that "today increasingly meaning is sustained through mechanisms of self-referentiality and the non-linguistic thing, the referent, fades into obscurity, playing less and less of a role in the delicate process of sustaining cultural meanings."[38] The operative question, then, is whether self-referentiality is of such monumentally greater significance today compared to, for instance, the age of print or tribal cultures, as to constitute an entirely new era. Frye's answer would be no.

If self-referentiality in language/discourse is not in fact the major factor demarcating the age of electronics from previous eras, the question becomes whether there may be other factors ignored or downplayed by Poster which do indeed distinguish clearly the electronics era from what preceded it—for example, Innis' historicist concept of time-space bias. And, of course, the bigger question: What difference does it make if we accede to Poster's position or to that of Innis?

Another obvious criticism, hinted at earlier, is that poststructuralism is itself "a discourse," and hence is implicated in structuring/concentrating power. As a riposte, Poster proposed that by introducing his concept of the mode of information into poststructuralist discourse he has lessened the "totalizing" tendency of poststructuralism, rendering it now merely in his words a "nontotalizing totalization."[39] This is because, he claims, despite important commonalties, each of the electronic media (telegraph, telephone, radio, television, computers, satellites) requires its own, detailed, unique exposition: "There is a multiplicity of discourses within the mode of information,"[40] he explained. The electronic mode of information, then, in his view, by covering variegated media, invalidates the charge of "grand narrative." However, this defense seems to contradict his main point, namely that the various electronic modes of communication individually and in combination have huge and uniform consequences: each and every one of these media, according to Poster, de-centers subjects, destroys truth as a meaningful idea, disconnects language from material reality, causes language to become more self-referential, de-authenticates "grand narratives," and annihilates the efficacy of reason. Do not these effects common to the various means of communicating electronically far outweigh the differences, thereby rendering the discourse on the electronic mode of information a "totalizing totalization"?

Even more problematic is the inconsistency in Poster's treatment of language and its relation to the media. On the one hand, Poster is virtually a technological determinist in associating three eras of media with three different modes of language. Ironically, his emphasis on the technological context was his self-consciously formulated response to accusations leveled at poststructuralism of linguistic reductionism. "My effort," he wrote, "in theorizing the mode of information, has been to counteract the textualist tendency by linking poststructuralist theory with social change, by connecting it with electronic communications."[41] In brief, Poster's cure for linguistic reductionism is a dose of technological determinism.

However, even this cannot resolve the more basic issue of self-referentiality. For once electronic media have transformed language from being representational into being self-referential, then nothing can actually be said with accuracy about anything existing outside language—including electronic media and the electronic mode of information. In order to have validity, any and all statements (including the string of books by Poster) about the mode of information would require an infusion of the *representational* properties of language. In other words, according to Poster's position, we should feel free to disregard everything he says—unless we assume him to occupy a position of omniscience (i.e., that of a "*transcendental ego*"), a position he also claims poststructuralism has discredited and neutralized. (In contrast Innis, and political economy generally, avoided the trap of self-referentiality first through reflexivity and second by claiming that there is a political economy of discourse, whereby knowledge structures affect power in the material world, even as the material world influences power structures; according to political economy, there is a two-way, nondeterministic interplay between medium and message.)

Finally, let us consider Poster's insistence that poststructuralists endeavor "to consider the context in which one is theorizing." For Poster, a poststructuralist is always aware of and reflects upon "the relative importance of the topic one is choosing to treat."[42] In other words, poststructuralists endeavor to adopt a position of theoretical relativism, as opposed to the absolutism of the "grand narrators." By "connecting one's theoretical domain to one's sociocultural world or to some aspect of it," he explains, "one ensures in advance that one's discourse does not emanate from a *transcendental ego*."[43] But just how successful is Poster (or can any writer be, for that matter), in avoiding "totalizations" emanating from a "transcendental ego"? The following excerpts from Poster's work speak for themselves:

> The intellectual's will to power is stashed in his or her text in the form of universal reason. The art of appropriating the universal was the main business of the Enlightenment. The philosophes were master impressionists whose collective textual voice ventriloquized that of humanity but spoke for a particular social class.[44]

As we bid farewell to the proletariat we must close the books on a whole epoch of politics, the era of the dialectic and the class struggle.[45]

Truth is not a transcendent unity.[46]

As just noted, Poster's very thesis regarding the electronic mode of information requires that he, Poster, *be* a transcendental ego, and the foregoing quotations exemplify that necessity.

Poststructuralism and Political Economy

Poster notes that Jürgen Habermas (often considered the leading contemporary exponent of the Frankfurt School) regards poststructuralism as being an essentially conservative or right wing philosophy due to its abandonment of the Enlightenment.[47] Poster himself remarked that "linearity and causality are the spatial and temporal orderings of the now-bypassed modern era."[48] As a result of abandoning the Enlightenment, poststructuralism is antithetical to political economy and to the pursuit of social justice. After all, how can one possibly do political economy if language is no longer representational, merely self-referential, and if causality is anachronous?

Poster's riposte, though, is interesting. He asserts, first, that since all discourses, all knowledge systems, including scientific knowledge systems, are implicated in power,[49] to redress domination and repression, discourses themselves (including scientific discourses) must be de-authenticated. Thus, for him, poststructuralism is the latest advance in critical theory. Poster concedes that in the industrial age, Marxist theory, centering on ownership of the means of production, was perhaps adequate to highlight patterns of domination. But with electronics, discourse has now superceded property as the primary site of domination, and so it now behooves contemporary critical theorists to reveal the language-based patterns of domination and subvert them. *Language must replace action.*

However, this position, too, deserves critical scrutiny. Are ownership and control of media really dwarfed in importance when compared to the linguistic consequences purported to be inherent in new media? Poster's technological determinism in this regard hinges on an affirmative answer, but the support he presents is unconvincing. He makes much of television advertising's imputation of nonsensical properties to products, for example, as an instance in which language loses representational properties in the electronic age. But actually, there is nothing inherent in the technology of television that requires it to be used for advertising at all, or if so used that its ads take on the characteristics outlined by Poster. Surely those issues are better approached through analyses of ownership, control, policy, and commodification—categories of political economy. Regarding the Johnson's floor wax commercial, Poster argues that linking ("articulating" in Grossberg's terms) floor wax and romance means that "the commodity has been given a semiotic value that is distinct from, indeed out of phase with, its use value and its exchange value." He continues: "The social effect of the ad (floor wax/romance) is not economic or psychological but linguistic: the TV viewer participates in a communication, is part of a new language system. *That is all.*"[50] From a political economy perspective, however, that is not all! Poster's analysis is naïve in the extreme. Floor wax is linked to romance in the commercial for the sole purpose of increasing the product's exchange value. Moreover, the purveyor of floor wax is able to accomplish the floor wax-romance "articulation" on account of the financial resources it commands, as well as the legal-technological-economic-financial milieu within which the television industry is structured. Viewers "participate" in a language system that is rife with political-economic causes and consequences.

More generally, the phenomena of self-referentiality, simulations, hyperrealities, electronic surveillance and simulacra, all addressed by Poster, point to the *heightened relevance* of political economy in the electronics age. *Who* is enabled to construct media simulations, why, and how are they so enabled? What is the nature of these simulations and whose interests do they promote? What aspects of material reality are obscured through simulations? Of course, Poster claims that we cannot fruitfully address material reality at all. But once we, in effect (and ironically given Poster's professed promotion of reflexivity and his ostensible concern for the marginalized), foreclose discussions on real-world power structures and powerplays by agreeing that language is totally self-referential, that hyperreality is "all there is" (to recall the old Peggy Lee song), then advertisers, PR professionals, propagandists, and others with communicatory power will certainly have won the day. Poster's poststructuralism negates the very possibility of critique; pseudoenvironments according to Poster are as real as we can get:

> In the [electronic] mode of information it becomes increasingly difficult, or even pointless, for the subject to distinguish a 'real' existing 'behind' the flow of signifiers and as a consequence social life in part becomes a practice of positioning subjects to receive and interpret messages.[51]
>
> This self-referentiality of signs upsets the representational model of language, the assurance of reason to contain meaning, and the confidence in the ability of logical argument to determine the truth. . . . The electronic mediation of communication in the postmodern lifeworld brings to the fore the rhetorical, figurative, performative, and self-reflexive features of language.[52]

Poster's poststructuralism, despite a professed concern for the marginalized, buttresses existing power and further marginalizes dissent. Who is best able to perform, to concoct pseudoenvironments, to use figurative and performative ploys to persuade? Professional communicators, of course. Who is better able to hire the services of media professionals than the wealthy? Marginalized groups such as environmentalists, lacking the big budgets required to concoct pseudoenvironments, need to draw on reason, logic, data, evidence, and a quest for truth—all of which Poster relegates to the dung heap of anachronous curiosities. Wide acceptance of poststructuralism as a paradigm would be a great boon to all professional persuaders and propagandists. In this light, poststructuralism can be seen as merely the latest instance of American scholarship skirting issues of social justice, and servicing established power.

HAROLD INNIS

Poster and Innis are both dedicated to the goal of developing reflexive capacities. For both, in the words of Poster, "the problem of communication theory begins with a recognition of necessary self-reflexivity, on the dependence of knowledge on its context."[53] For both, a method is needed to critically assess both "the authorial position of the theorist and the categories he or she develops."[54] For Poster, modernist social science, including political economy, is anathema to this project. This is because in science and social science the author's quest for objectivity invariably results in a position of omniscience—a totalitarian ("totalizing") posture, in his view. Hence, Poster flees the Enlightenment through deconstruction, or what he terms the self-referentiality of language in the electronic era. Innis, in contrast, although cognizant and wary of Enlightenment harms (mechanization of knowledge; loss of continuity, of meaning, and of an ethical base; decline in oral dialectic), never gave up on the Enlightenment and, ironically perhaps, came to view classicism as a major reference for developing a self-reflexive mindset.[55] In this context, Innis' media studies constituted an attempt to forge an inherently reflexive social science by developing a political-economic approach in which the concept of bias was prominent.

Bias

Guided by his classicist contemporaries at the University of Toronto,[56] Innis sought to investigate history by placing those interpreting history, and their biases, at the center of his analysis.[57] His concept of bias first appeared in a pre-communications studies paper of 1935, entitled "The Role of Intelligence."[58] It was a response to an article by E. J. Urwick, who had argued that the natural science paradigm is not suitable for the social scientist because, unlike the natural world, the social world is inherently unpredictable and ever-changing. The thoughts and actions of basically free-willed human beings, according to Urwick, are inherently unpredictable. The social scientist, too, he said, is infused with subjectivist tendencies. Hence, no human being can truly be objective while examining and interpreting the unpredictable subject of social behavior. For Urwick, "Life moves by its own immanent force, into an unknowable future."[59] Innis, though, challenged both the belief that human behavior ultimately is unpredictable, and Urwick's rejection of the scientific project. While agreeing that much behavior is spontaneous and that human beings (including social scientists) often act on the basis of engrained behavioral patterns involving degrees of unreflexive thought, Innis claimed that these thoughts and practices are themselves structurally conditioned. He called these engrained thoughts and practices, *biases*. Innis made an important assertion: while objectivity is impossible, the social scientist can develop the analytical tools needed to become aware of his/her own subjectivities, how they are constructed, and how and why they are unconsciously expressed again and again.[60]

Here the framework is established for the development of Innis' bias of communication. By examining how day-to-day lives are mediated by organizations and institutions—how key nodal points of social-economic power affect thoughts and practices—Innis understood that the social scientist can develop a needed self-awareness. By at least identifying these key mediators, Innis thought that the social scientist could take preliminary steps in the task of redressing the influences of his/her own biases and their subsequent implications for the state of knowledge.

Alarmed by the rapid growth of specialization in social science in the 1930s, Innis was concerned that the university was becoming the arbiter of instant solutions rather than an essential source of critical questions. Such concerns compelled him to pursue the question posed by philosopher James Ten Broeke—why do we attend to the things to which we attend?—and bias was the primary heuristic tool Innis developed in response.

Biases are organizational and conceptual orientations most generally expressed in terms of the two fundamental dimensions of human existence—time and space. Bias does not stem directly or solely from the medium itself but, rather, it is the outcome of how a given medium or complex of media is structured and used by already biased agents. In the context of capitalist modernity, a given medium—an institution, organization, or technology—may facilitate control over space (territory), and generally their strategic application tends to weaken interrelated capacities concerning time (duration, sustainability). Radio, television, and now the Internet, can be assessed as technologies which, for the most part, are structured to serve the spatial (i.e. "market share") interests of corporations and, in some cases, governments. Hence, for Innis, contemporary political-economic relations generally are sustained through the widening and deepening of historically structured relations involving, in the case of commercial applications, the immediate gratification and individualist biases normalized through mass media. Because bias can never be assessed in isolation of the historical, dialectical whole, the deleterious implications for the temporal conditions of life—for collective memory, for sustainable practices, for long-term considerations—constituted Innis' primary political concern.

For Innis, holistic, historical, and dialectical ruminations produced a pessimistic outlook when assessing the age of electronic communication. Efforts to control space could lead to a general and systemically replicating neglect of time. Rather than assessing a given medium as itself enabling or disabling some ways of thinking and acting relative to others (as with Poster's affiliation of decentered cultures and liberated identities), Innis focused on the balance or imbalance of a given society's constituent biases. In a way, Poster's political hopes relative to the Internet and related electronic media ironically reflect the progressive sentiments of the modernist social scientist as opposed to Innis' premodern, indeed classical emphasis on tension and balance. While Innis emphasized the dialectics of human action and its limits in terms of ecological and holistic contexts, Poster's veiled modernist bias asserts itself through his focus on individuals and marginalized communities.

Information and Knowledge

Poster argues that individuals in the electronics era are now finally experiencing the opportunity of liberation from Enlightenment-style grand narratives through the heightened possibility of subjective interpretations. In Poster's back-and-forth between an explicit subjectivist individualism and an implicit technological determinism, however, the cognitive processes lying behind the interpretation of information and experiences are neglected: he does not address, for instance, the forces, structures, and processes that help determine what information and experiences are available for interpretation, nor the pressures which guide interpreters. Innis, in contrast, assessed these issues directly using *monopolies of knowledge* and *time/space bias* as constructs.

Structurally, a *monopoly of knowledge* implies powerful forces at work in the production, distribution, and use of information. In a capitalist market system, in which the public service model is on the policy periphery and wealth is the primary determinant of who gets what information, those with financial resources tend to dominate. Such political-economic dimensions are not, of course, limited to mass media activities; among other nodal points of power they encompass scholarship also.[61]

Culturally, a monopoly of knowledge refers to *how* information is processed. Ideas about what is realistic and unrealistic, imaginable and unimaginable are generated through cultural norms and conventions ("biases"). Such norms are rife with political-economic influences and implications. The paucity of dialectical thinking in mainstream Western thought is but one important instance of culture shaping acceptable/unacceptable ways of thinking. Poster is naïve in his claim that communication mediated electronically negates socially constructed modes of processing information. He overlooks, for instance, the educational system and the requirements of employers in supporting particular ways of thinking and acting.

Technological Optimism and Pessimism

The same electronic technologies that Poster views to be prospectively liberating, Innis would have considered oppressive and potentially deadly. Innis declared:

> Intellectual man of the nineteenth century was the first to estimate absolute nullity in time. The present—real, insistent, complex, and treated as an independent system, the foreshortening of practical prevision in the field of human action—has penetrated the most vulnerable areas of public policy.[62]

For Innis, the application of prospectively liberating technologies tends to produce tragic results. Addressing the bias enacted through the contemporary mechanization of knowledge[63] and modernity's pernicious neglect of time, Innis would have argued that the Internet accelerates the peripheralization of reflexive thought. For him, an exponential growth of information would not be the formula for a self-reflexive civilization. Quite the opposite: "Enormous improvements in communication," observed Innis, "have made understanding [i.e. reflexivity] more difficult."[64] For Innis, the Internet would likely have been just one of many structurally biased mediators shaping how time and space are organized and conceptualized. In their annihilation of time and space, information and communication technologies (ICTs) and complementary structures would have been viewed as quite disturbing.

However, Innis would have examined new electronic technologies not only in relation to a complex of mediating dynamics. He would likely have viewed the poststructuralist preoccupation with identity and meaning as itself a kind of medium—an academic discourse perpetuating the modernist myth of progress, the ascendant neoliberal metanarrative, and present-mindedness. For Innis, electronic technologies and poststructuralist discourses, far from "opening a path of critique and possibly new politics,"[65] would have been understood as centralizing power by fetishizing the individual and universalizing the short-term as the predominant way of organizing and conceptualizing time.

CULTURAL STUDIES AND/OR POLITICAL ECONOMY?

At this juncture we would seem to have reached an impasse: despite surface similarities, there are fundamental antitheses between political economy (as practiced, for example, by Innis), and poststructuralist cultural studies, at least as represented by Poster, Grossberg, and Baudrillard. The inconsistencies between political economy and poststructuralism are attributable, at one level, to poststructuralism's insistence on moving from action to language, to its rejection of dialectical analyses, and to its persistent claim that the link between language and material reality is severed.

Fortunately, this book need not end on such a dour note. We would affirm that there are ample opportunities to integrate, or re-integrate, political economy and cultural studies. Three of these have been treated explicitly in the preceding chapters of part II. Another fecund way, though, of pursuing this reintegration would be to engage the question of technology and knowledge in the works of theorists explicitly dismissed by Poster for being "totalizing"—Habermas, Schiller, and Adorno, for example—and of others seldom if ever referred to by Poster—Raymond Williams, Armand Mattelart, Pierre Bourdieu and, of course, Harold Innis. I take up this question again, at a new level, in the Conclusion.

NOTES

1. Revised from an article originally coauthored with Edward Comor.
2. Mark Poster, *Cultural Theory and Poststructuralism: In Search of a Context* (Ithaca, NY: Cornell University Press, 1989), 6.
3. Mark Poster, *The Mode of Information: Poststructuralism and Social Context* (Chicago: University of Chicago Press, 1990), 7; emphasis added.
4. Poster, *The Mode of Information*, 6.
5. Poster, *Cultural Theory and Poststructuralism*, 82.
6. Poster, *The Mode of Information*, 6.
7. Poster, *The Mode of Information*, 6.
8. Poster, *Cultural Theory and Poststructuralism*, 126.

9. Poster, *Cultural Theory and Poststructuralism*, 126.

10. He writes: "Language is not simply a tool for expression; it is also a structure that defines the limits of communication and shapes the subjects who speak." Poster, *Cultural Theory and Poststructuralism*, 128.

11. "The habits of social analysis run deep. It is difficult to escape from old conceptual patterns, from the long-held assumption that in the field of society action has priority over language. The theorists who established the contours of the study of society—Marx, Weber, and more ambiguously Emile Durkheim—all gave precedence to action over language." Poster, *Cultural Theory and Poststructuralism,* 126.

12. "Poststructuralists point to various ways in which language materially affects the relation of the theorist to his or her discourse and the ways in which the social field is composed of linguistic phenomena." Poster, *Cultural Theory and Poststructuralism,* 4.

13. The older and more usual pairing is *thought vs. action*. Plato, through the parable of the cave, urged a movement from action to thought (contemplation of ideal forms). Marx promoted the opposite, writing: "The philosophers have only interpreted the world differently; the point is, however, to change it." Since language is a necessary tool for thought, Poster here is actually urging readers to become even further removed from action than the expression, "from action to thought," would imply, his poststructuralist position being light years from both Marx and Plato. See, generally, Hannah Arendt, *Between Past and Future* (1954, reprint, New York: Penguin, 2006), 13, 18.

14. Poster, *The Mode of Information*, 62–63.

15. Poster, *The Mode of Information*, 58.

16. Poster, *Cultural Theory and Poststructuralism*, 13.

17. Poster, *The Mode of Information*, 2.

18. Poster, *Cultural Theory and Poststructuralism*, 9.

19. Poster, *Cultural Theory and Poststructuralism*, 128.

20. Poster, *The Mode of Information*, 6.

21. Poster, *The Mode of Information*, 11.

22. Poster, *Cultural Theory and Poststructuralism*, 79–80.

23. Poster, *Cultural Theory and Poststructuralism*, 85.

24. Poster, *The Mode of Information*, 15.

25. Poster, *Cultural Theory and Poststructuralism*, 15.

26. Poster, *The Mode of Information*, 15.

27. Poster, *Cultural Theory and Poststructuralism*, 26.

28. Poster, *Cultural Theory and Poststructuralism*, 107. This definition can be compared to the one forwarded by Lazarsfeld and discussed in chapter 1.

29. Poster, *Cultural Theory and Poststructuralism*, 116.

30. Poster, *Cultural Theory and Poststructuralism*, 106.

31. Poster, *Cultural Theory and Poststructuralism*, 106.

32. Poster, *Cultural Theory and Poststructuralism*, 126.

33. Jody Berland, not addressing Poster specifically, argues that Innis differs from postmodernist positions in two major respects: first, he does not focus on representations as do postmodernists, and second he is much more materialist. Jody Berland,

"Space at the Margins: Critical Theory and Colonial Space After Innis," in *Harold Innis and the New Century,* 281–308.

34. Northrop Frye, *Anatomy of Criticism: Four Essays* (1957; reprint, Princeton, NJ: Princeton University Press, 1971), 17.

35. Frye, *Anatomy of Criticism*, 44.

36. Northrop Frye, *The Critical Path: An Essay on the Social Context of Literary Criticism* (Bloomington, IN: Indiana University Press, 1971), 24–25.

37. Thomas Kuhn, *The Structure of Scientific Revolutions* (2nd edition, Chicago: University of Chicago Press, 1962).

38. Poster, *The Mode of Information,* 13; emphasis added.

39. Poster, *Cultural Theory and Poststructuralism*, 7.

40. Poster, *Cultural Theory and Poststructuralism*, 139.

41. Mark Poster, *The Second Media Age* (Cambridge: Polity Press, 1995), 75.

42. Poster, *Cultural Theory and Poststructuralism*, 7–8.

43. Poster, *Cultural Theory and Poststructuralism*, 7–8.

44. Poster, *Cultural Theory and Poststructuralism*, 31.

45. Poster, *The Mode of Information*, 130.

46. Poster, *Cultural Theory and Poststructuralism*, 15.

47. Poster, *Cultural Theory and Poststructuralism*, 28, 62.

48. Poster, *Cultural Theory and Poststructuralism*, 90.

49. Poster, *Cultural Theory and Poststructuralism*, 26.

50. Poster, *The Mode of Information,* 59; emphasis added.

51. Poster, *The Mode of Information*, 15.

52. Poster, *The Mode of Information*, 10.

53. Poster, *The Second Media Age*, 74.

54. Poster, *The Second Media Age*, 75.

55. Innis preferred Plato to Aristotle. The former, by transcribing dialogues, preserved the oral dialectic in the written form and thereby "opposed the establishment of a finished system of dogma"—what Poster would term a "totalization." Innis added that Plato "would not surrender his freedom to his own books and refused to be bound by what he had written." See Harold Innis, *Empire and Communications* (1950; revised by Mary Q. Innis, Toronto: University of Toronto Press, 1972), 57. By contrast, according to Innis, "in Aristotle the power of the spoken word declined sharply and became a source of confusion. . . . The dead hand of the written tradition threatened to destroy the spirit of Western man." Harold Innis, "The Bias of Communication" (1949; reprint, Harold A. Innis, *The Bias of Communication*, Toronto: University of Toronto Press, 1972), 57. *Cf.* Ray Charron, "Postmodern Themes in Innis's Works," in *Harold Innis in the New Century, Harold Innis and the New Century: Reflections and Refractions,* edited by Charles Acland and W. Buxton, Montreal and Kingston: McGill-Queen's University Press, 1999), 309–21.

56. Eric Havelock, *Harold A. Innis: A Memoir* (Toronto: Harold Innis Foundation, 1982).

57. Alexander John Watson, *Marginal Man: The Dark Vision of Harold Innis* (Toronto: University of Toronto Press, 2006), 291.

58. Harold Innis, "The Role of Intelligence: Some Further Thoughts," *Canadian Journal of Economics and Political Science* 1 (August 1935): 280–88.

59. Edward J. Urwick, "The Role of Intelligence in the Social Process," *Canadian Journal of Economics and Political Science* 1 (February 1935): 76.

60. "The sediment of experience," Innis wrote, "provides the basis for scientific investigation." He added that "the habits or biases of individuals which permit prediction are reinforced in the cumulative bias of institutions and constitute [or should constitute] the chief interest of the social scientist." Innis, "The Role of Intelligence," 284.

61. See chapter 4.

62. Harold A. Innis, *Changing Concepts of Time* (1952; reprint, with Introduction by James W. Carey, Lanham, MD: Rowman and Littlefield Publishers, Inc., 2004), vi.

63. Innis generally used the phrase, "the mechanization of knowledge," as shorthand for the technology that facilitated growth of information ("useful facts") and the concomitant normalization of acritical, unreflexive intellectual pursuits driven forward by mostly commercial and administrative interests.

64. Innis, "Minerva's Owl" (1947; reprint, Harold Innis, *The Bias of Communication*, Toronto: University of Toronto Press, 1971), 31.

65. Mark Poster, *The Information Subject* (Amsterdam: G and B Arts International, 2001), 103.

Conclusion

The renowned split between political economy and cultural studies has been, in a sense, a distraction, a diversion, a *faux* debate. Attracting so much attention on account of the bitterness exuding from the combatants, the hostilities have diverted analysts from focusing on the more basic problematic—the bifurcation of critical cultural studies itself into cultural materialism and poststructuralism.[1] Pitting cultural studies (always in such instances represented as a unity) against political economy not only depicts the "enemy" as being outside the discourse (where it must remain, according to Grossberg), thereby making the fundamental debate "us vs. them" rather than "us vs. us," it also renders cultural studies (again, depicted as a unity) hard to pin down and hence to critique—because, for one thing, the ontologies of cultural materialism and poststructuralism are *so* antithetical. (Recall from chapter 3, for example, how celebrated cultural studies scholars on the one hand insisted that cultural studies is impossible to define as it varies according to who is doing the research on any particular day, but on the other they were sure of one thing: cultural studies is *not* political economy).[2]

One could be very cynical. Why are the founders of cultural studies (Hoggart, Williams, Thompson) bent so out of shape by poststructuralists so as to make it seem that *(a)* today's poststructuralists are following rather faithfully in the founders' footsteps, when such is clearly not the case, and *(b)* the founders of cultural studies created the field in order to put down the "economism" and "false consciousness" proposed by critical political economists, when again nothing could be farther from the truth?

Another question. Why do "critical" poststructuralists go on and on about oppression of gendered and racial minorities and speak of liberation through the abandonment of "grand narratives" and the authentication of individual perception and cognition when, at the same time, they propose (if not directly, then at least by implication) that oppression for one may be adulation for another and freedom to a third, reality being what one chooses it to be, linguistically speaking that is? Is not poststructuralism, in the end, despite its radical pretensions, really a paradigm or ideology for the status quo? Is not the claim that we all exist in language, that we cannot escape language, also an argument that we should refrain from tampering with the fundamental structures of society? Because, really, we can know nothing? These are certainly questions worth pondering.

In any event, I would like to conclude the present tome with a call to integrate, or reintegrate, political economy and cultural studies. Some ways of accomplishing this reintegration were suggested in chapters 5 to 7 and elsewhere: maintaining an awareness of the cultural biases of money; forwarding the time-space dialectic of Innisian medium theory; insisting on the dialectic of information; understanding culture as a whole way of life. Reintegrating critical political economy and cultural studies also means, most fundamentally, setting aside poststructuralist cultural studies. In fact, if poststructuralist cultural studies is disregarded, political economy and cultural studies (cultural materialism) are united already. They were never divorced, and hence need no reconciliation.

Why, then, is it of some human benefit to abandon poststructuralist cultural studies, or at least turn from its most extreme instances as represented here by Poster, Baudrillard, and Grossberg? One set of benefits flows simply from jettisoning a mode of thought which is falsified in self-reference and which is plagued by inconsistencies; if clarity of thought is in fact a benefit, casting aside poststructuralism is certainly an advantage.

Stuart Hall, who often seemed to have a foot testing the poststructuralist waters, inadvertently gave another one. He declared: "Postmodernism attempts to close off the past by saying that history is finished, therefore you needn't go back to it. There is only the present, and all you can do is be with it, immersed in it. . . . What it says is this: this is the end of the world. History stops with us and there is no place to go after this."[3] Harold Innis termed this kind of thinking *present-minded*, and he argued convincingly that contemporary scholarship, for this very reason, leads to a lack of understanding. John Ralston Saul, as we saw previously, made the same claim. To disregard poststructuralist positions, therefore, by implication, opens up possibilities for greater understanding.

Kevin O'Donnell, echoing Grossberg and Poster, has pointed to another potential benefit of casting aside poststructuralist thought. O'Donnell observed that a chief contention of poststructuralism is that "there is no way to escape language, no way to stand outside discourse *to get at pure, raw truth*."[4]

O'Donnell's qualification, "to get at pure, raw truth," which I have italicized, is of momentous importance, but that qualification is usually ignored in poststructuralist literature: both Baudrillard and Poster, for example, proposed that language and discourse are "all there is," that there is simply no way to escape language, *tout court*, never mind getting at "pure, raw truth." To agree with Poster and Baudrillard on this, however, is to subvert any and all quest for social justice simply because social justice pertains to lived conditions and our knowledge of lived conditions. Harold Innis, by contrast, while certainly agreeing that "pure, raw truth" is difficult if not impossible to attain on account of "biases" in our ways of perceiving and understanding, also insisted that we must continually strive through reflexivity to stand outside the biases of media and discourse sufficiently to at least glimpse truth, even if but as through a glass darkly, and that for him is precisely what the task and duty of scholarship is. Poststructuralism's allegation that there is no truth to seek ought be judged by poststructuralism's own standard, namely that all-encompassing statements cannot be true.

Consider as well the environmental implications of the strict poststructuralist insistence that we are forever trapped in language. A poststructuralist would be inclined to say that in principle the environment may impinge upon the life of each individual, community, society, and country. But all that is completely unknowable, for we live within language and cannot escape language. Environmental discourses for poststructuralists, therefore, are simply that—verbal structures concocted and engaged in by groups of people; and one such discourse is no better than any other. "This group over here speaks about global warming," a poststructuralist might remark, "and that group over there about species' extinctions. May they enjoy their dialogues! Only let us be sure there are other groups with *their* discourses to neutralize them. If there are not, then we run the risk of constructing 'grand narratives,' which means OPPRESSION, and the only way out of that deleterious situation would be to 'deconstruct' the discourses—certainly not to weigh their claims and predictions against observations in the material world because, as Baudrillard says, 'truth, reference and objective causes have ceased to exist.'[5] Everything is simulation nowadays, and everything is interpretation, and one person's interpretation of a simulation is no better or no worse than any other."

At the turn of the last century, there were two founding fathers of semiotics/semiology. The more influential was Ferdinand de Saussure. According to de Saussure, "signs," or words, are *unmotivated*, by which he meant there is nothing but convention or social agreement that gives a word its meaning. The meaning of signs (words), and of sentences ("syntagms"), de Saussure insisted, can be comprehended by studying the structure of language as it exists at present, without referring to either the history of the language (synchronic, as opposed to diachronic linguistics), or to the material world (internal, as opposed to external linguistics). De Saussure is the exact opposite of Raymond Williams, who insisted that one must study not only the history of meanings of words but relate those meanings to changes in the lived conditions. In de Saussure, then, we find the seeds of major contemporary poststructuralist contentions: that we live in language and cannot extricate ourselves from it, that the relation between language and outside reality is broken, and that we can safely disregard history.

The "road not taken"[6] was the semiology of the field's other founder, C. S. Peirce. Peirce grounded his semiotics in material reality, by insisting on a tripartite relationship among the sign (word), its object or referent in the material world, and the mental image of the person experiencing the sign. Meaning for Peirce, unlike de Saussure, comes not just from the structure of language, but also from one's experiences in the material world. According to Peirce, moreover, language bears an interactive (dialectical) relationship to material reality, as witnessed, for example, by the famous plethora of names Inuit people have for snow and Trobianders for yam.[7] Peirce made a direct connection between sign and referent, which is precisely what de Saussure rejected.

A major difference between Grossberg and Garnham, between Poster and Innis, between Baudrillard and Williams, between poststructuralists and political economists/cultural materialists, one suspects, is that the former in each case are at least implicitly descendants of de Saussure, and the latter of Peirce.

Raymond Williams, the preeminent inaugurator of cultural studies, like Harold Innis, has informed much of this book. It seems, then, only fitting to conclude by citing him once more. As his final remarks in *Culture and Society,* Williams wrote: "The human crisis is always a crisis of understanding. . . . There are ideas, and ways of understanding, with the seeds of life in them, and there are others, perhaps deep in our minds, with the seeds of a general death. Our measure of success in recognizing these kinds, and in naming them . . . may be literally the measure of our future."[8]

NOTES

1. Although the terminology differs, a related demarcation was made by Stuart Hall. In his article, "Cultural Studies: Two Paradigms," Hall distinguished between "culturalist" and "structuralist" modes. Derived from sociology, anthropology, and social history as influenced by Hoggart, Thompson, and Williams, the "culturalist mode" regards culture as a whole way of life; it is accessible through concrete (empirical) descriptions which capture the unities of commonplace cultural forms and

material experience. The "structuralist mode," on the other hand, is indebted to French linguistics, literary criticism, and semiotic theory, and conceives cultural forms as being "(semi)autonomous inaugurating 'discourses' susceptible to rhetorical and semiological analyses of cognitive constitutions and ideological effects." Vincent B. Leitch, "Birmingham Cultural Studies: Popular Arts, Poststructuralism, Radical Critique," *Journal of the Midwest Modern Languages Association* 24, no. 1 (spring 1991): 74. See also note 5, chapter 3.

2. In his contribution to the Colloquy, James Carey asserted: "I have never believed that the conflict between political economy and cultural studies, as I understand it, was an intellectual conflict. There are no intellectual differences beyond reconciliation, but there are political ones." Carey, "Abolishing the Old Spiritual World," *Critical Studies in Mass Communication* 12, no. 1 (1995): 87. Carey notwithstanding, in the present book it has been emphasized that while the *ostensible* political objectives of critical cultural studies and critical political economy are similar if not indeed identical, their different ontologies make their positions intellectually irreconcilable. Interestingly, in an article written at about the same time, and fundamentally contradicting his position referenced here, Carey insisted that economics is and must always be irreconcilable with communication studies: communication studies' methodological collectivism, he opined, is and must remain a counterpoint to economics' methodological individualism. See Carey, "Communications and Economics," in *Information and Communication in Economics,* ed. Robert E. Babe (Boston: Kluwer, 1994), 321–36.

3. Stuart Hall, "On Postmodernism and Articulation: An Interview with Stuart Hall," ed. Lawrence Grossberg (1986), in *Stuart Hall: Critical Dialogues in Cultural Studies,* ed. David Morley and Kuan-Hsing Chen (London: Routledge, 1996), 137, 134.

4. Kevin O'Donnell, *Postmodernism* (Oxford: Lion Publishing, 2003), 6.

5. Jean Baudrillard, *Simulations,* trans. Paul Foss, Paul Patton and Philip Beitchman (New York: Semiotext(e), 1983), 6.

6. See Paul Cobley, "Introduction," *The Communication Theory Reader,* ed. Paul Cobley (London: Routledge, 1996), 26–32. Cobley suggested that "the increased attention given to Peirce's work . . . often looks as though it might upset the whole applecart of post-structuralism. . . . [It] appears to offer a new perspective on how communication might be thought to refer to the real world."

7. Barrington Nevitt, *The Communication Ecology: Re-presentation versus Replica* (Toronto: Butterworths, 1982), 109–10.

8. Raymond Williams, *Culture and Society: 1780–1950* (1958; reprint, Harmondsworth: Penguin, 1984), 323.

References

Acland, Charles, and W. Buxton, eds. *Harold Innis and the New Century: Reflections and Refractions.* Montreal and Kingston: McGill-Queen's University Press, 1999.

Adorno, Theodor W. "On the Fetish Character in Music and the Regression of Listening." 1938. Pp. 26–52 in *The Culture Industry* by Theodor Adorno, edited with an Introduction by J. M. Bernstein. London: Routledge, 1991.

——. "The Stars Down to Earth: The *Los Angeles Times* Astrology Column." 1952–1953. Pp. 46–171 in *The Stars Down to Earth* by Theodor Adorno, edited with an Introduction by Stephen Crook. New York: Routledge, 2007.

——. "How to Look at Television. 1954. Pp. 136–53 in *The Culture Industry,* edited with an Introduction by J. M. Bernstein. London: Routledge, 1991.

——. *Negative Dialectics*, translated by Dennis Redmond. Originally published in German in 1966. www.efn.org/~dredmond/ndtrans.html (accessed December 15, 2007).

——. "Culture Industry Reconsidered." 1975. Pp. 85–92 in *The Culture Industry,* edited with an Introduction by J. M. Bernstein. London: Routledge, 1991.

——. "Free Time." 1977. Pp. 162–70 in *The Culture Industry,* edited with an Introduction by J. M. Bernstein. London: Routledge, 1991.

——. "The Schema of Mass Culture." 1981. Pp. 53–84 in *The Culture Industry,* edited with an Introduction by J. M. Bernstein. London: Routledge, 1991.

——. Transparencies on Film." 1981, 1982. Pp. 154–61 in *The Culture Industry,* edited with an Introduction by J. M. Bernstein. London: Routledge, 1991.

——. *The Culture Industry,* edited with an Introduction by J. M. Bernstein. London: Routledge, 1991.

Adorno, Theodor W., Else Frenkel-Brunswik, Daniel J. Levinson, and R. Nevitt Sanford. *The Authoritarian Personality.* 1950. Abridged. New York: Norton, 1982.

Agger, Ben. "Critical Theory, Poststructuralism, Postmodernism: Their Sociological Relevance." *Annual Review of Sociology* 17 (1991) www.uta.edu/huma/illuminations/agger2.htm (accessed June 10, 2008).

Alexander, Jeffrey C. "Analytical Debates: Understanding the Relative Autonomy of Culture." Pp. 1–30 in *Culture and Society: Contemporary Debates,* edited by Jeffrey C. Alexander and Steven Seidman. Cambridge: Cambridge University Press, 1990.

Anderson, Chris. *The Long Tail.* New York: Hyperion, 2006.

Angus, Ian. *A Border Within.* Montreal and Kingston: McGill-Queen's University Press, 1997.

———. *Primal Scenes of Communication.* New York: SUNY Press, 2000.

Arendt, Hannah. "Preface: The Gap Between Past and Future." 1954. Pp. 3–15 in *Between Past and Future.* New York: Penguin, 2006.

———. "The Crisis in Culture." 1954. Pp. 194–222 in *Between Past and Future.* New York: Penguin, 2006.

Associated Press. "George Gerbner, Studied TV Culture." *Washington Post,* 2 Jan. 2006, B4.

Babe, Robert E. "The Place of Information in Economics." Pp. 41–67 in *Information and Communication in Economics,* edited by Robert E. Babe. Boston: Kluwer Academic Publishers, 1994.

———, ed. *Information and Communication in Economics.* Boston: Kluwer Academic Publishers, 1994.

———. *Communication and the Transformation of Economics.* Boulder, CO: Westview Press, 1995.

———. "Paeans to Smythe." *Journal of Communication* 46, no. 1 (winter 1996): 179–82.

———. *Canadian Communication Thought: Ten Foundational Writers.* Toronto: University of Toronto Press, 2000.

———. *Culture of Ecology: Reconciling Economics and Environment.* Toronto: University of Toronto Press, 2006.

———. "The Political Economy of Knowledge: Neglecting Political Economy in the Age of Fast Capitalism (As Before)." *Fast Capitalism* 2, no. 1 (2006). www.uta.edu/huma/agger /fastcapitalism/2_1/index.html (accessed December 15, 2007).

———. "Innis and the News." *Javnost—the Public* 13, no. 3 (2006): 43–56.

———. "Harold Innis and the Paradox of Press Freedom." *Fifth Estate On-Line,* May 2007. www.fifth-estate-online.co.uk/criticsm/haroldinnisandtheparadox.html (accessed December 15, 2007).

———. "McLuhan and the Electronic Archives." Ottawa: Library and Archives Canada, 2007. www.collectionscanada.gc.ca/innis-mcluhan/002033-4010-e.html (accessed December 15, 2007).

———. *Media, Structures and Power: The Robert E. Babe Collection,* edited by Edward Comor. Toronto: University of Toronto Press, 2009.

Backhouse, Roger E. *The Ordinary Business of Life.* Princeton, NJ: Princeton University Press, 2002.

Bacon, Francis. *Novum Organum.* 1620. www.constitution.org/bacon/nov_org.htm (accessed December 15, 2007).

Bagdikian, Ben. *The Media Monopoly.* 6th ed. Boston: Beacon Press, 2000.

Bales, Kevin. *Disposable People: New Slavery in the Global Economy.* Berkeley, CA: University of California Press, 1999.

Bateson, Melissa, and Alex Kacelnik. "Risk-Sensitive Foraging: Decision-Making in Variable Environments." Pp. 297–342 in *Cognitive Ecology: The Evolutionary Ecology of Information Processing and Decision Making,* edited by Reuvan Dukas. Chicago: University of Chicago Press, 1998.

Baudrillard, Jean. "The System of Objects."1968. Pp. 13–31 in *Jean Baudrillard: Selected Writings.* 2nd edition, edited with an Introduction by Mark Poster. Stanford, CA: Stanford University Press, 2001.

———. "For a Critique of the Political Economy of the Sign." 1972. Pp. 60–100 in *Jean Baudrillard: Selected Writings.* 2nd edition, edited with an Introduction by Mark Poster. Stanford, CA: Stanford University Press, 2001.

———. *Simulations*, translated by Paul Foss, Paul Patton, and Philip Beitchman. New York: Semiotext[e], 1983.

———. *Jean Baudrillard: Selected Writings.* 2nd edition, edited with an Introduction by Mark Poster. Stanford, CA: Stanford University Press, 2001.

Beard, Charles A., and Mary Beard. *The Rise of American Civilization*. New York: Macmillan, 1930.

Becker, Gary. *The Economic Approach to Human Behavior.* Chicago: University of Chicago Press, 1976.

Beniger, James. *The Control Revolution: Technological and Economic Origins of the Information Society*. Cambridge, MA: Harvard University Press, 1986.

Bentham, Jeremy. *An Introduction to the Principles of Morals and Legislation.* 1781. www.utilitarianism.com/jeremy-bentham/index.html (accessed August 22, 2008).

Berger, Arthur Asa. *Media Analysis Techniques*. 3rd edition. Thousand Oaks, CA: SAGE Publications, 2004.

Berland, Jody. "Space at the Margins: Critical Theory and Colonial Space After Innis." Pp. 281–308 in *Harold Innis and the New Century: Reflections and Refractions,* edited by Charles Acland and W. Buxton. Montreal and Kingston: McGill-Queen's University Press, 1999.

Bernstein, J. M., ed. *The Culture Industry,* by Theodor W. Adorno. London: Routledge, 1991.

Bernstein, J. M. "Introduction." Pp. 1–25 in Theodor W. Adorno, *The Culture Industry,* edited by J. M. Bernstein. London: Routledge, 1991.

Bloom, Allan. *The Closing of the American Mind.* New York: Simon and Schuster, 1987.

Blumler, Jay, and Dennis McQuail. *Television in Politics: Its Uses and Influences.* London: Faber and Faber, 1968.

Blumler, Jay, and Elihu Katz, eds. *The Uses of Mass Communication.* Beverly Hills, CA: SAGE Publications, 1974.

Blundell, Valda, John Shepherd, and Ian Taylor. "Editor's Introduction." Pp. 1–17 in *Relocating Cultural Studies: Developments in Theory and Research.* London: Routledge, 1993.

Boulding, Kenneth. *The Image: Knowledge and Life in Society.* Ann Arbor, MI: University of Michigan Press, 1956.

———. *A Primer on Social Dynamics: History as Dialectics and Development.* New York: Free Press, Collier-Macmillan, 1970.

———. *Ecodynamics: A New Theory of Societal Evolution.* Beverly Hills, CA: SAGE Publications, 1978.

Bronowski, Jacob, and Bruce Mazlish. *The Western Intellectual Tradition: From Leonardo to Hegel.* New York: Harper and Row, 1960.

Calabrese, Andrew. "Toward a Political Economy of Culture." Pp. 1–12 in *Toward a Political Economy of Culture: Capitalism and Communication in the Twenty-First Century,* edited by Andrew Calabrese and Colin Sparks. Lanham, MD: Rowman and Littlefield Publishers, Inc., 2004.

Carey, James W. "Culture, Geography, and Communications: The Work of Harold Innis in an American Context." Pp. 73–91 in *Culture, Communication and Dependency: The Tradition of H. A. Innis,* edited by William H. Melody, Liora Salter, and Paul Heyer. Norwood, NJ: Ablex Publishing Corp., 1981.

———. *Communication as Culture: Essays on Media and Society.* Boston: Unwin Hyman, 1989.

———. "Communications and Economics." Pp. 321–36 in *Information and Communication in Economics,* edited by Robert E. Babe. Boston: Kluwer Academic Publishers, 1994.

———. "Abolishing the Old Spirit World." *Critical Studies in Mass Communication* 12, no. 1 (1995): 82–89.

———. "The Chicago School of Communication Research." Pp. 14–33 in *James Carey: A Critical Reader,* edited by Eve Munson and Catherine Warren. Minneapolis: University of Minnesota Press, 1996.

Chaffee, Steven, and John Hochheimer. "The Beginnings of Political Communication Research in the United States: Origins of the 'Limited Effects' Model." Pp. 75–104 in *Mass Communication Review Yearbook* 5, edited by Michael Gurevitch and Mark R. Levy. Beverly Hills, CA: SAGE Publications, 1985.

Chaffee, Steven H., and Everett M. Rogers, eds. *The Beginnings of Communication Study in America: A Personal Memoir,* by Wilbur Schramm. Thousand Oaks, CA: SAGE Publications, 1997.

Chandler, Daniel. "Why Do People Watch Television?" 1994. www.aber.ac.uk/media/Documents/short/usegrat.html (accessed December 15, 2007).

———. "Signs: Semiotics for Beginners." April 2006. www.aber.ac.uk/media/Documents/S4B/sem02.html (accessed December 15, 2007).

Charron, Ray. "Postmodern Themes in Innis's Works." Pp. 309–21 in *Harold Innis in the New Century: Reflections and Refractions,* edited by Charles Acland and W. Buxton. Montreal and Kingston: McGill-Queen's University Press, 1999.

Chomsky, Noam. "Force and Opinion." Pp. 351–406 in *Deterring Democracy.* Cambridge, MA: South End Press, 1991. www.zmag.org/chomsky/dd/dd-c12-s01.html (accessed December 15, 2007).

Christie, Ian R. *Wilkes, Wyvill and Reform: The Parliamentary Reform Movement in British Politics, 1760–1785.* London: Macmillan, 1962.

Coase, Ronald. "The Nature of the Firm." *Economica* 4 (1952): 386–405.

———. "The Problem of Social Cost." *Journal of Law and Economics* 3 (1960): 1–44.

Cobley, Paul. "Introduction." Pp. 1–32 in *The Communication Theory Reader,* edited by Paul Cobley. London: Routledge, 1996.

——. "Interpretation, Ideation and the Reading Process." Pp. 405–25 in *The Communication Theory Reader,* edited by Paul Cobley. London: Routledge, 1996.

Comor, Edward. "Harold Innis's Dialectical Triad." *Journal of Canadian Studies* 29:2 (Summer 1994): 111–27.

——. *Consumption and the Globalization Project: International Hegemony and the Annihilation of Time.* New York: Palgrave Macmillan, 2008.

——, ed. *Media, Structures and Power: The Robert E. Babe Collection.* Toronto: University of Toronto Press, 2009.

Connell, Ian. "Monopoly Capitalism and the Media." Pp. 69–98 in *Politics, Ideology and the State,* edited by Sally Hibbin. London: Lawrence and Wishart, 1978.

Cook, Deborah. *The Culture Industry Revisited: Theodor W. Adorno on Mass Culture.* Lanham, MD: Rowman and Littlefield Publishers, Inc., 1996.

Creighton, Donald. *Harold Adams Innis: Portrait of a Scholar.* Toronto: University of Toronto Press, 1957.

Crook, Stephen. "Introduction." Pp.1–45 in *The Stars Come Down to Earth,* by Theodor Adorno. 1994; reprint, New York: Routledge, 2007.

Crowley, David, and Paul Heyer, eds. *Communication and History: Technology, Culture and Society.* 5th ed. New York: Allyn and Bacon, 2007.

Czitrom, Daniel. *Media and the American Mind: From Morse to McLuhan.* Chapel Hill: University of North Carolina Press, 1982.

Daly, Herman E. *Steady State Economics,* 2nd ed. Washington, DC: Island Press, 1991.

de Saussure, Ferdinand. *Course in General Linguistics,* edited by Charles Bally and Albert Sechehaye, translated with an Introduction and notes by Wade Baskin. New York: McGraw-Hill, 1915. www2.sims.berkeley.edu/courses/is296a-3/s06/Saussure .pdf (accessed December 16, 2007).

Deacon, David, Michael Pickering, Peter Golding, and Graham Murdock. *Researching Communications: A Practical Guide to Methods in Media and Cultural Analysis.* London: Arnold, 1999.

Deibert, Ronald J. *Parchment, Printing, and Hypermedia: Communication in the World Order Transformation.* New York: Columbia University Press, 1997.

——. "Between Essentialism and Constructivism: Harold Innis and World Order Transformations." Pp. 29–52 in *The Toronto School of Communication Theory: Interpretations, Extensions, Applications,* edited by Rita Watson and Menahem Blondheim. Toronto and Jerusalem: University of Toronto Press and Hebrew University Magnes Press, 2007.

Delia, Jesse. "Communication Research: A History." Pp. 20–98 in *Handbook of Communication Science*, edited by Charles R. Berger and Steven Chaffee. Newbury Park, CA: SAGE Publications, 1987.

Derrida, Jacques. "Structure, Sign, and Play in the Discourse of the Human Sciences." 1966. Pp. 878–89 in *The Critical Tradition: Classic Texts and Contemporary Trends,* edited by David H. Richter. 2nd ed. Boston: Bedford/St. Martin's, 1998.

Dewey, John. *The Public and Its Problems*. Chicago: Swallow Press, 1927.

Di Norcia, Vincent. "Communications, Power and Time: An Innisian View." *Canadian Journal of Political Science* 13, no. 2 (1990): 336–57.

Drache, Daniel, ed. *Staples, Markets, and Cultural Change,* by Harold Innis. Montreal and Kingston: McGill-Queen's University Press, 1995.

Eagleton, Terry. "Base and Superstructure." Pp. 165–75 in *Raymond Williams: Critical Perspectives,* edited by Terry Eagleton. Cambridge: Polity Press, 1989.

———. *Figures of Dissent.* London: Verso, 2003.

Easthope, Anthony. *Literary Into Cultural Studies.* London: Routledge, 1991.

Eisenstein, Elizabeth. *The Printing Press as an Agent of Change: Communications and Cultural Transformations in Early-Modern Europe.* Cambridge: Cambridge University Press, 1980.

Elliot, T. S. *Notes Towards a Definition of Culture.* New York: Harcourt, Brace and Co., 1949.

Environmental Defense. "Global Warming Skeptics: A Primer," 2006. www.environmentaldefense.org/article.cfm?contentid=4870 (accessed December 16, 2007).

Ewen, Stuart. *PR! A Social History of Spin.* New York: Basic Books, 1996.

Fagan, Andrew. "Theodor Adorno." *The Internet Encyclopedia of Philosophy,* 2006. www.iep.utm.edu/a/adorno.htm (accessed December 15, 2007).

Fish, Stanley. *Is There a Text in this Class? The Authority of Interpretive Communities.* Cambridge, MA: Harvard University Press, 1980.

Fiske, John. *Understanding Popular Culture.* Boston: Unwin Hyman, 1989.

Fowler, Mark S. "Interview." *Reason Magazine,* November 1981. Excerpt available: http://findarticles.com/p/articles/mi _m1568/is_1998_Dec/ai_53260535/pg_4 (accessed August 21, 2008).

Friedman, Milton. *Essays in Positive Economics.* Chicago: University of Chicago Press, 1953.

Frye, Northrop. *Anatomy of Criticism: Four Essays.* 1957. Reprint, Princeton, NJ: Princeton University Press, 1971.

———. "The Language of Poetry." Pp. 43–53 in *Explorations in Communication,* edited by Edmund Carpenter and Marshall McLuhan. Boston: Beacon Press, 1960.

———. *The Critical Path: An Essay on the Social Context of Literary Criticism.* Bloomington, IN: Indiana University Press, 1971.

Galbraith, John Kenneth. *The New Industrial State.* Boston: Houghton Mifflin, 1967.

Gandy, Oscar H., Jr. "Colloquy." *Critical Studies in Mass Communication* 12, no. 1 (1995): 60–61.

Gardner, Gary. "The Challenge for Johannesburg: Creating a More Secure World." Pp. 3–23 in Worldwatch Institute, *State of the World 2002: Special World Summit Edition.* New York: W. W. Norton and Company, 2002.

Garnham, Nicholas. "Contributions to a Political Economy of Mass Communication." *Media, Culture and Society* 1, no. 2 (1979): 123–46.

———. "Toward a Theory of Cultural Materialism. *Journal of Communication* 33 (1983): 314–43.

———. "Political Economy and Cultural Studies: Reconciliation or Divorce?" *Critical Studies in Mass Communication* 12, no. 1 (1995): 62–71.

Geertz, Clifford. *The Interpretation of Cultures: Selected Essays.* New York: Basic Books, 1973.

Gerbner, George. *Against the Mainstream: The Selected Works of George Gerbner,* edited by Michael Morgan. New York: Peter Lang, 2002.

Ginsberg, Benjamin. *The Captive Public: How Mass Opinion Promotes State Power.* New York: Basic Books, 1986.

Golley, Frank Benjamin. *A History of the Ecosystem Concept in Ecology: More Than the Sum of the Parts.* New Haven, CT: Yale University Press, 1993.

Goodwin, Andrew. "The Uses and Abuses of In-discipline." Pp. xiii–xxxix in Richard Hoggart, *The Uses of Literacy,* edited by Andrew Goodwin. New Brunswick, NJ: Transaction Publishers, 1998.

Gordon, Anita, and David Suzuki. *It's A Matter of Survival.* Toronto: Stoddart, 1990.

Goudie, Andrew. *The Human Impact on the Natural Environment.* 5th ed. Cambridge, MA: MIT Press, 2000.

Gouliamos, Kostas. *Sacred Fallacies: Essays on Political Communication and Culture.* Athens: Gavrilides Publishing House, 2004.

Grant, George. *Time as History.* 1969. Reprint, edited with an Introduction by William Christian. Toronto: University of Toronto Press, 1995.

Grossberg, Lawrence. *We Gotta Get Out of this Place: Popular Conservativism and the Postmodern Culture.* New York: Routledge, 1992.

———. "The Formations of Cultural Studies: An American in Birmingham." Pp. 21–66 in *Relocating Cultural Studies: Developments in Theory and Research,* edited by Valda Blundell, John Shepherd, and Ian Taylor. London: Routledge, 1993.

———. "Cultural Studies vs. Political Economy: Is Anybody Else Bored with this Debate?" *Critical Studies in Mass Communication* 12, no. 1 (1995): 72–81.

———. "Rereading the Past From the Future." *International Journal of Cultural Studies* 10, no. 1 (March 2007): 125–33.

———. "Aims and Scope." *Cultural Studies,* 2007. www.tandf.co.uk/journals/routledge/09502386.html (accessed December 16, 2007).

Guback, Thomas, ed. *Counterclockwise: Perspectives on Communication,* by Dallas W. Smythe. Boulder, CO: Westview Press, 1994.

Hackett, Robert. *News and Dissent: The Press and the Politics of Peace in Canada.* Norwood, NJ: Ablex Publishing Corporation, 1991.

Hall, Stuart. "Encoding/Decoding." Pp. 128–38 in *Culture, Media, Language,* edited by Stuart Hall, Dorothy Hobson, Andrew Lowe, and Paul Willis. London: Hutchinson, 1980.

———. "Race, Articulation and Societies Structured in Dominance." Pp. 305–45 in *Sociological Theories: Race and Colonialism.* Paris: UNESCO, 1980. www.ukzn.ac.za/ccs/files/Race,%20articulation%20and%20societies%20structured%20in%20dominance.pdf (accessed December 15, 2007).

———. "Cultural Studies: Two Paradigms." *Media, Culture and Society* 2 (1980): 57–72.

———. "The Rediscovery of 'Ideology': Return of the Repressed in Media Studies." Pp. 56–90 in *Culture, Society and the Media,* edited by Michael Gurevitch, Tony Bennett, James Curran and Janet Woolacott. London: Methuen, 1982.

———. "On Postmodernism and Articulation: An Interview with Stuart Hall," in *Stuart Hall: Critical Dialogues in Cultural Studies*, ed. David Morley and Kuan-Hsing Chen. London: Routledge, 1996.

——. "Cultural Studies and its Theoretical Legacies." Pp. 277–94 in *Cultural Studies,* edited by L. Grossberg, C. Nelson, and P. Treichler. London: Routledge, 1992.

Hardt, Hanno. *Critical Communication Studies: Communication, History and Theory in America.* London: Routledge, 1992.

Hartley, John. *A Short History of Cultural Studies.* London: SAGE Publications, 2003.

Havelock, Eric. *Harold A. Innis: A Memoir.* Toronto: Harold Innis Foundation, 1982.

Hayles, N. Katherine. *How We Became Posthuman: Virtual Bodies in Cybernetics, Literature, and Informatics.* Chicago: University of Chicago Press, 1999.

Held, David. "Introduction," *Critical Theory: Horkheimer to Habermas.* Cambridge: Polity Press, 1980.

Herman, Edward S., and Noam Chomsky. *Manufacturing Consent: The Political Economy of the Media.* 1988. Revised edition, New York: Pantheon, 2002.

——. "Reply to Kurt and Gladys Engel Lang." *Political Communication* 21 (2004): 103–07.

Heyer, Paul. *Communications and History: Theories of Media, Knowledge, and Civilization.* New York: Greenwood Press, 1988.

——. *Harold Innis.* Lanham, MD: Rowman and Littlefield Publishers, Inc., 2003.

Hoggart, Richard. *The Uses of Literacy.* 1957. Reprint, edited with an Introduction by Andrew Goodwin and a Postscript by John Corner. New Brunswick, NJ: Transaction Publishers, 1998.

——. "Adult Education: The Legacy and the Future," lecture in celebration of the fiftieth anniversary of the University of Glasgow's Department of Adult and Continuing Education, 18 October 2001. www.gla.ac.uk/adulteducation/latestnews/RichardHoggart.html (accessed June 9, 2008).

Horkheimer, Max, and Theodor W. Adorno. *Dialectic of Enlightenment.* New York: Continuum, 1991; originally published in German in 1944; first English translation, 1972.

Hughes, Robert. *The Shock of the New: Art and the Century of Change.* London: BBC, 1980.

Hume, David. "On the First Principles of Government," in *Essays, Moral, Political, and Literary.* 1742. Reprint, edited by Eugene F. Miller, Indianapolis, IN: Liberty Fund, 1987. www.econlib.org/library/LFBooks/Hume/hmMPL4.html (accessed December 15, 2007).

Inglis, Fred. *Raymond Williams.* London: Routledge, 1995.

Innis, Harold A. "The Teaching of Economic History in Canada. 1929. Pp. 3–16 in *Essays in Canadian Economic History,* edited by Mary Q. Innis. Toronto: University of Toronto Press, 1956.

——. "The Work of Thorstein Veblen." 1929. Pp. 17–26 in *Essays in Canadian Economic History,* edited by Mary Q. Innis. Toronto: University of Toronto Press, 1956.

——. *The Fur Trade in Canada: An Introduction to Canadian Economic History.* 1930. New edition based on the revised edition prepared by S. D. Clark and W. T. Easterbrook, with a foreword by Robin W. Winks. Toronto: University of Toronto Press, 1967.

——. "Government Ownership and the Canadian Scene." 1933. Pp. 78–96 in *Essays in Canadian Economic History*, edited by Mary Q. Innis. Toronto: University of Toronto Press, 1956.

——. "The Role of Intelligence: Some Further Thoughts." *Canadian Journal of Economics and Political Science* 1 (August 1935): 280–88.

——. "The Role of the Social Scientist." 1935. Pp. 429–38 in *Staples, Markets and Cultural Change: Selected Essays, Harold A. Innis*, edited by Daniel Drache. Montreal and Kingston: McGill-Queen's University Press, 1995.

——. "The Passing of Political Economy." 1938. Pp. 438–42 in *Staples, Markets, and Cultural Change,* edited by Daniel Drache. Montreal and Kingston: McGill-Queen's University Press, 1995.

——. *The Cod Fisheries: The History of an International Economy.* 1940. Revised edition, Toronto: University of Toronto Press, 1954.

——. "The Canadian Situation." 1940, 1952. Unpublished.

——. *Political Economy in the Modern State.* Toronto: The Ryerson Press, 1946.

——. "Minerva's Owl." 1947. Pp. 3–32 in *The Bias of Communication.* Toronto: University of Toronto Press, 1971.

——. "Adult Education and Universities." 1947. Pp. 203–14 in *The Bias of Communication,* Toronto: University of Toronto Press, 1971.

——. "A Critical Review." 1948. Pp. 190–202 in *The Bias of Communication.* Toronto: University of Toronto Press, 1971.

——. "The Bias of Communication." 1949. Pp. 33–60 in *The Bias of Communication,* with an Introduction by Marshall McLuhan, Toronto: University of Toronto Press, 1971.

——. "Technology and Public Opinion in the United States. 1949. Pp. 156–89 in *The Bias of Communication.* Toronto: University of Toronto Press, 1971.

——. "Industrialism and Cultural Values." 1950. Pp. 132–41 in *The Bias of Communication.* Toronto: University of Toronto Press, 1971.

——. *Empire and Communications.* 1950. Reprint with Foreword by Marshall McLuhan. Toronto: University of Toronto Press, 1972.

——. "A Plea for Time." 1951. Pp. 61–91 in *The Bias of Communication.* Toronto: University of Toronto Press, 1971.

——. "The Problem of Space." 1951. Pp. 92–131 in *The Bias of Communication.* Toronto: University of Toronto Press, 1971.

——. "The English Publishing Trade in the Eighteenth Century." 1951. Pp. 142–55 in *The Bias of Communication.* Toronto: University of Toronto Press, 1971.

——. *The Bias of Communication.* 1951. Reprint, with an Introduction by Marshall McLuhan. Toronto: University of Toronto Press, 1971.

——. "Adult Education and Universities." 1951. Pp. 471–81 in *Staples, Markets and Cultural Change: Selected Essays, Harold A. Innis*, edited by Daniel Drache. Montreal and Kingston: McGill-Queen's University Press, 1995.

——. "The Concept of Monopoly and Civilization." 1951. Pp. 384–89 in *Staples, Markets and Cultural Change: Selected Essays, Harold A. Innis,* edited by Daniel Drache. Montreal and Kingston: McGill-Queen's University Press, 1995.

———. *Changing Concepts of Time.* 1952. Reprint, with an Introduction by James W. Carey. Lanham, MD: Rowman and Littlefield Publishers, Inc., 2004.
———. *Essays in Canadian Economic History*, edited by Mary Q. Innis. Toronto: University of Toronto Press, 1956.
———. *The Idea File of Harold Innis,* edited by William Christian. Toronto: University of Toronto Press, 1980.
———. *Innis on Russia: The Russian Diary and Other Writings,* edited with a preface by William Christian. Toronto: The Harold Innis Foundation, 1981.
———. *Staples, Markets, and Cultural Change: Selected Essays, Harold A. Innis,* edited by Daniel Drache. Montreal and Kingston: McGill-Queen's University Press, 1995.
Innis, Mary Q., ed. *Essays in Canadian Economic History,* by Harold A. Innis. Toronto: University of Toronto Press, 1956.
Jacobs, Jane. *Systems of Survival: A Dialogue on the Moral Foundations of Commerce and Politics*. New York: Vintage, 1994.
Jansen, Sue Curry. "Walter Lippmann, Straw Man of Communication Research." Pp. 71–112 in *The History of Media and Communication Research: Contested Memories,* edited by David W. Park and Jefferson Pooley. New York: Peter Lang, 2008.
Jarvis, Simon. *Adorno: A Critical Introduction.* Cambridge: Polity Press, 1998.
Jay, Martin. *The Dialectical Imagination: A History of the Frankfurt School and the Institute of Social Research 1923–1950.* 1973. Reprint, Berkley, CA: University of California Press, 1996.
Jevons, William Stanley. *The Theory of Political Economy*, 3rd ed. London: Macmillan and Co., 1888.
Johnson, Richard. "What Is Cultural Studies Anyway?" *Social Text* 16 (Winter 1986–1987): 38–80.
Katz, Adam. "Postmodern Cultural Studies: A Critique." *Cultural Logic* 1, no. 1, (Fall 1997): 1–16.
Katz, Elihu. "Foreword: The Toronto School and Communication Research." Pp. 1–5 in *The Toronto School of Communication Theory: Interpretations, Extensions, Applications,* edited by Rita Watson and Menahem Blondheim. Toronto and Jerusalem: University of Toronto Press and The Hebrew University Magnes Press, 2007.
Katz, Elihu, and Paul F. Lazarsfeld. *Personal Influence: The Part Played By People in the Flow of Mass Communication*. 1955. Reprint, New York: Free Press, 1964.
Katz, Elihu, Jay Blumler, and Michael Gurevitch. "Uses of Mass Communication by the Individual." Pp. 11–35 in *Mass Communication Research: Major Issues and Future Directions*, edited by W. P. Davidson and F. Yu. New York: Praeger, 1974.
Kellner, Douglas. "Critical Theory and the Culture Industries: A Reassessment." *Telos* 62 (1984–85): 196–206.
Knudtson, Peter and David Suzuki. *Wisdom of the Elders*. Toronto: Stoddart, 1992.
Kuhn, Thomas. *The Structure of Scientific Revolutions.* 2nd ed., Chicago: University of Chicago Press, 1962.
Lang, Kurt and Gladys Engel Lang. "Noam Chomsky and the Manufacture of Consent for American Foreign Policy." *Political Communication* 21 (2004): 93–101.

——. "Response to Herman and Chomsky." *Political Communication* 21 (2004): 109–11.

Lazarsfeld, Paul Felix. "Administrative and Critical Communications Research." 1941. Pp. 166–73 in *Mass Communication and American Social Thought,* edited by John Durham Peters and Peter Simonson. Lanham, MD: Rowman and Littlefield Publishers, Inc., 2004.

Lazarsfeld, Paul, Bernard Berelson, and Hazel Gaudet. *The People's Choice.* New York: Duell, Sloan and Pearce, 1944.

Lears, T. J. Jackson. "From Salvation to Self-Realization: Advertising and the Therapeutic Roots of the Consumer Culture 1880–1930." Pp. 74–86 in *The Culture of Consumption,* edited by Richard Wightman Fox and T. J. Jackson Lears. New York: Pantheon, 1983.

Lee, Richard E. *Life and Times of Cultural Studies: The Politics and Transformation of the Structures of Knowledge.* Durham, NC: Duke University Press, 2003.

Leitch, Vincent B. "Birmingham Cultural Studies: Popular Arts, Poststructuralism, Radical Critique." *Journal of the Midwest Modern Languages Association* 24, no. 1 (Spring 1991): 74–86.

Lent, John A., ed. *A Different Road Taken: Profiles In Critical Communication.* Boulder, CO: Westview Press, 1995.

Lerner, Daniel. *The Passing of Traditional Society: Modernizing the Middle East.* New York: Free Press, 1958.

Lippmann, Walter, *Public Opinion.* 1922. Reprint. New York: Free Press, 1965.

Littlejohn, Stephen. *Theories of Human Communication.* 4th edition. Belmont, CA: Wadsworth, 1992.

Lower, Arthur. "Harold Innis As I Remember Him." *Journal of Canadian Studies* 20, no. 4 (1986): 3–11.

Lowery, Shearon and Melvin DeFleur. *Milestones in Mass Communication Research,* 2nd ed. White Plains, NY: Longmans, 1983.

Lubken, Deborah. "Remembering The Straw Man: The Travels and Adventures of *Hypodermic.*" Pp. 19–42 in *The History of Media and Communication Research,* edited by David W. Park and Jefferson Pooley. New York: Peter Lang, 2008.

Lux, Kenneth. *Adam Smith's Mistake: How a Moral Philosopher Invented Economics and Ended Morality.* Boston: Shambhala Publications, 1990.

Lyons, Oren. "An Iroquois Perspective." in *American Indian Environment: Ecological Issues in Native American History*, ed. C. Vecsey and R. Venables. Syracuse, NY: Syracuse University Press, 1980.

Macey, David. *The Penguin Dictionary of Critical Theory.* London: Penguin Books, 2000.

Macpherson, C. B. *Property: Mainstream and Critical Positions.* Toronto: University of Toronto Press, 1978.

Mandelbaum, Michael. *The Meaning of Sports: Why Americans Watch Baseball, Football and Basketball and What They See When They Do*. New York: Public Affairs, 2004.

Markowitz, Gerald, and Daniel Rosner. *Deceit and Denial: The Deadly Politics of Industrial Pollution*. Berkeley, CA: University of California Press, 2002.

Massolin, Philip A. "Academic Modernization and the Decline of Higher Learning: The University Question in the Later Scholarship of Harold Innis." *Canadian Journal of Communication* 23: 1 (1998). www.cjc-online.ca/viewarticle.php?id=445 (accessed 15 Dec. 2007).

Maxwell, Richard. "Political Economy Within Cultural Studies." Pp. 116–38 in *A Companion to Cultural Studies,* edited by Toby Miller. Oxford: Blackwell Publishing, 2001.

McChesney, Robert W. *Rich Media, Poor Democracy.* New York: The New Press, 1999.

———. "The Political Economy of Communication and the Future of the Field." *Media, Culture and Society* 22, no. 1 (2000): 109–16.

McCombs, Maxwell and Donald Shaw. "The Agenda-setting Function of Mass Media." *Public Opinion Quarterly* 36 (1971): 176-87.

McCracken, Grant. *Culture and Consumption: New Approaches to the Symbolic Character of Consumer Goods and Activities.* Bloomington, IN: Indiana University Press, 1988.

McCright, Aaron M., and Riley E. Dunlap. "Defeating Kyoto: The Conservative Movement's Impact on U.S. Climate Change Policy." *Social Problems* 50, no. 3 (2003): 348–73.

McLuhan, Marshall. *The Gutenberg Galaxy: The Making of Typographic Man.* Toronto: University of Toronto Press, 1962.

———. *Understanding Media: The Extensions of Man.* New York: Mentor, 1964.

———. *Culture is Our Business.* New York: McGraw Hill, 1970.

———. "Introduction." Pp. vii–xvi in *The Bias of Communication,* by Harold A. Innis. Toronto: University of Toronto Press, 1971.

———. "Foreword," Pp. v–xii in *Empire and Communications,* by Harold A. Innis. Toronto: University of Toronto Press, 1972.

McLuhan, Marshall, and Eric McLuhan, *Laws of the Media: The New Science.* Toronto: University of Toronto Press, 1988.

McLuhan, Marshall, and Harley Parker. *Through the Vanishing Point: Space in Poetry and Painting.* New York: Harper and Row, 1968.

McLuhan, Marshall, and Bruce R. Powers. *The Global Village: Transformations in World Life and Media in the 21st Century.* New York: Oxford University Press, 1989.

McLuhan, Marshall, with Wilfred Watson. *From Cliché to Archetype.* New York: Pocket Books, 1971.

McRobbie, Angela. "Post-marxism and Cultural Studies: A Post-script." Pp. 719–30 in *Cultural Studies,* edited by L. Grossberg, C. Nelson, and P. Treichler. New York: Routledge, 1992.

Meehan, Eileen R. "Commodity, Culture, Common Sense: Media Research and Paradigm Dialogue." *The Journal of Media Economics* 12, no. 2 (1999): 149–63.

Menzies, Heather. *No Time: Stress and the Crisis of Modern Life.* Vancouver: Douglas and McIntyre, 2005.

Mirowski, Philip. *More Heat Than Light: Economics as Social Physics, Physics as Nature's Economics.* Cambridge: Cambridge University Press, 1989.

Mitchell, Wesley C. *Types of Economic Theory,* Vol. 1, edited by Joseph Dorfman. New York: Kelley, 1967.

Mosco, Vincent. *The Political Economy of Communication.* Thousand Oaks, CA: SAGE Publications, 1996.

Mullen, Andy. "Twenty Years at the Margins: The Herman-Chomsky Propaganda Model, 1988–2008." *Fifth Estate-Online,* January 2008. /www.fifth-estate-on-line .co.uk/comment/twentyyears.html (accessed January 16, 2008).

Munson, Eve, and Catherine Warren, eds. *James Carey: A Critical Reader.* Minneapolis, MN: University of Minnesota Press, 1996.

Murdock, Graham. "Across the Great Divide: Cultural Analysis and the Condition of Democracy." *Critical Studies in Mass Communication* 12, no. 1 (March 1995): 89–95.

Neill, Robin. *A New Theory of Value: The Canadian Economics of H. A. Innis.* Toronto: University of Toronto Press, 1972.

Nevitt, Barrington. *The Communication Ecology: Re-presentation versus Replica.* Toronto: Butterworths, 1982.

Nohrestedt, Stig A. "Ruling by Pooling." Pp. 118–27 in *Triumph of the Image: The Media's War in the Persian Gulf—A Global Perspective,* edited by Hamid Mowlana, George Gerbner, and Herbert I. Schiller. Boulder, CO: Westview Press, 1992.

Nye, Joseph, and William Owens. "America's Information Edge." *Foreign Affairs* (March/April 1996): 20–36.

O'Connor, Alan. *Raymond Williams.* Lanham, MD: Rowman and Littlefield Publishers, Inc., 2006.

O'Connor, Brian, ed. *The Adorno Reader.* Oxford: Blackwell Publishers, Ltd., 2000.

O'Donnell, Kevin. *Poststructuralism.* Oxford: Lion Publishing, 2003.

O'Neill, John. "Value Pluralism: Incommensurability and Institutions." Pp. 75–88 in *Valuing Nature: Economics, Ethics and Environment,* edited by John Foster. London: Routledge, 1997.

Ong, Walter. *Orality and Literacy: Technologizing the Word.* New York: Methuen, 1982.

O'Sullivan, Tim, John Hartley, Danny Saunders, Martin Montgomery, and John Fiske. *Key Concepts in Communication and Cultural Studies,* 2nd Edition. London: Routledge, 1994.

Parker, Ian. "Innis, Marx, and the Economics of Communication." *Queen's Quarterly* 84 (1977): 535–63.

Peck, Janice. "Why We Shouldn't Be Bored with the Political Economy versus Cultural Studies Debate." *Cultural Critique* 64 (2006): 92–125.

Pencak, William. "Harold Innis, Thorstein Veblen, and In-formation." Pp. 155–165 in *Semiotics and Information Sciences,* edited by Paul Perron, Marcel Danesi, Jean Umiker-Sebeok, and Anthony Watanabe. Toronto: LEGAS, 2000.

Peters, John Durham. "Introduction." Pp. 13–20 in *Mass Communication and American Social Thought: Key Texts 1919–1968,* edited by John Durham Peters and Peter Simonson. Lanham, MD: Rowman and Littlefield Publishers, Inc., 2004.

Picard, André. "Blue-plate Specials Indeed a Swell Deal: It's Now Official: Those Food Portions Are Getting Larger, But We're Heaping It On at Home Too." *Globe and Mail,* January 25, 2006, A6.

Pietrzyk, Kamilla. *Exit From the Myopic Social Movement Strategy in the Age of the Internet.* M.A. Thesis, Faculty of Information and Media Studies, The University of Western Ontario, 2007.

Ponting, Clive. *A Green History of the World: The Environment and the Collapse of Great Civilizations.* New York: Penguin, 1991.

Pool, Ithiel de Sola. "Communication and Development." Pp. 106–110 in *Modernization: The Dynamics of Growth,* edited by M. Weiner. Washington, DC: Voice of America, 1966.

Pooley, Jefferson. "Fifteen Pages That Shook the Field: *Personal Influence,* Edward Shils, and the Remembered History of Mass Communication Research." *The Annals of the American Academy of Political and Social Science* 608 (November, 2006): 130–56.

———. "The New History of Mass Communication Research." Pp. 43–69 in *The History of Media and Communication Research: Contested Memories,* edited by David W. Park and Jefferson Pooley. New York: Peter Lang, 2008.

Poster, Mark. *Cultural Theory and Poststructuralism: In Search of a Context.* Ithaca, NY: Cornell University Press, 1989.

———. *The Mode of Information: Poststructuralism and Social Context.* Chicago: University of Chicago Press, 1990.

———. "The Mode of Information and Postmodernity." Pp. 173–92 in *Communication Theory Today,* edited by David Crowley and David Mitchell. Stanford, CA: Stanford University Press, 1994.

———. *The Second Media Age.* Cambridge: Polity Press, 1995.

———. "Introduction." Pp. 1–12 in *Jean Baudrillard: Selected Writings,* by Jean Baudrillard. 2nd edition. Stanford, CA: Stanford University Press, 2001.

———, ed. *Jean Baudrillard: Selected Writings.* 2nd edition. Stanford, CA: Stanford University Press, 2001.

———. *The Information Subject.* Amsterdam: G and B Arts International, 2001.

———. "Network Digital Information Humachines: A Conversation with Mark Poster." *Qui parle* 14 (Fall/Winter, 2003).

Raphael, D. D., and A. L. Macfie. "Introduction." Pp. 1–52 in *The Theory of Moral Sentiments,* by Adam Smith, edited by D. D. Raphael and A. L. Macfie. Indianapolis, IN: Liberty Press, 1982.

Real, Michael R. "The Super-Bowl: Mythic Spectacle." Pp. 92–117 in *Mass-Mediated Culture,* by Michael R. Real. Englewood Cliffs, NJ: Prentice Hall, 1977.

Robins, Kevin, and Frank Webster. "The Communications Revolution: New Media, Old Problems." *Communication* 10, no.1 (1987): 71–89.

Rogers, Everett M. *A History of Communication Study: A Biographical Approach.* New York: Free Press, 1994.

Rogers, Everett M., and Floyd Shoemaker. *Communication of Innovations: A Cross Cultural Approach.* New York: Free Press, 1971.

Ruderman, Richard S. "Odysseus and the Possibility of Enlightenment." *American Journal of Political Science* 43, no. 1 (January 1999): 138–61.
Ruggles, Myles. *Automating Interaction: Formal and Information Knowledge in the Digital Network Economy*. Foreword by Robert E. Babe. Cresskill, NJ: Hampton Press, 2005.
Sachs, Wolfgang. *Planet Dialectics: Explorations in Environment and Development.* New York: Zed Books, 1999.
Samuels, Warren J. *The Classical Theory of Economic Policy*, with an Introduction by Herman Finer. Cleveland, OH: World Publishing Company, 1966.
——. "The Chicago School of Political Economy: A Constructive Critique." Pp. 1–18 in *The Chicago School of Political Economy,* edited by Warren J. Samuels. New Brunswick, NJ: Transaction Publishers, 1993.
Sardar, Ziauddin, and Borin Van Loon. *Introducing Cultural Studies.* St. Leonards: Allen and Unwin, 1998.
Saul, John Ralston. *Voltaire's Bastards: The Dictatorship of Reason in the West.* Toronto: Penguin, 1992.
——. *The Unconscious Civilization.* Toronto: Anansi, 1995.
Schramm, Wilbur. "The Nature of Communication between Humans." Pp. 3–53 in *The Process and Effects of Mass Communication,* edited by Wilbur Schramm and Donald F. Roberts. Revised, Urbana, IL: University of Illinois Press, 1971.
——. *The Beginnings of Communication Study in America: A Personal Memoir*, edited by Steven H. Chaffee and Everett M. Rogers. Thousand Oaks, CA: SAGE Publications, 1997.
Scitovsky, Tibor. *The Joyless Economy: The Psychology of Human Satisfaction.* Oxford: Oxford University Press, 1976.
Seligman, Ben B. *Main Currents in Modern Economics: Economic Thought Since 1870.* Glencoe, IL: Free Press of Glencoe, 1962.
Simon, Julian. "The Grand Theory." Chapter 4 of *The Ultimate Resource II: People, Materials, and Environment* (Princeton, NJ: Princeton University Press, 1998). www.juliansimon.com/writings/Ultimate_Resource/TCHAR04B.txt (accessed August 22, 2008).
Simpson, Christopher. *Science of Coercion: Communication Research and Psychological Warfare 1945–1960.* Oxford: Oxford University Press, 1994.
Slack, Jennifer Daryl. "The Theory and Method of Articulation in Cultural Studies." Pp. 112–27 in *Stuart Hall: Critical Dialogues in Cultural Studies,* edited by David Morley and Kuan-Hsing Chen. London: Routledge, 1996.
Smith, Adam. *The Theory of Moral Sentiments.* 1759. Reprint edited by D. D. Raphael and A. L. Macfie. Indianapolis, IN: Liberty Press, 1982.
——. *An Inquiry into the Nature and Causes of the Wealth of Nations.* 1776. Modern Library Edition edited by Edwin Cannan with an Introduction by Max Lerner. New York: The Modern Library, 1937.
Smythe, Dallas W. *Dependency Road: Communications, Capitalism, Consciousness, Canada.* Norwood, NJ: Ablex Publishing Corporation, 1981.
——. *Counterclockwise: Perspectives on Communication,* edited by Thomas Guback. Boulder, CO: Westview Press, 1994.

Sorell, Tom. "Tobacco Company Sponsorship Discredits Medical but Not all Research—Ethical Debate: Should Industry Sponsor Research?" *British Medical Journal,* 1 August, 1998. www.findarticles.com/p/articles/mi_m0999/is_n7154_v317/ai_21023727 (accessed December 15, 2007).

Stamps, Judith. *Unthinking Modernity: Innis, McLuhan and the Frankfurt School.* Montreal and Kingston: McGill-Queen's University Press, 1995.

Stigler, George. "The Economics of Information." *Journal of Political Economy* 69, no. 3 (June 1961): 213–25.

Stigler, George, and Gary Becker. "De Gustibus Non Est Disputandum." *American Economic Review* 67, no. 2 (1977): 76–90.

Sussman, Gerald and John Lent. "Introduction: Critical Perspectives on Communication and Third World Development." In *Transnational Communications: Wiring the Third World,* edited by Gerald Sussman and John A. Lent. Newbury Park, CA: SAGE Publications, 1991.

Suzuki, David. *Metamorphosis: Stages in Life.* Toronto: Stoddart, 1987.

Suzuki, David, and Holly Dressel. *From Naked Ape to Superspecies: A Personal Perspective on Humanity and the Global Eco-Crisis.* Toronto: Stoddart, 1999.

Suzuki, David and Amanda McConnell. *The Sacred Balance: Rediscovering Our Place in Nature.* Vancouver: David Suzuki Foundation and Greystone Books, 1997.

Thompson, E. P. *The Making of the English Working Class.* 1963. Revised, Harmondsworth: Pelican, 1972.

———. *Witness Against The Beast: William Blake and the Moral Law.* Cambridge: Cambridge University Press, 1993.

———. *The Romantics: England in a Revolutionary Age.* New York: The New Press, 1997.

Turner, Graeme. *British Cultural Studies: An Introduction.* Cambridge, MA: Unwin Hyman, 1990.

Urwick, Edward J. "The Role of Intelligence in the Social Process." *Canadian Journal of Economics and Political Science* 1 (February 1935): 64–76.

Veblen, Thorstein. "The Intellectual Pre-eminence of Jews in Modern Europe." 1919. Pp. 467–79 in *The Portable Veblen,* edited by Max Lerner. New York: Viking Press, 1950.

Von Hayek, F. A. "The Use of Knowledge in Society." *American Economic Review* 35, no. 4 (1945): 519–30.

Watson, Alexander John. *Marginal Man: The Dark Vision of Harold Innis.* Toronto: University of Toronto Press, 2006.

Watson, Rita, and Menahem Blondheim, eds. *The Toronto School of Communication Theory: Interpretations, Extensions, Applications.* Toronto and Jerusalem: University of Toronto Press and The Hebrew University Magnes Press, 2007.

Weatherford, Jack. *The History of Money: From Sandstone to Cyberspace.* New York: Crown Publishers, Inc., 1997.

Webster, Frank. *Theories of the Information Society.* London: Routledge, 1995.

Wells, Jennifer. "In the New Economy, 'Free Becomes Inevitable,'" *Globe and Mail,* May 5, 2008, B1, B4

Wernick, Andrew. "No Future: Innis, Time, Sense, and Postmodernity." Pp. 261–80 in *Harold Innis and the New Century, Reflections and Refractions,* edited by Charles Acland and W. Buxton. Montreal and Kingston: McGill-Queen's University Press, 1999.

Wiener, Norbert. *The Human Use of Human Beings: Cybernetics and Society.* 1950. Reprint, New York: Avon Books, 1967.

Weizsäcker, Carl Friedrich. *The Unity of Nature.* New York: Farrar, Straus and Giroux, 1980.

Wikipedia. "Cultural Studies," n.d. http://en.wikipedia.org/wiki/Cultural_studies (accessed December 15, 2007).

Williams, Raymond. *Culture and Society 1780–1950.* 1958. Reprint, Harmondsworth: Penguin Books, 1984.

———. *The Long Revolution.* 1961. Reprint, Peterborough, Canada: Broadview Press, 2001.

———. *Communications.* 1962. Revised edition, Harmondsworth: Penguin, 1971.

———. "Literature and Sociology: In Memory of Lucien Goldman." 1971. Pp. 11–30 in *Problems in Materialism and Culture.* London: Verso, 1997.

———. "Base and Superstructure in Marxist Cultural Theory." 1973. Pp. 32–49 in *Problems in Materialism and Culture.* London: Verso, 1997.

———. *Television: Technology and Cultural Form.* Glasgow: Fontana/Collins, 1974.

———. *Keywords: A Vocabulary of Culture and Society.* 1976. Revised, Oxford: Oxford University Press, 1983.

———. *Marxism and Literature.* Oxford: Oxford University Press, 1977.

———. "Means of Communication as Means of Production." 1978. Pp. 50–63 in *Problems in Materialism and Culture.* London: Verso, 1997.

———. *Problems in Materialism and Culture.* 1980. Reprint. London: Verso, 1997.

———. *The Year 2000.* New York: Pantheon, 1983.

Willis, Andrew. "EnCana's Breakup a Boon for Bay Street." *Globe and Mail,* May 13, 2008, B17.

Winner, Langdon. *Autonomous Technology: Technics-out-of-Control as a Theme in Political Thought.* Cambridge, MA: MIT Press, 1977.

Winter, James. *Lies the Media Tell Us.* Montreal: Black Rose Books, 2007.

World Commission on Environment and Development. *Our Common Future.* New York: Oxford University Press, 1987.

Worster, Daniel. *Nature's Economy: A History of Ecological Ideas.* 2nd edition. Cambridge: Cambridge University Press, 1994.

Zinn, Howard. *A People's History of the United States.* 1980. Reprint, New York: HarperPerennial, 2005.

Index

About the Author

Robert E. Babe is professor of media studies at the University of Western Ontario, where he was the holder of the Jean Monty/BCE Chair in Media Studies. He received his Ph.D. in economics from Michigan State University in 1972. He has taught at several universities. He is author, coauthor, or editor of many articles, book chapters, technical reports, and books, including *Telecommunications in Canada: Technology, Industry and Government* (1990), *Communication and the Transformation of Economics* (1995), *Canadian Communication Thought: Ten Foundational Writers* (2000), *Culture of Ecology: Reconciling Economics and Environment* (2006), and *Media, Structures and Power: The Robert E. Babe Collection* (2009). He is recipient of the prestigious OCUFA award for excellence in university teaching. He has been consultant and expert witness before several regulatory tribunals. When not writing, Robert Babe may be found exploring back roads of southwestern Ontario on his motorcycle or enjoying the aquatic of life of Pigeon Lake near Bobcaygeon.

www.ingramcontent.com/pod-product-compliance
Ingram Content Group UK Ltd.
Pitfield, Milton Keynes, MK11 3LW, UK
UKHW041631031026
15587UKWH00001B/212

9 780739 123669